Rethinking Empowerment

Rethinking Empowerment looks at the changing role of women in developing countries and rejects the established notion that empowerment is best understood and pursued at a local level. It calls for a new approach, one that adopts a more nuanced, feminist interpretation of power and empowerment and recognises that local empowerment is always embedded in regional, national and global contexts. It must both pay attention to institutional structures and politics and acknowledge that empowerment is both a process and an outcome. Moreover, the book warns that an obsession with measurement rather than process can undermine efforts to foster transformative and empowering outcomes. It concludes that power must be restored as the centrepiece of empowerment. Only then will the term and its advocates provide meaningful ammunition for dealing with the challenges of an increasingly unequal, and often sexist, global/local world.

This edited collection will be essential reading for undergraduates and graduates in politics, development studies and gender studies as well as for specialists in these fields. In addition to chapters focusing on Latin America and predominantly Islamic countries, it contains case studies on Chile, Turkey, India, Kenya, Cameroon and Tanzania.

Jane L. Parpart is Professor of History, International Development Studies and Women's Studies at Dalhousie University, Canada. **Shirin M. Rai** is Reader in Politics at the University of Warwick, UK. **Kathleen Staudt** is Professor of Political Science at the University of Texas at El Paso, USA.

Routledge/Warwick Studies in Globalisation

Edited by Richard Higgott and published in association with the
Centre for the Study of Globalisation and Regionalisation,
University of Warwick

What is globalisation and does it matter? How can we measure it? What are its policy implications? The Centre for the Study of Globalisation and Regionalisation at the University of Warwick is an international site for the study of key questions such as these in the theory and practice of globalisation and regionalisation. Its agenda is avowedly interdisciplinary. The work of the Centre will be showcased in this new series.

This series comprises two strands:

Warwick Studies in Globalisation addresses the needs of students and teachers, and the titles will be published in hardback and paperback. Titles include:

Globalisation and the Asia-Pacific
Contested Territories
Edited by Kris Olds, Peter Dicken, Philip F. Kelly,
Lily Kong and Henry Wai-chung Yeung

Regulating the Global Information Society
Edited by Christopher Marsden

Banking on Knowledge
The Genesis of the Global Development
Network
Edited by Diane Stone

Historical Materialism and Globalisation
Essays on Continuity and Change
Edited by Hazel Smith and Mark Rupert

Civil Society and Global Finance
Edited by Jan Aart Scholte with Albrecht Schnabel

Towards a Global Polity
Edited by Morten Ougaard and Richard Higgott

New Regionalisms in the Global Political Economy
Theories and Cases
Edited by Shaun Breslin, Christopher W. Hughes,
Nicola Phillips and Ben Rosamond

Routledge/Warwick Studies in Globalisation is a forum for innovative new research intended for a high-level specialist readership, and the titles will be available in hardback only. Titles include:

1 Non-State Actors and Authority in the Global System
Edited by Richard Higgott, Geoffrey Underhill and
Andreas Bieler

2 Globalisation and Enlargement of the European Union
Austrian and Swedish Social Forces in the
Struggle over Membership
Andreas Bieler

3 Rethinking Empowerment
Gender and Development in a
Global/Local World
Edited by Jane L. Parpart, Shirin M. Rai and
Kathleen Staudt

4 Globalising Intellectual Property Rights
The TRIPs Agreement
Duncan Matthews

Rethinking Empowerment

Gender and development in a global/local world

**Edited by
Jane L. Parpart, Shirin M. Rai
and Kathleen Staudt**

London and New York

First published 2002
by Routledge
2 Park Square, Milton Park, Abingdon, Oxon, OX14 4RN

Simultaneously published in the USA and Canada
by Routledge
270 Madison Ave, New York NY 10016

Routledge is an imprint of the Taylor & Francis Group

Transferred to Digital Printing 2006

Selection and editorial material © 2002 Jane L. Parpart, Shirin M. Rai
and Kathleen Staudt
Individual chapters © 2002 the contributors

Typeset in Baskerville by Taylor & Francis Books Ltd

British Library Cataloguing in Publication Data
A catalogue record for this book is available from the British Library

Library of Congress Cataloging in Publication Data
A catalog record for this book has been requested

ISBN 0–415–27769–8

Contents

Contributors

Shaheen Sardar Ali is Professor, Faculty of Law, University of Peshawar, Pakistan and Reader, School of Law, University of Warwick, UK. Currently, she is Minister for Health, Population, Welfare and Women's Development, Government of the North West Frontier Province of Pakistan. She is Chairperson of the National Commission on Women in Pakistan. She has an LLM and a PhD in international human rights law from the University of Hull, UK. Her areas of research and publication include Islamic law, gender issues, human rights and international law, minority rights and child rights. Her recent book, published by Kluwer Law International, is entitled *Gender and Human Rights in Islam and International Law: Equal before Allah; Unequal before Man?*.

Pauline Gardiner Barber is Associate Professor of Social Anthropology, Women's Studies and International Development Studies at Dalhousie University, Canada. Dr Gardiner Barber's research explores issues of culture and political economy, expressed locally and in globalizing forms. Her published work discusses livelihoods, culture and class politics in industrial Cape Breton and the Philippines. She has been involved in gender and development projects in relation to sustainable livelihoods, primarily in the Philippines and Indonesia. She is currently researching the discursive and social class implications of Philippine gendered labour migration, transnationalism and diaspora. She is writing a monograph entitled: *No/Maids: Silent Subjects of Philippine Migration*.

Marella Bodur is currently a doctoral candidate and a sessional lecturer in the Department of Political Science at Carleton University, Canada. She received her BA in English Language and Literature and her MA in Political Science and International Relations from Boğaziçi University, Istanbul, Turkey. Her main research interests are gender and politics in the Middle East and the relationship between social movements, feminism and democracy. She is currently completing her dissertation on women's movements and democracy in Turkey.

Vandana Desai is Lecturer in Development Studies at the Department of Geography, Royal Holloway, University of London. She is director for the Masters course on 'The Geography of Third World Development'. She has carried out research on a wide spectrum of NGO activities. She is currently interested in the subtle strategies adopted by women to cope with global restructuring and the formation of informal networks and their impact on the dynamics of household relations. She has published *Community Participation and Slum Housing: A Study of Bombay* (1995) and the *Companion to Development Studies* (2001) (Arnold Publications).

Susan Franceschet currently teaches political science at Acadia University in Nova Scotia, Canada. She recently received her PhD in Political Science from Carleton University. Her dissertation explores the changing patterns of women's politics in Chile in the context of democratisation. She has published an article on this work in the *International Feminist Journal of Politics*.

Josephine Lairap-Fonderson is currently a research fellow at the University of Amsterdam's Department of Political Science. She is working on her PhD dissertation on 'Micro credit and women's empowerment in Kenya and Cameroon'.

Jane L. Parpart is Professor of History, International Development Studies and Women's Studies at Dalhousie University, Canada. She has had extensive experience with gender and development issues in Asia and Africa. Her primary interest is the connection between development theorizing, gender issues and development theory and practice, along with a long-standing interest in urban problems in Africa, particularly in regard to gender and class. She is currently working on a study of the middle class in Bulawayo, Zimbabwe, especially notions of modernity, progress and development. She has published *Feminism/Postmodernism/Development* (Routledge, 1995) with co-editor, Marianne Marchand, and *The 'Man' Question in International Relations* (Westview, 1998) with co-editor, Marysia Zalewski.

Reena Patel is Lecturer at the School of Law, University of Warwick, UK. She teaches in the areas of gender and law, and comparative perspectives on gender, law and development. Her doctoral thesis explores women's land rights in India, to be published as *Legal Entitlements, Perceptions and Women's Access to Land in Rural India* (forthcoming). Her research interests lie within the area of gender, law and development.

Shirin M. Rai is Reader in the Department of Politics and International Studies at the University of Warwick. Her research interests are in the area of feminist politics, democratisation, globalisation and development studies. She has written extensively on issues of gender, governance and democratisation. Her relevant publications include (all as co-editor): *Women in the Face of Change: Soviet Union, Eastern Europe and China* (Routledge, 1992); *Women and the State* (Taylor & Francis, 1996); and *Global Social Movements* (Macmillan, 2000). She has also written two books and several articles on Chinese politics. Her latest monograph is *Gender and the Political Economy of Development* (Polity Press, 2002). She is series editor (with Wyn Grant) for Perspectives on Democratization with Manchester University Press.

Lisa Ann Richey is Researcher at the Centre for Development Research in Copenhagen, Denmark. She was a post-doctoral Fellow at Harvard University where she carried out research in the Kilimanjaro Region of Tanzania, examining the relationship between gender, household wealth, meanings of modernity and perceptions and use of family planning. This research followed upon her PhD dissertation on family planning and population policy in Tanzania, received in 1999 from the University of North Carolina at Chapel Hill. She is currently researching comparative population issues in Uganda and Tanzania. She also teaches on the relationship between donor priorities, international discourse on gender and development, and local-level interventions in Africa at the Centre of African Studies, Copenhagen University.

Kathleen Staudt is Professor of Political Science at the University of Texas at El Paso. She is Faculty Co-ordinator for the Institute for Community-Based Teaching and Research, and Director of the Center for Civic Engagement. She is a scholar-activist, is involved in various community organisations (including cross-border organisations) and has published eleven books and many articles and chapters. These include, among others, *Policy, Politics and Gender* (Kumarian Press, 1998) and the edited collection *Women, International Development and Politics: The Bureaucratic Mire* (Temple, 1997).

Nelly P. Stromquist (PhD Stanford University) is Professor of International Development Education at the University of Southern California. She has considerable experience in formal and non-formal education, particularly in Latin America and West Africa. Her research interests focus on issues of gender equity, educational policies and practices and adult literacy – themes that she examines from a critical theory perspective. She has published widely; her most recent works include authoring *Literacy for Citizenship: Gender and Grassroots in Brazil* (SUNY, 1997), editing *Women in the Third World: An Encyclopedia of Contemporary Issues* (Garland, 1998) and co-editing (with Michael Basile) *Politics of Educational Innovations in Developing Countries* (Garland, 1999).

Gillian Youngs is an international political economist and has taught in the UK and Hong Kong. She currently lectures at the Centre for Mass Communication Research, University of Leicester, UK. Her publications include *International Relations in a Global Age: A Conceptual Challenge* (Polity Press, 1999) and the edited collection *Political Economy, Power and the Body: Global Perspectives* (Macmillan, 2000). She has published on concepts and theories of globalisation, feminist approaches to and women's use of the Internet in international contexts, and linkages between technological and cultural processes. Her practice-based research has included involvement in the UNESCO/Society for International Development Women on the Net project. She is co-editor of *International Feminist Journal of Politics* and associate editor of *Development*.

Acknowledgements

This book has been in the making for almost four years. Over this period many conversations have been had, via new and old technology, and over dinners, lunches and teas; conversations that have no doubt strengthened the book, but also developed our ideas, and clarified some of our doubts. Working in three different countries with different work schedules, teaching and research commitments and deadlines, all three of us have managed to work closely together with each other, and also with our contributors.

We would like to thank Richard Higgott and the Centre for the Study of Globalisation and Regionalisation for funding a workshop in 1998 on Gender and Empowerment that built on the panel organised by Jane on the same theme at the International Studies Association Conference in Toronto in 1997. Both the workshop and the panel helped us to identify the issues that we wished to see discussed in the book.

All of us would like to thank our contributors for the work they have put into their chapters and for their patience with us as we have struggled to put the book together. We hope they will agree that the book is stronger for the revisions. From all the chapters we learnt a great deal, as is reflected in the introduction. We would also like to thank Susan Rolston for doing such a wonderful job of the final editing work and for pursuing each missing reference with determination tempered with good humour. Many thanks to the Routledge production staff and to the politics and international studies section, particularly Heidi Bagtazo and her assistant, Grace McInnes. Many thanks also to our external reviewer, who provided constructive suggestions and encouraging support for the concept and the book.

Jane would like to thank the many colleagues around the world who have contributed to her thinking on gender and empowerment, particularly participatory approaches to empowerment. The chapter on PRA has been presented in such diverse places as Uganda, Denmark, South Africa and Trinidad as well as Canada. It has benefited from close scrutiny, critical comments and suggestions for improvements, not only from fellow academics but also from practitioners (including the growing number of people who manage to do both). She is particularly grateful to Diana Rivington at CIDA and Neeru Shrestha at the International Development Research Centre in Ottawa for arranging stimulating meetings with their colleagues. She would also like to thank friends and colleagues from Dalhousie University, Stellenbosch University, the University of Zimbabwe, Aalborg University and the University of Copenhagen for their support and suggestions. Above all, she is grateful to Kathy and Shirin for their helpful and insightful comments, their ongoing friendship and unstinting support. Finally, Jane would like to thank her husband, Tim Shaw, for his support and patience, and their four children, Laura, Lee, Amanda and Ben and their spouses/partners, for reminding her that family, as well as work, is essential to human happiness.

Kathy would like to thank her good colleagues over many years, Jane and Shirin, for their friendship and consistent analytic attention to gender and class. She also thanks her children, Mosi and Asha, for reminding her about the important things in life. She is grateful to her institution and to her transnational regional community for the many opportunities to act strategically for change. Community partners ALWAYS provide 'reality checks' for non-grounded academic thinking and writing.

Shirin would like to thank Jane and Kathy for all the work they put in, especially toward the end of the project, when she was immersed in other work, and for all that she learnt from such professional and supportive friends. To work with the editors of *Women and the State in Africa* has been a dream come true! She also thanks her family – Jeremy Roche, and Arjun and Sean Rai-Roche – and friends, and thanks her students for conversations, all of which continue to enrich her life and her thinking.

This has been a complex and challenging project. Indeed, at points we all wondered if we would manage to succeed. We have, and are extremely grateful to have participated in such a fruitful collaboration and are proud of the result.

JP, SR, KS
2001

Abbreviations

ACHR	American Covenant on Human Rights
AMM	Annapurna Mahila Mandal – grassroots NGO in India
ASEAN	Association of Southeast Asian Nations
BERDSCO	Benevolent Community Education and Rural Development Society (Cameroon)
CBD	Community Based Distribution (Tanzania)
CEAAL	Council for Adult Education in Latin America
CEDAW UN	Convention on the Elimination of All Forms of Discrimination against Women
CIC	Grupo Iniciativo Chile – women's NGO network in Chile
CIDEM	Centros de Información de los Derechos de la Mujer – Chilean women's rights information centres
CPD	Concertación por la Democracia – Chilean political party
CSW	United Nations Committee on the Status of Women
CWDS	Centre for Women's Development Studies (India)
DAWN	Development Alternatives with Women for a New Era
DGIS	Directorate General of International Co-operation in the Netherlands
ECHR	European Convention on Human Rights and Fundamental Freedoms
EZ	Empowerment Zones
GAD	Gender and Development
GATE	Girls' Access to Education Project (Nepal)
GEM	Gender Empowerment Measure
HSA	Hindu Succession Act (India)
HDI	Human Development Index
HDR	UNDP Human Development Reports
HUD	Housing and Urban Development (US)
ICCPR	International Covenant on Civil and Political Rights
ICESCR	International Covenant on Economic, Social and Cultural Rights
ICPD	The International Conference on Population and Development (Cairo 1994)
ICT	Information and communication technologies

ILO	International Labour Organization
IMF	International Monetary Fund
INSTRAW	International Research and Training Institute for the Advancement of Women
IPPF	International Planned Parenthood Federation
KAD-ER	The Association for Support and Training of Women (Istanbul)
KSSGM	Directorate General on the Status and Problems of Women (Turkey)
KWFT	Kenyan Women Finance Trust
NAFTA	North American Free Trade Agreement
NCW	National Commission for Women (India)
NGO	Non-governmental organization
NORAD	Norwegian Agency for Development Co-operation
OIC	Organization of Islamic Conference
OVC	Overseas Contract Workers
PRA	Participatory Rural Appraisal
PRI	Panchayati Raj Institutions – (Indian local government institutions)
PRODEMU	Fundación para la Promoción y Desarrollo de la Mujer – to promote women's leadership skills in Chile
REPEM	Women's Education Network
ROSCA	Rotating savings and credit association
SAP	Structural Adjustment Programme
SERNAM	Servicio Nacional de la Mujer – state agency for improving women's position in Chile
SEWA	Self-employed Women Association (India)
SID	Society for International Development
SIDA	Swedish International Development Authority
SPARC	Society for the Promotion of Area Resource Centres (India)
TAWMA	Tanzanian Women's Media Association
UDHR	Universal Declaration of Human Rights
UIDHR	Universal Islamic Declaration of Human Rights
UMATI	Uzazi na Malezi Bora Tanzania
UN	United Nations
UN/DAW	United Nations Division for the Advancement of Women
UNDP	United Nations Development Programme
UNESCO	United Nations Educational, Scientific and Cultural Organization
UNICEF	United Nations International Children's Fund
UNIFEM	United Nations Voluntary Fund for Women
UNRISD	United Nations Research Institute for Social Development
USAID	United States Agency for International Development
WDC	Women's Development Collective (Malaysia)
WED	Women in Enterprise Development

WEEL	Women's Economic Empowerment and Literacy Project (Nepal)
WEP	Women's Employment Promotion Project
WID	Women in Development
WoN	Women on the Net Project (UNESCO)
WTO	World Trade Organization
WWB	Women's World Banking

Part I
Theory and praxis

1 Rethinking em(power)ment, gender and development

An introduction

Jane L. Parpart, Shirin M. Rai and Kathleen Staudt

Empowerment has become a popular, largely unquestioned 'good' aspired to by such diverse and contradictory institutions as the World Bank, Oxfam and many more radical non-government organizations (NGOs). Initially, the term was most commonly associated with alternative approaches to development, with their concern for local, grassroots community-based movements and initiatives, and their growing disenchantment with mainstream, top-down approaches to development. More recently, empowerment has been adopted by mainstream development agencies as well, albeit more to improve productivity within the status quo than to foster social transformation. Empowerment has thus become a 'motherhood' term, comfortable and unquestionable, something very different institutions and practices seem to be able to agree on. Yet this very agreement raises important questions. Why is empowerment acceptable to such disparate bedfellows? What can empowerment mean if it is the watchword of such different and often conflicting development approaches and institutions? How can such a fluid, poorly defined term address issues of women's empowerment in a still largely male dominated world?

We are not the only scholars raising these questions. Empowerment, especially for women, has been on the minds of a number of scholars and practitioners, most notably Haleh Afshar (1998), Jo Rowlands (1997), Naila Kabeer (1994) and Srilatha Batliwala (1994). However, most interrogations of the term have focused on ways to improve its effectiveness at the local level. The emphasis has been on grassroots, participatory methods and their empowerment potential for the 'poorest of the poor' (especially women). While a welcome antidote to the development community's long-standing preference for state-led, top-down development, we believe this focus on the local also has profound limitations. In particular, it tends to underplay or ignore the impact of global and national forces on prospects for poor people's (especially women's) empowerment, and encourages a rather romantic equation between empowerment, inclusion and voice that papers over the complexities of em(power)ment, both as a process and a goal.

We propose a new approach to women's empowerment, focusing on four issues. First, since even the most marginalized, impoverished communities are affected by global and national forces, we believe empowerment must be analysed in global and national as well as local terms. Global forces, whether economic, political or cultural, are both marginalizing some and enhancing the power of others. But no one is left untouched. Moreover, this is a highly gendered process. To ignore the multilevel, interrelated character of these struggles, even in poor, marginalized communities, is to misunderstand empowerment in our increasingly interconnected global/local world.

Second, understanding and facilitating women's empowerment requires a more nuanced analysis of power. Empowerment is not simply the ability to exert *power over* people and resources. Drawing on Foucault's writings, we argue that empowerment involves the exercise rather than possession of power. This approach reminds us that empowerment cannot transcend power relations; it is enmeshed in relations of power at all levels of society. At the same time, such an analysis allows us to open up development praxis to scrutiny by feminist theories of power in order to explore issues of structure and agency. In agreement with Rowlands, we believe empowerment must be understood as including both individual conscientization (*power within*) as well as the ability to work collectively, which can lead to politicized *power with* others, which provides the *power to* bring about change.

Third, although empowerment is a process whereby women and men experience as well as challenge and subvert power relationships, it takes place in institutional, material and discursive contexts. Whether gaining skills, developing consciousness or making decisions, individual empowerment takes place within the structural constraints of institutions and discursive practices. Groups become empowered through collective action, but that action is enabled or constrained by the structures of power that they encounter. We believe much closer attention must be paid to the broad political and economic structures, cultural assumptions and discourses, notions of human rights, laws and practices in which women and men seek to survive and even flourish in marginalized communities around the world.

Finally, we believe empowerment is both a process and an outcome. It is a process in that it is fluid, often unpredictable, and requires attention to the specificities of struggles over time and place. Empowerment can also be seen as an outcome that can be measured against expected accomplishments. Attempts to measure outcomes are important as a means for keeping development practitioners and policy-makers honest. At the same time, we caution against a too ready assumption that the achievement of stated goals is proof of individual or group empowerment (see Kabeer 1999).

Rethinking Empowerment brings together scholar/activists who are concerned with women's empowerment but believe it can only be understood and facilitated if we bring these four dimensions into both analysis and praxis. To that end, several chapters address the way new social movements and multilateral institutions use and abuse the concept and practice of empowerment. They remind us that empowerment approaches are always embedded in institutional structures and must be understood at that level. At the same time, certain development practices and issues have become associated with the empowerment approach, most notably education, micro credit, grassroots participatory approaches, land rights and representation. A number of chapters explore these 'solutions', arguing against an uncritical acceptance of their empowerment potential. They call for a careful, contextual analysis framed in the broad forces at play in national, regional and global contexts. Finally, although all chapters link the global, national and the local, several authors take up the challenge of thinking about the empowerment potential of cyberspace, global migration patterns and an increasingly international, proactive civil society.

Empowerment and power

In order to think about em(power)ment in new ways, we need to explore its diverse and complex history. While Paulo Freire (1973) did not use the term, his emphasis on education as a means for conscientizing and inspiring individual and group challenges to social inequality provided an important backdrop for social activists concerned with empowering the poor and marginalized (Stromquist, this volume). Intellectuals and activists in the South, and to a lesser extent the North, drew on Freire and others to expand the concept of empowerment. Social activists concerned with poverty issues saw empowerment as a local, grassroots endeavour, designed to inspire the poor to challenge the status quo. On the other hand, business and personnel managers generally thought of empowerment as a means for improving productivity within established structures. Mainstream development agencies adopted this interpretation in the 1990s, when they too began to use the language of empowerment, participation and people's development. Thus, empowerment seems to fit many shoes.

How can we explain this seeming paradox? How can empowerment have such different meanings and consequences? The explanation may lie in the fluidity of the term 'power'. To empower implies the ability to exert *power over*, to make things happen. It is an action verb that suggests the ability to change the world, to overcome opposition. It has a transformatory sound, an implicit promise of change, often for the better. Consequently, empowerment has often been the watchword of crusaders trying to make the world a better, more equitable place. But this change is often seen as requiring a revolution or, at the very least, fundamental social transformation (Wolf 1999: 4–8; Scott 1990). Others hold a more benign view of power, one that emphasizes the potential for rational discussion and evolutionary change within modern societies. Associated with liberal arguments about modernization and democracy, this approach assumes even marginalized people can bring about change by mobilizing to convince the powerful of the need for change. While apparently different, both perspectives are captured by the notion that power is largely the ability to exert *power over* institutions, resources and people (Held *et al.* 1999).

In order to understand the limitations of these approaches to empowerment and power, we need to explore some of the more nuanced notions of power that have emerged since the 1970s. Steven Lukes rejects the notion that power is simply control over institutions and resources, and argues instead that power is wielded by controlling the agendas and thinking of others (1974: 23–4). Michel Foucault moves the analysis further. Rejecting the notion that power is something held by individuals or groups (and not others), he argues that it permeates society. It is fluid, relational and exists only in the everyday relationships of people, both individually and in institutions. Such power can lead to repressive practices that are expressed in disciplined bodies, actions and thoughts/discourses. While much of Foucault's work has centred on the disciplinary, disempowering nature of modern power, he recognizes that relations of power inspire resistance as well (Foucault 1979, 1991; McNay 1992). In this regard, we find Akhil Gupta and James Ferguson's reading of Foucault useful, especially their argument that Foucault did not see resistance 'in a disembodied duel with power' (1997: 19), but rather as a complex interaction. People are empowered and changed through resisting disciplinary power relations, but this very action/agency may also strengthen their incorporation into the status quo. While this analysis illuminates the workings of power (and empowerment) at the individual and institutional level, Foucault has less to say about the impact of larger political and economic structures. Moreover, his analysis is relentlessly European and male-focused. A more feminist and global analysis is required if we are to rethink women's empowerment in comparative perspective.

Since the 1980s, feminists have in fact contributed important insight to these debates. Most feminists have started from querying the concept of power as simply *power over* people and resources. An arena of politics that has been particularly important for understanding the concept of public power as *power over* has been that of the state. Feminist scholars have addressed this issue in terms of both the institutional power of the state to privilege some (male) interests over other (female) ones and its capacity to maintain gender inequalities (MacKinnon 1987). They have also examined the question of state power in the context of the state's monopoly of violence and its claim to the legitimate use of this violence. Third World feminists in particular have sought to engage with state-based resources and agencies, and to theorise from their experiences of such engagements (Parpart and Staudt 1989; Agnihotri and Mazumdar 1995; Rai and Lievesley 1996). Attempting to address some of the differences among feminist analyses of state-based power, Tetreault, among others, has sought to explore whether state/institutions can become 'authorised' as opposed to being in power by demonstrating 'over and over' the 'hard resources' of 'expertise, eloquence, judgement and competence' (Tetreault and Teske 2000: 276). In doing so she has sought to reinforce Hannah Arendt's distinction between power and authority, and ultimately a feminist vision of public power. Others have rejected the domain of state power, seeing it as unimportant to feminist politics (Allen 1990). Participation in institutional and public political life is therefore empowering for some and disempowering for others.

Those who found the preoccupations with the state unsatisfactory and disempowering have found Foucauldian theory useful for challenging the dominant assumption that power is a possession exercised over others within familiar boundaries of state, law or class. They have been attracted to his focus on bodies as sites of power and to his notion of power as fluid, relational and embedded in struggles over meanings/discourses (Hekman 1996). Others have used the expanded boundaries of power that Foucauldian thought opens up to query the concept of empowerment itself. Anna Yeatman, for example, worries that the term is reproducing the hierarchy between the powerful protector (the state, the elite) and the powerless (i.e. women, children and the poor), who are seen as helpless, passive and needy. She would rather use the term 'empowering', which is interchangeable with 'capacitating' or 'enabling' (1999). Other feminists argue that Foucault's vision of power encourages a relativist position where all transformative politics become suspect (Fraser 1989; Hartsock 1990).

Individual and collective participation has, as noted above, been an important foundational concept for analysing empowerment. Participation in challenges to hegemonic systems and discourses has often inspired both greater self-understanding and political action in women's private and public lives. Involvement in the politics of subversion is thus empowering in itself, even if it fails to transform immediately dominant power relations. As Patricia Hill Collins points out, 'change can also occur in the private, personal space of an individual woman's consciousness. Equally fundamental, this type of change is also empowering' (1991: 111). However, feminist scholars have also worried about the differential burdens of participation (Phillips 1999). Working-class women and women from some ethnic and religious groups do not have the resources of time and money to be empowered through participation in collective action, or the costs of their participation is disproportionately high. From a different perspective Third World and black feminist scholars and activists have also reminded us that individual conscientization does not necessarily lead to progressive politics. The language of women's empowerment has been used by right-wing political groups and parties to inspire Hindu women to resist the 'pseudo-secularism' of the male, Westernized elites who have granted Muslim and other minorities 'concessions' not available to the Hindu majority (Butalia and Sarkar 1996). While this rhetoric has inspired Hindu women's agency in defence of the *dharma* (faith), such empowerment obviously poses important questions for other communities, as well as for Hindu women who do not subscribe to this interpretation of empowerment.

We believe these different approaches/arguments need to, and can, be brought together if we are to think about empowerment in new ways. Foucault's exposition of power allows us to move away from more traditional notions of power as the ability to exert *power over* structures, people and resource. It reminds us that power is fluid, relational and connected to control over discourses/knowledge. It is therefore an important insight for feminist analyses of power and empowerment. However, we would also insist upon focusing on the relationship between structures and agency, of challenge and transformation which transcend the bounds of discursive 'normality' (see also Deveaux 1996: 230–7). This allows feminists to make judgements about the nature of their experience of structures and discourses of power, and their own political judgements and actions. It also allows us to incorporate notions of power that recognize the importance of individual consciousness/understanding (*power within*), and its importance for collective action (*power with*) that can organize and exert *power to* challenge gender hierarchies and improve women's lives (see also Rowlands 1997: 13). These insights inform our analysis of empowerment, power and gender as it relates both to broad questions of development and gender equality, and to specific empowerment interventions. For this, we must explore the intersection between development, power and empowerment, both in theory and practice.

Empowerment, power and development

Various interpretations of power and empowerment have influenced the thinking and practice of development practitioners and theorists. The development enterprise was introduced in the 1940s as a very top-down affair. It was seen as a technical problem that could be solved by transferring Northern knowledge to Southern clients. This was regarded as an unproblematic, noble endeavour. By the 1970s, however, the failure of many development projects inspired critiques, most notably from South America. These scholars accused Northern capital of deliberately marginalizing the South, of creating dependency to ensure a source of raw materials and markets for their manufactured goods. They called for self-reliance and the transformation of the world system (Amin 1974; Wallerstein 1979). While holding different conceptions of capital, both perspectives agree that *power* is defined by control *over* resources, people and institutions.

More recent critiques have retained this critical stance towards the Northern development establishment, but emphasize the power of development discourse to define development as a technical 'problem' requiring intervention by Northern expertise. This process, they argue, has effectively silenced the voices and knowledge of marginalized peoples around the world. They call for a new approach, one based on equitable and respectful partnership and collaboration between the North and the South, with due attention to local knowledge and accumulated wisdom in the periphery (Crush 1995; Escobar 1995; Friedmann 1992). Some critics of this approach, while acknowledging the power of discourse, remind us that even the apparently 'powerless' can sometimes turn development discourse to their own ends, using it as a basis for their demands (Cooper and Packard 1997). For both critiques, the relationship between structure, discourse and agency is critically important – though conceived of differently.

These critiques have found allies in the work of small-scale alternative development organizations, most notably NGOs that take pride in working outside and even challenging 'the system'. These organizations have tended to focus on local communities and have been deeply influenced by the participatory, people-first approach to development of Robert Chambers (1997). His set of practical, assessable methods for grassroots, participatory development, characterized as participatory rural appraisal (PRA), has become the staple methodology for alternative development practitioners (see Parpart, this volume). Understandably this methodology and approach initially found little support among established development agencies with their government-to-government agreements and their concern to protect established power structures.

At the level of individual development, Amartya Sen's work on human capabilities stresses empowerment as both a means and an end. It is a process of developing individual capacities through gaining education and skills in order to empower individuals to fight for a better quality of life (1990, 1995). Sen sees poverty as an indication of the inability of people to meet their basic needs, whether physical or more intangible, through participation, empowerment and community life (Dreze and Sen 1989). Sen criticizes development economics for emphasizing quantity, such as longevity, rather than the quality of lives led (Crocker 1995: 156). He points out that women in particular face social as well as physical problems and that 'the remedies sought have to take note of the nature of the constraints involved and extent to which they can be removed' (Dreze and Sen 1989: 44). While one may quarrel with Sen's lack of attention to the political processes required for equitable resource distribution, he raises some important issues for the study of empowerment. However, he too assumes that human empowerment is best carried out at the local communities where most people live their lives (Rai, 2002). Though Sen's focus on capabilities provides a framework for the study of empowerment, feminists need to be wary of his argument about the universal right to development and his lack of attention to the political processes required for equitable resource distribution that could lead to general empowerment.

While mainstream development agencies remained, for the most part, rather sceptical of these arguments, their many failures have led some practitioners to question top-down, state-led development practice. Neo-liberal sympathisers have taken these failures as proof of the need to reduce the size and function of the state, leaving development to the wisdom of market forces. This has been argued with increasing force as the globalization of world markets reduces the relevance of states around the world (Hoogvelt 1997). At the same time, growing doubts about state capacity and commitment to development goals in the South have led to demands for good governance, democracy and economic liberalization. These demands are seen as requiring institutional reform based on accountability, democracy and grassroots participation in governance, including recognition of the importance of 'listening to and learning from the poor' (World Bank 1999: 153). In their efforts to operationalize these goals, mainstream development agencies have adopted many of the techniques of alternative development practices. The language of participation and empowerment has entered mainstream development discourse. Increasingly projects must express sensitivity to community concerns and a willingness to work with the poor. Even the current preoccupation with knowledge-based development is often cast in terms of participation, empowerment and partnership within specific, small-scale communities (Rugh and Bossert 1998; World Bank 1998). Thus, the language of empowerment, whatever the development perspective, remains largely rooted in the local – it is seen as the business of grassroots, small-scale communities. This is largely true for considerations of women's empowerment as well.

Empowerment, gender and development

Scholars and activists concerned with women, gender and development have both contributed to and been influenced by these debates. Development initially was a largely gender-blind endeavour, but by the 1970s some practitioners had recognized the need to help women, albeit largely within the status quo. The limitations of this approach inspired a shift to gender in the 1980s, and a growing awareness that deeply held attitudes about femininity and masculinity influenced gender relations and reinforced women's subordination. This gender and development (GAD) approach highlighted the role of culture as well as socio-economic inequalities in women's subordination (Young 1993; Sen and Grown 1988), but remained largely captured by Western notions of development, with their focus on economic solutions to development problems (Hirshman 1995).

By the late 1980s, activists and theorists from the South, and to a lesser extent from the North, began to discuss the need for a new approach, one that highlights the need for women to become empowered so they can challenge patriarchal and political-economic inequalities. Gita Sen and Caren Grown introduced the term in their landmark book, *Development, Crises and Alternative Visions: Third World Women's Perspectives* (1988). They offered a vision of empowerment rooted in a commitment to collective action growing out of the specific problems and contexts facing women (and men) in the South, whether economic, political or cultural. While rather utopian in tone, the book calls for a collective vision, a set of strategies and new methods for mobilizing political will, empowering women (and poor men) and transforming society. The authors put considerable faith in the transformative potential of 'political mobilization, legal changes, consciousness raising, and popular education' (1988: 87). Caroline Moser (1989, 1993) expanded on the term, particularly in regard to development planning, and did much to publicize its importance and its international roots.

Writings on empowerment and gender as an approach to development have continued to emerge in the alternative development literature, especially from the South. In 1994, for example, Srilatha Batliwala warned that 'empowerment', which had virtually replaced terms such as poverty alleviation, welfare and community participation, was in danger of losing its transformative edge. She called for a more precise understanding of both power and empowerment, one that sees power 'as control over material assets, intellectual resources, and ideology' (1994: 129). For Batliwala, empowerment is 'the process of challenging existing power relations, and of gaining greater control over the sources of power' (1994: 130). It requires political action and collective assault on cultural as well as national and community power structures that oppress women and some men. Thus, while acknowledging the need to improve the lives of grassroots women, Batliwala insists that women's empowerment must include transformative political action as well.

Naila Kabeer (1994) also insists on the centrality of empowerment for the struggle to achieve gender equality. Drawing on the work of Lukes (1974), she criticizes the liberal and Marxist emphases on *power over* resources, institutions and decision-making, adding Lukes's (1974) argument that power also consists of being able to control discussions/discourses and agendas. She argues, however, for a more feminist approach to power, one that emphasizes the transformative potential of *power within*. This power is rooted in self-understanding that can inspire women (and some men) to recognize and challenge gender inequality in the home and the community (1994: 224–9). Like Batliwala, she emphasizes collective, grassroots participatory action – the *power to* work *with* others 'to control resources, to determine agendas and to make decisions' (1994: 229). More concerned with action than theory, she continues to explore practical, measurable ways to empower women, especially at the local level (Kabeer 1999).

Jo Rowlands (1997, 1998) brings a broader analytical perspective to the discussion of gender and empowerment. Drawing on Foucault and feminist writings, she argues that 'empowerment is more than participation in decision-making; it must also include the processes that lead people to perceive themselves as able and entitled to make decisions' (1997: 14). It is personal, relational and collective. She recognizes that empowerment is not just a gender issue but also a development issue affecting women and men. While acknowledging the complexity and difficulties of empowerment as a concept and a practice, she remains convinced that the key to empowerment lies in mobilizing marginalized people, especially women. She cautions, however, that empowerment is a process rather than an end product, neither easily defined nor measured. At the same time, she believes 'there is a core to the empowerment process ... which consists of increases in self-confidence and self-esteem, a sense of agency and of "self" in a wider context, and a sense of *dignidad* (being worthy of having a right to respect from others)' (1997: 129–30).

Initially, mainstream development agencies concerned with women ignored the language of empowerment, but as top-down development failed to alleviate poverty in the 1990s, especially among women, the discourse began to change. Empowerment entered the lexicon of mainstream women/gender and development discourse. For example, the Beijing Platform for Action states emphatically that women's empowerment is 'fundamental for the achievement of equality, development and peace' (UN 1996: para.13). The Canadian International Development Agency's (CIDA) *Policy on Gender Equality* includes women's empowerment as one of the eight guiding principles for its policy goals (1999). While mainstream development agencies generally emphasize the reformative rather than the transformative nature of empowerment (World Bank 1995), at the level of discourse, both alternative development practitioners and mainstream empowerment advocates increasingly use the language of empowerment when discussing women/gender and development, albeit largely within the rubric of small-scale, grassroots community development (Friedmann 1992; Craig and Mayo 1995).

This seeming congruence of policy and approach obscures the difficulties faced by those trying to understand, implement and measure women's empowerment. While the very instability of the term has its advantages – for empowerment varies by context and condition – that same fluidity impedes our understanding and implementation of empowerment. Some practitioners and scholars focus on personal empowerment. Indeed, Caroline Moser places self-reliance and internal strength at the centre of empowerment. For her, empowerment is the ability 'to determine choices in life and to influence the direction of change, through the ability to gain control over crucial material and non-material resources' (1993: 74–5). Others emphasize collective empowerment, noting the fragility of individual efforts (Kabeer 1994). Always concerned with transforming ideals into practice, Moser remains sceptical about the willingness of mainstream development agencies to embrace the grassroots, participatory small-scale methods of the empowerment approach in a meaningful way (1993: 87–99). Moreover, as Kabeer points out, attempts to measure (and direct) empowerment are often based on the assumption that 'we can somehow predict the nature and direction that change is going to assume. In actual fact, human agency is indeterminate and hence unpredictable in a way that is antithetical to requirements of measurement' (1999: 462).

Rethinking Empowerment is in many ways a response to these challenges for we believe the tension between agency and structures, and their interrelationships, lies at the heart of the empowerment debate. While Moser is correct in pointing out that any challenge to structural power will alienate the mainstream development agencies, one also needs to reflect upon how the capacitating/agency of women (and poor men) can be achieved without some transformation of existing power relations. Anne Phillips has addressed this question by pointing out that today few would expect to be able to eliminate (as opposed to ameliorate) structural inequalities embedded in the production regimes of capitalism. The focus of the debate should be on inequality of distribution (1999: 17). Only then can the issue of capacity enhancement be directly linked to redistribution of resources. Negotiations with, and challenges to, the state (and global forces) then become an important part of collective action leading to women's empowerment. This factors in the agency of political actors as much as it pays attention to structural power. David Marquand, for example, argues that only an empowered and active citizenry can make any progress towards social equality (1997: 41). The two aspects need to be held together, sometimes in tension, to understand the nature of change through the politics of collective (and individual) action at all levels of political institutions – local, national and global. Thus, we believe empowerment for women (and men) cannot be understood only at the local level. It requires attention to the specific historical struggles of women and men within the structures and discourses of power operating at micro-, meso- and macro-levels.

Empowerment: local, national and global

While the focus on the local remains central to most advocates of empowerment, some members of the development studies community have become increasingly concerned with the role of national and global politics (Stiles 2000). We believe these discussions need to be brought together. The growing power of global corporate and financial forces in an increasingly unequal world has inspired new thinking about potential solutions to the disempowerment and marginalization of peoples around the world. Some see globalization as a potential tool for empowerment. From this perspective, globalization and economic liberalization go hand in hand, providing benefits for women, the poor and the world; the uneven, gendered character of much globalization is rarely acknowledged (Held *et al.* 1999). A more nuanced view of globalization acknowledges the fact that free trade and global shifts in productivity have led to casualization and feminization of certain labour sectors, resulting in additional burdens on women and tensions within the family for women as gender relations get reconfigured. However, it also points to the opening of opportunities for women, albeit often affected by race and class. Professional women inhabiting the world of international finance or involved in international bureaucratic machineries are positioned very differently from white Russian women looking to improve their life chances by consenting to become 'catalogue brides', and still more differently from Filipina domestic workers in Canada and elsewhere (Gardiner Barber, this volume). Globally, women own little of the world's property; and therefore tend to be involved in the globalization process through their access to labour markets rather than financial or production markets. They are providers of services, often poorly paid and rarely in control of the huge financial and export flows of global enterprises (Marchand and Runyan 2000).

Yet within the limits of women's opportunities, some possibilities for empowerment exist. We need to analyse the impact of gendered roles for women within markets if we are to understand the possibilities and the challenges facing women in this context. Women's specific positioning in markets poses questions about the nature and functioning of markets, the values and behaviour that they generate and the controls and mechanisms of accountability that are required to participate (Lairap-Fonderson, this volume; Freeman 2001). We also have to know what market factors intensify a consciousness of rights and a willingness to undertake collective and individual actions to improve women's position in the global workforce (Gardiner Barber, Lairap-Fonderson and Desai, this volume). Questions need to be raised about how women can be empowered to take advantage of the markets they can access, or to push open the doors of those they cannot.

If globalization is about markets, it is also about space. James Rosenau, for example, writes of 'globalization as boundary-eroding' and 'localization as boundary-strengthening' (1997: 81). On the one hand, new technologies allow the possibility of thinking about the world as one. Some argue that this 'overcoming' of space through communication technology is producing new identities as well as opportunities for men and women (Youngs, this volume). At the same time, technology is spatially located itself – more urban than rural, more accessible for the middle classes than for the poor, and more accessible for men than women. This is not to minimize the importance of these advances, only to caution about the limits of their possibilities. Globalization can also enhance 'boundary-strengthening' when it is perceived as hegemonic cultural domination. As Paul Lubeck argues, the rise of Islamism under globalization can be seen both as a reaction against the dominant political power of the USA, and as an integration of the wider, global Islamic community through communication, travel and trade (2000: 153). For Muslim women, participation in a global community of Islam can be both a problem and an opportunity, as demonstrated by Shaheen Sardar Ali's chapter (this volume). Thus, global/local space raises important questions for thinking about women's empowerment.

A third aspect of the globalization debate is governance, although again this is rarely a gendered discussion. Some 'globalists' argue that the state's regulatory role is being taken over by multilateral organizations. They look to international organizations and legal instruments for solutions, pinning their hopes on the regulatory effect of the United Nations, the World Court and bodies such as the World Trade Organization (WTO), the World Bank and the International Monetary Fund (IMF). However, recent protests at the WTO meeting in Seattle and the World Bank/IMF meeting in Washington reveal a growing scepticism about this option. Although some authors argue that recent protests demonstrate the capacity of citizen activists to reign in global institutions (Liebowitz 2000: 41; Finnegan 2000; Naim 2000; Staudt *et al.* 2001), others believe these global organizations are no longer accountable to citizens of nation states, but more to global civil society.

Increasingly, scholars and activists are looking to the nation state for solutions. In *The Work of Nations*, as Robert Reich points out, the only governance mechanism we have left for corporate nationality is increasingly irrelevant (1992). Nation states, of course, vary markedly in their ability and/or desire either to confront and/or negotiate with global forces, corporations and finance. And within states, considerable variation exists in the degree to which democratic accountability exists to all or most people, who are never monolithically equal in political and power terms. Class, geography and gender are notable factors determining access to and/or experience with state power. Nevertheless, national politics is increasingly seen as a key arena for struggles against poverty and marginalization. Not surprisingly, good governance and the empowerment of citizens and groups so they can ensure responsible governance, is beginning to become a more central issue for some empowerment scholars and activists, including the contributors to this book (see also Stiles 2000; Staudt 1998).

At the same time, it is important to remember that states have historically institutionalized male interests (see, for example, Charlton *et al.* 1989; Parpart and Staudt 1989; Rai and Lievesley 1996). This is reflected in the small numbers of women in decision-making positions in state structures – a mere tenth or less of women legislators is the global norm (UNDP 1995; Staudt 1996). Such minority positioning often constrains women legislators from raising strategic issues for women. Challenges to this situation are being pursued at two levels. First, greater participation of women in national political bodies is argued for as part of the processes of democratization (Rai, this volume). Second, some call for mainstreaming gender in both national and global policy-making and institutional politics (see McBride-Stetson and Mazur 1995; Rai, 2002). Empowerment in this context depends upon the space women are able to create within political structures, as well as the issues they are able to raise (or not) in their own strategic interests. We need much more careful, historically specific analyses of women's attempts to develop political strategies and networks that challenge male power structures and improve state responsiveness to women's issues, both locally and nationally (Cockburn 1999). Globalizing issues of governance, as well as networking globally to challenge hegemonic institutional politics within the local/national space are also critically important elements in the struggles for women's empowerment.

Conclusion

These debates and discussions raise a number of issues that need to be dealt with when considering empowerment, gender and development. One of the key issues underpinning any discussion of empowerment must be a clearer definition/understanding of power. While the authors in this book do not subscribe to a particular definition of power and empowerment, they do reject the simple dichotomy between those who have *power over* people, resources and institutions and those who do not (i.e. the powerless). They all consider the importance of language and meanings, and the need to think about identities and cultural practices when considering women's empowerment. More or less explicitly, the chapters in this collection take the position that women's empowerment requires understanding of the many ways that power can be understood and acted upon, and the importance of incorporating feminist insights into their analysis.

However, the authors approach the question of power in several ways. Kathy Staudt, for example, explores the way official institutions employ discourses of empowerment but often fail to translate them into action. Thus, women's empowerment may have entered the discourse, but it has failed to offer women *power over* those institutions or *power to* demand fundamental change. She calls for collective political action, for *power with* others through politics, as a means for moving empowerment from rhetoric to action. Reena Patel demonstrates how women's lack of economic and political power limits their *power to* use land legislation in order to gain *power over* one of the most critical resources in India, namely land. She believes women will never become empowered until they gain more control over this resource. Marella Bodur and Susan Franceschet highlight the potential empowerment emerging from women's organizations, from the *power* gained by working *with* other women. Others focus on power *within*, on the need for individual empowerment, both of an emotional and material kind. Vandana Desai emphasizes the subtle strategies of informal politics, whereby women seek small but important changes in their personal lives. She points out that triumphs in personal power, *power within*, can lead to individual empowerment and ultimately to involvement in formal political activism, or *power with* and *power to* as well.

Some of the authors draw more explicitly on the feminist theoretical literature about the gendered nature of power. Josephine Lairap-Fonderson uses a Foucauldian framework to explore the empowerment potential (or not) of micro credit projects. While emphasizing the disciplinary and relational character of micro credit, particularly the constraints placed on borrowers through regulations and restrictions of lending institutions, she acknowledges its potential for resistance as well. Jane Parpart calls for integrating attention to discourse, knowledge and power into the thinking and methodology of participatory rural appraisal (PRA). Shaheen Sardar Ali reminds us that an insistence upon universal rights for women might not be in the best interests of Muslim women. As Muslim states, for example, are more apt to support demands for equity (to be equal within differences) than equality, which suggests sameness, women in these states need to take this into account when strategising about empowerment and rights. Thus, cultural practices, and disputes over meanings/discourses, are central for considering women's em(power)ment. Legal instruments, even international legal instruments, that ignore this fact are no more apt to empower women than development projects and policies framed around Northern conceptions of gender and development.

Second, while the local is important as a focus for discussions on empowerment, the chapters in this book reflect our belief that the local is embedded in the global and national, and vice versa. The interconnectedness of the three levels provides a framework for our interrogation of empowerment, gender and development. The chapters take up this argument from different positions. Desai and Parpart focus on the local. Richey and Lairap-Fonderson evaluate the empowerment potential (or lack) of some national, but also local, development projects. Rai examines the potential of national political representation for women's empowerment, while Franceschet and Bodur investigate the empowerment potential of women's organizations within nation states. Staudt and Stromquist range widely across continents, but generally focus on relations between nations in their consideration of development institutions and education's empowerment potential. Youngs, Gardiner Barber and Ali adopt a deliberately global perspective, framing their analysis of cyberspace, international migration and international legal covenants in the global/local context we live in. However, these chapters, and the others, connect their analyses to all three levels. The disciplining and disruptive power of national states is, for example, evident in Parpart's chapter on PRA and in Desai's on grassroots NGOs in Bombay. Rai's chapter focuses on the ways in which national debates on women's representations have been influenced by international and local political struggles and discourses. Youngs reminds us that cyberspace cannot be understood unless we remember that travelling in cyberspace requires technology that is situated in space and requires certain resources and expertise.

Gardiner Barber traces the links between international global changes, national economic policies and the daily lived experiences and opportunities of Filipina women. Thus, the dynamic interconnectedness of the three levels is an essential component for evaluating women's empowerment in this collection.

Third, the empowerment literature has focused on consciousness-raising and individual and group action/agency without perhaps paying enough attention to the ways in which institutional structures and politics frame, constrain and enable these activities. We believe the institutional, material and discursive framework within which individual and group agency can develop must be taken seriously. This does not mean that the process of implementing 'empowerment' policies and projects, and the agency involved, is less important. It does, however, point to the need to situate individual and group action/agency within the material, political and discursive structures in which it operates. Thus, the book calls for careful, historically situated analyses of women's struggles to gain power in a world rarely of their own choosing.

All of the chapters take up this challenge, albeit often in somewhat different ways. Stromquist suggests that formal educational institutions do not offer women as much potential for empowerment as do autonomous women's organizations committed to women's empowerment. Thus, for her, participation and consciousness-raising are often more important than institutional structures for determining women's agency. However, Rai's study of women's political representation points to the importance of working within institutional politics while remaining aware of the limitations inherent in working within male-dominated political bodies. Desai reminds us of the importance of individual struggles through informal politics, and the structural and cultural constraints within which these take place. The issue of cultural constraints and the impact of liberalizing economies on women's options – political, economic and social – is illustrated in several chapters including those by Patel, Ali, Gardiner Barber and Lairap-Fonderson.

Finally, we see empowerment to be as much a process as an outcome. At times the two are indistinguishable; at others, outcome becomes part of the process itself, and at still others, the process is the outcome. Staudt, for example, focuses on specific outcomes of empowerment politics that can be documented by economic, budgetary and spatial indicators. Her chapter reminds us of the importance of seeking evidence of empowerment, both to keep development practitioners honest and to evaluate appropriate strategies for pursuing women's strategic interests. Other chapters point to the difficulty of measuring women's empowerment. Desai reminds us that subtle and often unexpected strategies have the potential but not the certainty of empowerment. On the other hand, chapters by Ali and Patel suggest that seemingly empowering legal instruments do not always guarantee women's empowerment. Parpart suggests that participatory processes themselves need to be scrutinized and theorized if they are to be effective and transformative. Rai warns readers that the process of debates among women can lead to dangerous divisions within the women's movement, and Parpart points out that the process of participation and voice is not always empowering. Thus, while conceptual clarity demands some distinction between process and outcome, and attempts to evaluate outcomes are important, the chapters in *Rethinking Empowerment* suggest that we need to see empowerment not simply as measurable or quantifiable. Indeed, both the process and supposed outcomes of empowerment are perhaps best seen as untidy and unpredictable rather than linear, inevitable and easily understood.

In conclusion, we believe these issues provide lenses for rethinking the concept and practice of empowerment. They offer a way to make the term and the practice of empowerment strategies for women more rigorous, effective and perhaps complex. Women's groups, movements and feminist scholars would then be able to reflect upon the interconnectedness that the term requires if it is to be more than a 'motherhood' term. *Rethinking Empowerment* is thus a critique of the existing debates on empowerment as well as a contribution to the debates and practice on women's strategizing for empowerment. We hope it will push the analysis of women's empowerment in ways that both strengthen the concept and enhance attempts to operationalize women's empowerment in an increasingly complex, global/local world.

References

Afshar, Haleh (ed.) (1998) *Women and empowerment: Illustrations from the Third World*, New York: St Martin's Press.

Agnihotri, I. and V. Mazumdar (1995) 'Changing terms of political discourse: Women's movement in India, 1970s–1990s', *Economic and Political Weekly* XXX(29): 1869–78.

Allen, J. (1990) 'Does feminism need a theory of the state?', in S. Watson (ed.) *Playing the State*, London: Verso.

Amin, Samir (1974) *Accumulation on a World Scale*, trans. Brian Pearce, New York: Monthly Review Press.

Batliwala, Srilatha (1994) 'The meaning of women's empowerment: New concepts from action', in G. Sen, A. Germain and L.C. Chen (eds) *Population Policies Reconsidered: Health, Empowerment and Rights*, Boston: Harvard University Press, pp. 127–38.

Butalia, U. and T. Sarkar (eds) (1996) *Women and Right-wing Movements: Indian Experiences*, London: Zed Books.

Canadian International Development Agency (CIDA) (1999) *Policy on Gender Equality*, Ottawa: CIDA.

Chambers, R. (1997) *Whose Reality Counts? Putting the First Last*, London: Intermediate Technology Publications.

Charlton, S.E., J. Everett and K. Staudt (1989) *Women, the State and Development*, Albany, NY: SUNY/Albany Press.

Collins, Patricia Hill (1991) *Black Feminist Thought: Knowledge, Consciousness, and the Politics of Empowerment*, New York: Routledge.

Cockburn, C. (1999) *The Space between Us: Negotiating Gender and National Identities in Conflict*, London: Zed Press.

Cooper, F. and R. Packard (eds) (1997) *International Development and the Social Sciences*, Berkeley: University of California Press.

Craig, C. and M. Mayo (eds) (1995) *Community Empowerment*, London: Zed Press.

Crocker, D.A. (1995) 'Functioning and capability: The foundations of Sen's and Nussbaum's development ethic', in J. Glover and M. Nussbaum (eds) *Women, Culture and Development: A Study of Human Capabilities*, Oxford: Clarendon Press.

Crush, J. (ed.) (1995) *Power of Development*, London: Routledge.

Deveaux, Monique (1996) 'Feminism and empowerment: A critical reading of Foucault', in S. Hekman (ed.) *Feminist Interpretations of Michel Foucault*, University Park, PA: Pennsylvania State University Press.

Dreze, J. and A. Sen (1989) *Hunger and Public Action*, Oxford: Clarendon Press.

Escobar, A. (1995) *Encountering Development: The Making and Unmaking of the Third World*, Princeton: Princeton University Press.

Finnegan, William (2000) 'After Seattle: Anarchists get organized', *The New Yorker*, April 17: 40–51.

Foucault, Michel (1991) *The Foucault Reader: An Introduction to Foucault's Thought*, ed. P. Rabinow, Harmondsworth: Penguin.

—— (1979) *Discipline and Punish: The Birth of the Prison*, Harmondsworth: Penguin.

Fraser, Nancy (1989) *Unruly Practices: Power, Discourse and Gender in Contemporary Social Theory*, Minneapolis, MN: University of Minnesota Press.

Freeman, C. (2001) 'Is local:global as feminine:masculine? Rethinking the gender of globalization', *SIGNS* 26(4): 1007–37.

Freire, Paulo (1973) *Education for Critical Consciousness*, New York: Seabury Press.

Friedmann, J. (1992) *Empowerment: The Politics of Alternative Development*, London: Zed Press.

Gupta, A. and J. Ferguson (eds) (1997) *Culture, Power, Place: Explorations in Critical Anthropology*, Durham, NC: Duke University Press.

Hartsock, Nancy (1990) 'Foucault on power: A theory for women?', in Linda Nicholson (ed.) *Feminism/Postmodernism*, New York: Routledge.

Hekman, Susan (1996) *Feminist Interpretations of Michel Foucault*, University Park, PA: Pennsylvania State University Press.

Held, D., A.M. McGrew, D. Goldblatt and J. Perraton (1999) *Global Transformation: Politics, Economics, Culture*, Cambridge: Polity Press.

Hirshman, M. (1995) 'Women and development: A critique', in M. Marchand and J. Parpart (eds) *Feminism/Postmodernism/Development*, London: Routledge.

Hoogvelt, A. (1997) *Globalization and the Postcolonial World: The New Political Economy of Development*, London: Macmillan.

Kabeer, N. (1999) 'Resources, agency, achievements: Reflections on the measurement of women's empowerment', *Development and Change* 30: 435–64.

—— (1994) *Reversed Realities: Gender Hierarchies in Development Thought*, London: Verso.

Liebowitz, Debra (2000) 'Explaining absences, analyzing change, looking toward the future: U.S. women's participation in transnational feminist organizing in North America', presented at ISA, Los Angeles.

Lubeck, Paul (2000) 'The Islamic revival, antinomies of Islamic movements under globalization', in Robin Cohen and Shirin Rai (eds) *Global Social Movements*, London: Athlone Press.

Lukes, S. (1974) *Power: A Radical View*, London: Macmillan.

McBride-Stetson, D. and A. Mazur (eds) (1995) *Comparative State Feminism*, London: Sage Press.

MacKinnon, C. (1987) *Feminism Unmodified: Discourses on Life and Law*, Cambridge, MA: Harvard University Press.

McNay, L. (1992) *Foucault and Feminism: Power, Gender and Self*, Cambridge: Cambridge University Press.

Marchand, M. and A. Sisson Runyan (2000) *Gender and Global Restructuring: Sightings, Sites and Resistances*, London: Routledge.

Marquand, D. (1997) *The New Reckoning: Capitalism, States and Citizens*, Cambridge: Cambridge University Press.

Moser, C. (1993) *Gender Planning and Development: Theory, Practice and Training*, London: Routledge.

—— (1989) 'Gender planning in the Third World: Meeting practical and strategic gender needs', *World Development* 17(11): 1799–825.

Naim, M. (2000) 'The FP interview: Lore's war', *Foreign Policy* 118: 29–55.

Parpart, J. and K. Staudt (1989) *Women and the State in Africa*, Boulder, CO: Lynne Rienner Press.

Phillips, Anne (1999) *Which Equalities Matter?*, Cambridge: Polity Press.

Rai, Shirin (2002) *Gender and International Political Economy: From Nationalism to Globalization*, Cambridge: Polity Press.

Rai, S. and G. Lievesley (1996) *Women and the State: International Perspectives*, London: Taylor & Francis.

Reich, Robert (1992) *The Work of Nations*, New York: Vintage Press.

Rosenau, James (1997) *Along the Domestic–Foreign Frontier: Exploring Governance in a Turbulent World*, Cambridge: Cambridge University Press.

Rowlands, J. (1998) 'A word of the times, but what does it mean?: Empowerment in the discourse and practice of development', in H. Afshar (ed.) *Women and Empowerment*, New York: St Martin's Press.

—— (1997) *Questioning Empowerment: Working with Women in Honduras*, Oxford: Oxfam Publications.

Rugh, A. and H. Bossert (1998) *Involving Communities: Participation in the Delivery of Education Programs*, Washington, DC: Creative Associates International.

Scott, J. (1990) *Domination and the Arts of Resistance*, New Haven: Yale University Press.

Sen, Amartya (1995) 'Gender inequality and theories of justice', in J. Glover and M. Nussbaum (eds) *Women, Culture and Development*, Oxford: Oxford University Press.

—— (1990) 'Gender and cooperative conflicts', in Irene Tinker (ed.) *Persistent Inequalities*, New York: Oxford University Press.

Sen, G. and C. Grown (1988) *Development, Crises and Alternative Visions: Third World Women's Perspectives*, New York: Monthly Review Press.

Staudt, K. (1998) *Policy, Politics and Gender: Women Gaining Ground*, Hartford, CT: Kumarian Press.

—— (1996) 'Political representation: Engendering politics', in *Background Papers: Human Development Report 1995*, New York: UNDP.

Staudt, K., S. Rai and J. Parpart (2001) 'Protesting world trade rules: Can we talk about empowerment?', *SIGNS* 26(4): 1251–7.

Stiles, Ken (2000) *Global Institutions and Local Empowerment: Competing Theoretical Perspectives*, London: Macmillan.

Tetreault, M.A. and R.L. Teske (eds) (2000) *Conscious Acts and the Politics of Social Change: Feminist Approaches to Social Movements, Community and Power*, Volume One, Columbia: University of South Carolina Press.

United Nations (1996) *Platform for Action and the Beijing Declaration*, Fourth World Conference on Women, Beijing, China, 4–15 September 1995.

United Nations Development Program (UNDP) (1995) *The Human Development Report 1995*, Oxford: Oxford University Press.

Wallerstein, I. (1979) *The Capitalist World Economy*, Cambridge: Cambridge University Press.

Wolf, Eric (1999) *Envisioning Power: Ideologies of Dominance and Crisis*, Berkeley: University of California Press.

World Bank (1999) *World Development Report, Knowledge for Development*, Oxford: Oxford University Press.

—— (1998) *Assessing Aid: What Works, What Doesn't, and Why*, Oxford: Oxford University Press.

—— (1995) *World Bank Participation Source Book*, Washington, DC: World Bank Environment Department Papers.

Yeatman, Anna (1999) *Activism and the Policy Process*, London: Allen & Unwin.

Young, K. (1993) *Planning Development with Women: Making a World of Difference*, London: Macmillan.

2 Education as a means for empowering women

Nelly P. Stromquist

Education has often been seen as one of the keys to empowerment. This chapter presents the concept of empowerment from an educational perspective, namely, how it has been applied in formal schooling with young students and in non-formal education programmes, with mostly adult populations. It offers a wide scope, appraising efforts in various parts of the world, particularly in Asia and Latin America – a reflection of the existing literature, which is often available only in the form of conference papers or institutional reports. As we explore the applications of the empowerment concept in the educational arena, we consider the objectives it has sought, the forms it has taken and the instructional modes it has utilized. This chapter also presents and evaluates several case studies of educating for empowerment.

Revisiting the concept of empowerment

The concept of empowerment has special resonance within the women's movement today. Although its origins are unclear, the evidence points to an Asian rather than a Western inception, perhaps best reflected in the publication by Gita Sen and Karen Grown, *Development, Crisis, and Alternatives*, widely distributed at the Third World Women's Conference in Nairobi in 1985. An exhaustive interrogation of the ideas and actions in the USA's feminist movement reveals no such concept in almost forty years of the movement's efforts to reframe and advance the condition of women in society (DuPlessis and Snitow 1998; see also Ware 1970). Contrary to popular belief, the concept of empowerment did not formally originate with Freire. His ideas of conscientization are totally compatible with the notion of empowerment, but conscientization (or deep awareness of one's socio-political environment) is really a precursor to the development of empowering skills and feelings. In fact, the word 'empowerment' still has no fixed translation in Spanish, some preferring *potenciamiento*, others *poderío*, and yet others the neologism *empoderamiento*.

At times the concept has been used in an all-encompassing manner that has amounted to co-optation. For instance, one can find in the educational literature claims that attending classes is 'empowering', that story-telling is 'empowering', that motherhood is 'empowering'. While there are multiple definitions of empowerment, I prefer to use one I proposed several years ago (Stromquist 1995). Empowerment consists of four dimensions, each equally important but none sufficient by itself to enable women to act on their own behalf. These are the cognitive (critical understanding of one's reality), the psychological (feeling of self-esteem), the political (awareness of power inequalities and the ability to organize and mobilize) and the economic (capacity to generate independent income) (Stromquist 1995).

Educational settings have the potential to foster all four dimensions but require the educational programme to be designed explicitly to achieve each of those ends. While the interlocking nature of these dimensions can contribute to making empowerment irreversible, the path to the development of an empowered woman is not easy. It necessitates persistent and long-term interventions in order to break old patterns of low self-worth and dependence, and to foster the construction of new personalities with a realistic understanding of how gender functions in their society and strategies for its modification.

Empowerment within formal schooling

In recent years, especially those following the Fourth World Conference on Women (in Beijing, 1995), several governments have taken steps to modify the textbooks used in primary and secondary schooling, and, to a lesser extent, to provide teachers with gender-sensitive training. The former effort has typically involved the introduction of more inclusive language and images that offer a more balanced representation of women and men in society; the latter sought to make teachers aware of how their own sexist attitudes affect classroom practices and performance/career expectations for girls and boys. Training has also provided teachers with new pedagogical strategies to foster gender equality in the classroom.

Most of the interventions in the formal school system have, unfortunately, been sporadic, superficial and far from comprehensive in content. Even in pilot projects characterized by careful interventions, the training of teachers has usually meant at most three days over the course of a school year (Lazarte and Lanza 2000; Cortina and Stromquist 2000). Curriculum changes have generally brought explicit references to the roles men and women have played in history and play (and should play) in contemporary society. Deeper treatments of sexual stereotypes and sexism in education have been minimal, in part because they are often contested. In Argentina, for example, the Catholic Church successfully blocked the nationwide introduction of a gender-sensitive curriculum (Bonder 1999). In Mexico, conservative sectors of the Catholic Church have also led the fight against sex education in the schools (Bayardo 1996). Similar interventions have occurred in Peru and the Dominican Republic. To my knowledge, no country has designed, much less implemented, a graduated curriculum for the introduction of gender suitable to the age and experience levels of girls and boys at each grade of schooling.

Girls' access to schooling in many developing countries is so low that the term empowerment has been used to mean mere participation in the formal system. This is problematic because it assumes that the experience and knowledge attained in schooling automatically prepare girls to assess their worth and envisage new possibilities. It ignores the reproductive function of formal schooling, particularly in more traditional societies. Is a gender-sensitive education the same as an empowering education? Does it make sense to apply the term to young girls by virtue of their presence in formal institutions? I think it can, but only when important modifications have fitted the concept to the age of the student and to the nature of the institution in which she finds herself, and only if special measures to empower students take place.

Typical of governmental programmes that describe themselves as empowering, this statement describes a sex education programme offered by an Asian government:

> [The program content covers] communication with the opposite sex, selection of marriage partner, married life, family planning, and marital problems …. The sex and family education are [designed so that learners] perform their duties and roles as a good person and member of family as well as society …. Through sex education, male and female students will realize how to appropriately act their roles with their sex counterparts.
>
> (Singussawin and Ratansing 1999: 5)

Judging from the above description, this sex education programme, far from being empowering, seems designed to prepare girls and boys to accept more readily established traditional gender roles.

Other programmes seem to have more potential for empowerment. The Girls' Access to Education (GATE) Project in Nepal aims to provide literacy, health knowledge and skills to girls of ages ten to fourteen who had never entered school or who had been forced to drop out. The curriculum includes health and sanitation, reproductive health, nutrition, environmental health, adolescent psychology, population and health, and empowerment. Specifically under the category of 'empowerment', it covers 'awareness of girls' trafficking, importance of girls' schooling, domestic violence and sexual abuse' (World Education 1999: 4). The GATE curriculum thus contains elements that can build critical awareness of gender issues in girls. However, the extent to which the empowerment component meshes with or amplifies the other curriculum themes remains unclear.

To achieve empowerment through education, several concepts must be introduced at appropriate levels. When referring to primary and secondary schooling, empowerment should enable girls (children and adolescents) to develop the knowledge and skills to nullify and counter sexual stereotypes and conceptions of masculinity and femininity that limit the social potential of women. Empowering girls should mean offering them courses with content that not only attacks current sexual stereotypes but also provides students with alternative visions of a gender-free society. These courses should also provide them with education, not only on the anatomical and physiological aspects and consequences of sex, but also on the social aspects framing sexual relations. Schools engaged in efforts to foster the empowerment of girls should enable them to increase their participation in class, to learn not to be intimidated by boys and to speak their own minds. In that way, girls would be able to explore a more complete range of life options and develop fuller personalities. An empowering education in the schools would reduce the creation of masculine norms among boys, thus decreasing their desire to be superior to girls, to avoid dealing with emotions, to set themselves as different in nature from girls and to engage in sexual 'conquests'. This empowering education, as noted earlier, would have to be sensitive to the age of the students, introducing knowledge and information that is progressively tailored to the increased age of the girls and boys. Students in formal schooling are capable of developing the cognitive and psychological dimensions of empowerment. The other two – political and economic – will most likely have to wait until they are adults. However, formal schooling can establish the basis for these dimensions.

At older ages of schooling – when (some) women are attending university – the possibilities for empowerment may be stronger because: (1) university access in most countries is expanding and universities provide increasingly better-designed programmes on gender and women's studies, and (2) being older, university students are more mature and (some) can reflect on the implications of complexity of their surrounding society. Women's studies programmes started in the USA in 1972, in Western Europe in the 1980s and in Eastern Europe in the 1990s. Latin America initiated these programmes in the mid-1980s. Similar programmes emerged a few years later in Asia and Africa.

Gender and women's studies programmes have made it possible for students to gain a greater understanding of how gender forces operate in society. These programmes have influenced the development and dissemination of new theoretical and methodological approaches dealing with the nature of gender, national development and social change. Further, many of the graduates of these programmes have been able to embark on careers that have made a difference in the way gender functions in institutions. In many developing countries, women's studies graduate programmes have joined state machineries working on equality for women.

However, two major weaknesses still handicap these programmes. First, they attract a very small proportion of university students. Many young women, seeing the increased representation of women in all spheres of society, do not recognize the need for such knowledge. Their regular programme of studies may be too demanding to accommodate additional courses, and women's studies are rarely integrated into regular academic programmes. Universities, as institutions, have not been very responsive to women's studies as a new field. Indeed, after almost thirty years of existence, the field is only weakly institutionalized in many universities. Women's studies usually does not have departmental status. It typically depends on the sponsorship of a related department, whose needs and priorities often lie elsewhere.

Empowerment among adult women

To talk of the empowerment of adult women, we must examine the work of women-led non-governmental organizations (NGOs), entities that render concrete the women's movement through their educational actions and political demands. However, the full functions and impacts of women-led NGOs have received academic attention only recently (Alvarez 1990; Yudelman 1993). Although women-led NGOs vary depending on the functions they fulfil (from providing assistance for basic needs to transforming attitudes and behaviours) and the geographical area they cover (from neighbourhoods to the national level), these organizations provide key examples of mobilization and articulation around gender issues. Women-led NGOs have existed throughout Latin American and in several places in India since the early 1970s. They appeared in Africa and other parts of Asia in the mid-1980s. Not surprisingly, some NGOs tend to be more professional and politicized than others. Many women-led NGOs are multiclass movements, comprising a middle-class leadership with low-income women among their most important beneficiaries, seeking objectives that permeate all social classes.

It is with adult women outside of formal education that empowerment at present reaches its highest forms. Not only are adults more capable of reflective thought – typically derived from family, work and other everyday experiences – but they can also acquire new knowledge in less restrictive and more creative settings, such as those provided by non-formal education programmes.

Being a synthesis of new knowledge, dialogical communication and a reflection on personal experience, empowerment develops best initially at local levels, in small groups and in women-only settings. Moore notes that 'activists need a social and cultural space within the prevailing order – a more or less protected enclave' for them to grow intellectually (1978: 482). A similar point can be made for women who are developing their gender awareness. The importance of new spaces for learning has also been noted in the political literature. Selbin (1998: 2, citing Hakim Bey) describes these spaces as 'temporary autonomous zones from which people seek opportunity, a moment in which they endeavour to take control, perhaps for the first time, of their lives'.

Educational interventions of an empowering nature must perforce challenge patriarchal ideologies. As Patel illustrates from her own experience in India, the empowering organization must locate the geopolitical region in which it wants to work. Women must set aside a separate time and space for themselves to question collectively their situation and develop their critical thinking about it, prioritize issues to tackle and acquire skills that enhance women's individual and collective autonomy (Patel 1996). The creation of these alternative social spaces for the discussion of gender issues has been extremely useful. In Kenya, for instance, women's organizations have enabled women to refuse forced marriages or genital mutilations, to argue against male control over their sexuality and to protest violence against women. Precursors to these political stands have been gender sensitization, legal awareness and civic education programmes – all conducted in women-only groups and within women-led NGOs (Nzomo 1994).

The alternative spaces provided by these women-led NGOs promote systematic learning opportunities through the workshops (courses of short duration on specific themes) they offer on topics of great relevance to women's advancement: gender subordination, reproductive health, domestic violence, gender and legislation, gender and politics, and others. They also make possible a wide range of informal learning, which occurs through processes such as mobilization and organization, or through less intense activities such as role modelling, participation in global networks, lobbying, monitoring, and testing one's leadership. Literacy, a high-profile topic for women, often results in empowerment of a psychological nature. However, much of the gain in self-confidence and more autonomous practices at the family level seem to derive not merely from learning to code and decode print (which seldom seems to reach anticipated levels). Rather it arises from classroom experiences that provide the opportunity for women to discuss problems with others and exchange viewpoints in their relatively frequent meetings for literacy training (for more on this see Stromquist 1997).

An example of the political character of empowerment-focused educational programmes comes from the Women's Development Collective (WDC) in Malaysia, which describes empowerment 'as a process of changing the balance of power, i.e., between the powerful and powerless, haves and have-nots, and men and women'. The WDC defines power as control over resources and ideology in social, economic and political contexts. The WDC's main non-formal education programmes are: gender and feminist analysis, health and safety at work, understanding and use of laws, and leadership and organizing. According to the WDC, empowerment should not merely promote critical awareness; it should enhance the ability to act for change. In reflecting upon its work, WDC raises questions such as 'What criteria can we develop to assess how empowering a particular strategy or intervention is? Is consciousness and mobilization greater than providing access to concrete schemes and resources in an empowerment process?' (Abdullah 1999: 3).

Learning processes in the empowerment of adult women

Internal (psychological and cognitive) as well as collective processes (political, organizational, economic) are involved in the acquisition of feelings and practices of empowerment among adult women. Below we review some of the elements that promote such empowerment.

Recognising oppression at the personal level

Awareness of the existence of oppression at the personal level requires recognition of oneself as a victim in particular circumstances or in recurrent social transactions. Although some observers argue that self-recognition as a victim moves a person into a passive role, the contrary can be asserted. Far from producing a defeatist attitude, the understanding of oneself as a victim is the first step toward redressing the inequity of social and economic treatment.

The complex set of conditions and interlocking forces that affect women has been explored by the women's movement through efforts of gender consciousness-raising. Ware defines conscientization as a 'close examination of the individual lives of group members to determine how society must be changed to eliminate the oppression to which all women can testify' (1970: 109). Consciousness-raising has been the method most utilized for women to recognize and challenge their subordination and marginalization. The term has a distinct trajectory within Marxist thought and certainly influenced feminists who came from within the political left. In use since 1969 in the women's movement, conscientization also owes its origins to the industrial experience of US workers. The acquaintance by the women's movement of Paulo Freire's conscientization methods (which also call for dialogical circles but focus on social class rather than gender issues) came much later. Ware, one of many who participated in the early consciousness-raising efforts of women in the USA, describes the process as:

> A greatly improved descendant of the T-groups that industrial psychologists instituted to effect a working team out of a group of men in competition for promotion. In the original T-group, the personal problems of the men were seen as obstacles to be eradicated. In the women's movement, consciousness-raising focuses on women, i.e., social problems as the central issues on which political attention should be directed.
>
> (1970: 109)

Gender consciousness-raising efforts serve to render the personal public and hence to seek collective responses. Since consciousness-raising promotes a belief in women's autonomy as subjects, it fosters among participants a sense of their independent worth and needs. It enables women to see themselves as individuals with agency beyond their responsibilities for home and family. More bluntly, such consciousness-raising efforts seek to instil in women an awareness of their role and needs as citizens, not just as mothers or wives. NGO work in the area of empowerment has identified as a common difficulty the task of helping women think of themselves, independent of family obligations.

Developing resilience

A notion of resilience is particularly relevant to the increased empowerment of women. This concept, which emerged in the context of US education to describe the ability of certain Afro-American children to succeed in their education while facing numerous obstacles, refers to the ability to persist, not to be overwhelmed by the seemingly insurmountable difficulties – to 'bounce back'. Linda Winfield, one of its original proponents, defines resilience as 'protective mechanisms that modify the individual's response to risk situations and operate at turning points during his or her life' (1994: 3). She sees resilience also as synonymous with 'coping, persistence, adaptation, long-term success despite adverse circumstance' (1994: 3). Resilience here is taken as the ability to persist in one's goals despite being ridiculed for such attempts.

Facing conflict productively

An important feature of empowerment is learning to deal with conflict. Since empowerment is oriented toward social change, conflict is likely to emerge at two levels: externally, with the surrounding institutions that maintain the established order in society, and internally, by positioning women's needs and desires against those expressed by their close family/household members. Conflict can be exploited as a means to create critical awareness and a strategy to strengthen collective action. Conflict should not be avoided but should be employed judi- ciously. Well-managed conflict develops negotiating skills, allowing women to state their rights with determination and controlled sentimentality.

In several Latin American countries, Chile being a case in point, access to contraception, legalized therapeutic abortion, and divorce are demands by the women's movement to which the Catholic Church is strongly opposed (Dandavati 1996). Indeed, women's empowerment is reflected in their persistent demands for these rights despite strong opposition and in their willingness to engage in the proscribed practices.

Resolving rivalries among women

A central objective of empowerment is to create gender solidarity among women. While various motives can bring women together, at the group level women often either distrust each other or engage in personal rivalry. This rivalry is itself a product of women's socialization, which leads them to see men as superior and, conversely, women as inferior and as competitors for the small socio-political space open to them. Practitioners who have engaged in systematic efforts to enhance the skills of women leaders find that rivalry among women is one of the most resistant impediments to the development of empowering strategies. Thus, some women leaders tend to disqualify and even to express strong opposition to other women leaders to prevent them from attaining important public positions or representa- tive office. In a Chilean experiment to develop greater skills among women leaders, feelings of rivalry were explicitly brought into the curriculum and women learned to be conscious of their attitudes toward other women holding leadership positions, and to be aware of their persistence in thinking that alliances with powerful men were more effective than working with women. As a result, women leaders learned to develop more alliances with other women (Valdes 2000).

Engaging in political thinking

The empowerment of women implies the dissolution of power structures that function to the nearly exclusive benefit of men. To accomplish tangible changes in power configurations, women find that they must learn to think tactically and strategically, that they must learn how the formal political processes work and that they must acquire negotiating and monitoring skills.

These political skills can be learned through discussion of past events and through various simulation exercises. However, the most effective learning occurs through actual engagement in change and mobilization efforts within specific groups. This has also been the case among women-led NGOs, as will be seen below.

Types of empowering knowledge

New, accurate knowledge about gender, politics and ideology is indispensable in the creation of empowerment. However, not every 'empowerment' project provides knowledge that is actually empowering. Typical topics in courses addressed to women, particularly low-income women, include agricultural skills, skills for production, family planning and literacy. In government-sponsored programmes, one often finds social improvement courses on family healthcare, family food and nutrition, sewing and crafts.

These programmes, especially in the African countries, tend to be reformist, incremental and conservative (Ityavyar and Obiajunwa 1992). If the topics covered are presented in a way that de-links them from the dynamics associated with patriarchy, sexuality, colonialism and power, chances are that the new knowledge will not be empowering. It would have failed to place that knowledge in the context of women's conditions and the need for challenging asymmetrical gendered power. Usually, empowerment is fostered through knowledge of issues such as health, work, legislation, politics, domestic violence, sexual harassment and rape. However, this training requires competent facilitators who can help participants, through class exercises and discussions, to connect the personal with the social and the political.

In the area of human rights, women have been empowered by providing them with knowledge of the Universal Declaration of Human Rights (UDHR) and the United Nations Convention on the Elimination of All Forms of Discrimination against Women (CEDAW) (see chapter by Ali). Legislation, however limited in scope, is always ahead of implementation. Therefore, knowledge of the laws creates spaces for action, promotes their implementation and ultimately helps to inject a rights-based approach to development.

Leadership training

In several ways, empowerment is very much connected with leadership training. This is well illustrated by a programme for training women leaders in Chile. The training programme focused on setting up supportive networks for these women, promoting a variety of leadership styles and, very importantly, trying to reduce their feelings of exaggerated stereotypical identity as women (referred to in Spanish as *identidad*), which is a consequence of gender socialization (Valdes

2000). Women were trained to acknowledge their own individuality or, in the programme's words, to develop their capacity for 'individuation', defined as 'the ability to have a singularized self-perception, with an individual project, able to distinguish oneself from the collective affiliation or social instances that give one's identity'. This individuation was fostered through the development of skills to make proposals, to capture collective needs and identities, to face conflict and demands, to propose solutions, to question whomever was deemed to need questioning and to develop a critical gender vision. The training programme also enhanced the capacity to recognize one's desires, to understand the diversity of positions/perspectives as a source of conflict and to develop skills to negotiate and to resolve. A fundamental feature of this leadership programme has been its attempt to clarify the link between women's individual problems and difficulties, and those that exist at the national level (Valdés 2000).

Innovative pedagogies

Making a distinction between the instructional order (what is to be learned) and the regulative order (the context in which the new knowledge is learned), Zúñiga (1999) maintains that many non-formal education programmes provide a rigid instructional order, as they emphasize the transmission of specific knowledge, abilities and attitudes. However, they also offer a relaxed regulative order, characterized by flexible interaction, with open and friendly social relations between trainers and trainers. This regulative order is further supported by the use of social dynamics that favour group learning and collective work. Zúñiga's point, thus, is that despite strong directives about curriculum content, the relaxed transactional approaches that characterize these non-formal education programmes account for their popularity with women participants.

Several innovative instructional methods have been tried in non-formal education programmes for women. These include the use of songs, simulation exercises, games, role playing and popular theatre. A Philippine programme in existence for several years has identified three phases in the implementation of empowering methods in the classroom: (1) working with the women's awareness of and adjustment to social realities, (2) challenging their received knowledge, and (3) linking their new learning to their practical experience. They work these phases through three essential instructional strategies: story telling, which seeks to teach the women 'how to understand forests but also trees, branches, and leaves'; learning from polemics (fostering constant arguments within the classroom); and constantly providing feedback (de Vela 1999).

The contributions of informal learning

The women-led NGOs foster the crucial political dimension of empowerment through informal learning. As noted earlier, these types of knowledge and skills are learned most effectively through interaction among women in non-threatening physical and social spaces. Among economically disadvantaged women – whose levels of formal education are low – a major obstacle to action, as perceived by the women, is their inability to speak correctly. This is especially true for indigenous women who are often afraid to express themselves (CEIMME 1995). The positive effects of these spaces for developing women's confidence for presenting views and opinions cannot be overstated.

It is widely understood that women must organize if they are to create a political force and that they must mobilize if they are to expand their political power. Below, we examine the specificities of organizing and mobilizing, and how empowerment contributes to and is simultaneously enhanced by these two processes.

Organizing

By joining women-led grassroots groups, particularly NGOs, women identify common experiences and conditions, and consequently develop shared identities. As Oxhorn observes (1998: 7), 'shared identities, the ability for self-organization and even a history of collective struggle are sources of power which can enable disadvantaged groups to challenge the status quo'. Organizing, in the context of aggregating demand in systematic and orderly ways, implies the adoption of some form of structure and process shared by the group. This means creating collectivities with leaders and followers, establishing ways of doing things and obtaining financial and knowledge resources for successful operations.

To become organized, women must feel empowered enough to want to act autonomously, on their own agendas. In the process of becoming organized and acting as a group, the sense of empowerment is further increased. Organization at the local level is essential to accomplish immediate aims linked to the household and the community, but women have learned that they must be organized beyond the local to increase their capacity to interact with the state. The organization of women's groups constantly faces new challenges since the new relations being formed between the women's movement, political parties and civil society can seldom rely on established models and new social experimentation is needed. Additional challenges for women today are those brought by the phenomena of economic and technical globalization (see Youngs, Gardiner Barber and Staudt in this volume).

Mobilizing

In a sense a person must first become part of some collective group to develop a collective identity; but developing a sense of collective identity also leads women to mobilize. After analysing the work of several successful movements for land redistribution in Latin America, Grindle (1996) observes that one commonality among them has been independent and sustained mobilization. This is doubly applicable to women's groups, whose movements not only seek vindication of claims to personal rights but strive for social transformation as well.

Through collective struggle, collective identities are created and refined as new sources of political power. This is especially important because women have not engaged, and most likely will not engage, in physical struggle to achieve objectives of equity and gender justice. Most political mobilizations of women tend to be based on non-traditional female roles, but, as political action continues, the range of issues is expanded to reach transformative levels. In several instances, mobilization by women has escalated from demands for basic neighbourhood services to redefining their rights as citizens. These shifts toward more complex and broader types of social demands can be observed in the work of groups that began as mothers' clubs in Brazil, neighbourhood groups in India and communal kitchens in Peru. Through the experience in organization and mobilization that participation in NGOs provides, women attain a sense of personal and collective empowerment.

Mobilization serves as a means to create a political agenda as well as to demand the implementation of that agenda. It requires a belief in one's ability to influence others. The act of mobilizing creates opportunities for women to develop skills and discover new talents. As Winfield observes (1994: 3), 'self-efficacy and self-esteem are learned through positive social interaction and successful accomplishment of tasks'.

It is well recognized that women will not be able to enhance their political power without mobilization and that part of this mobilization must include coalition building. At the same time, consolidation of small efforts into larger groups for feminist action tends to expand women's political agendas, which at times may introduce topics about which there is no consensus. Examples of such issues are the priority given to sexual orientation and the extent to which the women's movement should work independently of support from either the state or international development agencies.

Combining the cognitive and the economic dimensions of empowerment

Because many adult women depend financially on their families and men, empowerment for that group must have an economic component. Therefore, a number of non-formal education programmes for women combine the provision of emancipatory gender knowledge with the supply of productive skills, management skills or micro credit. These programmes report high levels of psychological and economic empowerment among their participants.

Evidence from the experience of non-formal education that targets poor women in Latin America indicates that the most successful efforts have been those which offer both a material and a subjective dimension, i.e. those that consider improving the quality of life of women and their families by increasing economic resources of the household as well as seeking to enhance the women's self-esteem (Ruiz Bravo 1992). This has meant providing women with material resources (credit, food) in addition to the symbolic and cognitive resources (education, information, training).

A project in the Philippines, Women in Enterprise Development (WED), defines empowerment as 'a process of enabling an individual to gain access to and control of resources, optimally utilize the resources and enjoy the benefits that accrue due to the efforts exerted' (Lim 1999: 4). The WED project aims at developing entrepreneurship; increasing productivity, income and managerial capabilities of the learners; and promoting and improving health and nutrition habits through adult education/functional literacy (Lim 1999: 6). The project's literacy sessions are used to enable women to 'understand and be aware of the undesirable situations they are in and the cause of the oppressing conditions' (1999: 7). In WED, the cognitive aspect of empowerment is a small component relative to greater inputs of entrepreneurship, credit, markets and technical assistance.

Two additional examples of how empowerment is being implemented through an economic dimension come from the Women's Economic Empowerment and Literacy Project (WEEL) in Nepal, in which women participate in savings and credit groups to improve their livelihoods. This project links literacy and training curricula. It does not provide skills for the actual production of goods, but rather skills in marketing, product feasibility and management, record keeping, accounting and the like (Shrestha 1999). The other example comes from Pro Mujer in Bolivia, which provides women with a holistic array of courses, including reproductive health, communal organization and leadership, productive and marketing skills, and micro-financial services (involving individual loans usually ranging from US$50 to US$100) (Pro Mujer *c.* 1999). According to its own evaluations, 64 per cent of the women in this programme have gone on to occupy community leadership positions, and 67 per cent have reported increased revenues.

Institutional development and support

The empowerment skills women gain enable them to create more effective social movements. These, in turn, support the empowerment of more women. The social movements must operate simultaneously on two fronts. As Dandavati (1996: 141) explains: 'social movements struggle to maintain their autonomy and yet be political actors and work with political parties and the state'. In the years in which the contemporary women's movement has been active, crucial support has been obtained from several institutions, most of them operating within the non-governmental sector.

In the Latin American context, it is essential to recognize the supportive role of the Council for Adult Education in Latin America (Consejo de Educación de Adultos para América Latina, CEAAL), which functions as the main umbrella for NGOs working on popular education in the region. In the 1980s, women-led NGOs complained of the lack of gender perspective in mixed (comprising men and women) NGOs. Since 1990, largely as a result of this criticism, CEAAL has undergone three changes in its organization: it has incorporated a gender perspective in its programming, developed greater sensitivity to social movements and engaged in more systematic gender research.

Since the early 1980s, a group within CEAAL, but with financial and decision-making autonomy, has been the Women's Education Network (Red Popular de Educación entre Mujeres, REPEM). Comprising approximately 180 NGOs working on gender and education, REPEM's work has grown rapidly from facilitating the creation of a regional communication and information network to assuming leadership in the advocacy of women's adult education in the world. This was demonstrated by its key role in the official documentation produced at the 1996 Fifth World Conference of Adult Education in Hamburg, Germany. The conference's Plan of Action acknowledges the importance of education for women's empowerment and calls for governments to endorse the role of women-led NGOs in the process of adult education. At the present time REPEM is lobbying and monitoring governments in the region in order to ensure that the Hamburg agreements become a reality. Again, the work of REPEM is very much a product of the acquisition of empowerment skills, many of which were gained through participation in workshops organized by women-led NGOs and their multiple organization and mobilization efforts.

In the past ten years, the United Nations Education, Scientific and Cultural Organization (UNESCO) has encouraged the production of gender-sensitive materials in programmes dealing mostly with non-formal education for adult women in Asia and Africa. These efforts have involved removing sex-stereotyped images and replacing them with representations of men performing domestic tasks and women in professional roles or as traders and farmers. This has led, in Africa, to the production of booklets with simple stories of:

> the lives of common people in Africa in the language that they understand. Free of difficult and confusing technical terms, full of anecdotes, local humor and parlance, they stand a good chance of being able to [be] read. More importantly, these booklets help young women and men reflect on their situation. True, they don't give answers because there are no ready-made answers. But they do help provoke thoughts and ideas and provide alternatives to help people further explore the issues so close to their realities.
>
> (Aksornkool 1999)

Many attempts by governments to improve the condition of women, however, involve the use of 'culturally acceptable' strategies. This, at one level, sounds reasonable but at another becomes quite contradictory. Often, it translates concretely into the avoidance of conflict and the presentation of very bland material that scarcely challenges either patriarchal ideologies or the existing sexual division of labour. Changes in the social relations of gender necessitate modifying cultural norms, values and practices. So, while empowerment should lead to the identification of cultural aspects that need to be changed and to strategies for achieving this transformation, most new efforts and materials produced through governmental programmes, even in ostensibly modern and democratic countries, avoid dealing with such potentially disruptive social modifications.

Conclusion

Subjective changes, such as increased levels of critical understanding, self-esteem and confidence, are crucial for the development of stronger, more assertive personalities. The cognitive and psychological dimensions of empowerment have been attained through access to gender-sensitive materials and teachers in the case of young women in the formal school system, and through participation in various kinds of workshops in non-formal education settings in the case of adult women. On those occasions, significant knowledge and skills are acquired to create new identities and autonomous agency among women, and even to develop a new democratic culture.

Formal education can 'empower' girls, but the concept takes a different form given the age of the students and the institutional parameters in which their learning takes place and in which 'useful knowledge' is defined. Unfortunately, in most nations, very little systematic learning occurs in schools to empower girls from a gender perspective.

At this moment, women-led NGOs, primarily in developing countries, have enabled women to realize the full dimensions of empowerment – not only the cognitive and psychological but also the economic and political dimensions. Though non-formal education programmes cannot always provide the best mix of experiences to foster thorough-going empowerment, the social spaces they create, the activities they promote and the flexibility they enjoy in dealing with new knowledge, and the forms by which it is conveyed, are contributing substantially to the emergence of 'empowered' women as individuals and groups.

Globalization forces today, which position states as competitors in the market rather than as providers of social welfare, may provide disincentives for government to engage in empowering initiatives for women and other disadvantaged social groups. The options left open are neither numerous nor well endowed. It is here that work based on hope, persistence and self-reliance emerges as crucial.

References

Abdullah, Maria Chin (1999) 'The women's development collective', paper presented at the International Seminar on Literacy for Women's Empowerment in the 21st Century, 10–14 December, Bangkok: UNESCO.

Aksornkool, Namtip (1999) Personal communication, 10 December, UNESCO.

Alvarez, Sonia (1990) *Engendering Democracy in Brazil. Women's Movements in Transition Politics*, Princeton: Princeton University Press.

Bayardo, Barbara (1996) 'Sex and the curriculum in Mexico and the United States: A heavy burden in ignorance', in Nelly P. Stromquist (ed.) *Gender Dimensions in Education in Latin America*, Washington, DC: Organization of American States, pp. 157–86.

Bonder, Gloria (1999) 'La equidad de género en las políticas educativas: La necesidad de una mirada reflexiva sobre premisas, experiencias y metas', Mimeo.

Centro de Estudios e Investigación sobre el Maltrato a la Mujer Ecuatoriana (CEIMME) (1995) *Mujer Indígena y Participación Política*, Quito: CEIMME.

Cortina, Regina and Nelly P. Stromquist (eds) (2000) *Distant Alliances: Promoting Education for Girls and Women in Latin America*, New York: RoutledgeFalmer.

Dandavati, Annie (1996) *The Women's Movement and the Transition to Democracy in Chile*, New York: Peter Lang.

de Vela, Tesa (1999) 'Empowerment in the Philippines', paper presented at the International Seminar on Literacy for Women's Empowerment in the 21st Century, 10–14 December, Bangkok: UNESCO.

DuPlessis, Rachel and Ann Snitow (eds) (1998) *The Feminist Memoir Project. Voices from Women's Liberation*, New York: Three Rivers Press.

Grindle, Merilee (1996) *State and Countryside Development Policy and Agrarian Politics in Latin America*, Baltimore: Johns Hopkins University Press.

Ityavyar, D.A. and S. N. Obiajunwa (1992) *The State and Women in Nigeria*, Jos, Nigeria: Jos University Press.

Lazarte, Cecilia and Martha Lanza (2000) 'La equidad de género en las políticas educativas Bolivianas: Experiencias y desafios', in R. Cortina and N.P. Stromquist (eds) *Distant Alliances*, New York: RoutledgeFalmer.

Lim, Myrna (1999) 'The empowering dimensions of literacy: A Philippine NGO experience', paper presented at the International Seminar on Literacy for Women's Empowerment in the 21st Century, 10–14 December. Bangkok: UNESCO.

Moore Jr. Barrington (1978) *Injustice: The Social Bases of Obedience and Revolt*, White Plains: M.E. Sharpe.

Nzomo, Maria (1994) 'Empowering women for democratic change in Kenya: Which way forward?', in *Empowerment of Women in the Process of Democratization. Experiences of Kenya, Uganda, and Tanzania*, Dar es Salaam: Friedrich Ebert Stiftung.

Oxhorn, Philip (1998) 'Social inequality, civil society, and the limits of citizenship in Latin America', paper presented at the annual meeting of the Latin American Studies Association, 24–6 September, Chicago.

Patel, Sheela (1996) 'From a seed to a tree: Building community organization in India's cities', in Shirley Walters and Linzi Manicomm (eds) *Gender in Popular Education. Methods for Empowerment*, London: Zed Books, pp. 87–101.

Pro Mujer (*c.* 1999) *Programas para la mujer*, brochure, La Paz: Pro Mujer.

Ruiz Bravo, Patricia (1992) *Género, educación y desarrollo*, Santiago: UNESCO/OREALC.

Selbin, Eric (1998) 'Social justice in Latin America. Dilemmas of democracy and revolution', paper presented at the annual meeting of the Latin American Studies Association, 24–5 September, Chicago.

Shrestha, Chij (1999) 'Linking non-formal education to development. Women's Economic Empowerment and Literacy (WEEL) Program', paper presented at the International Seminar on Literacy for Women's Empowerment in the 21st Century, 10–14 December, Bangkok: UNESCO.

Singussawin, Oumboon and Koontolrat Ratansing (1999) *Country Report on Women Education in Thailand*, Bangkok: Department of Curriculum and Instructional Development, Ministry of Education, Mimeo.

Stromquist, Nelly (1997) *Literacy for Citizenship. Gender and Grassroots Dynamics in Brazil*, Albany: State University of New York Press.

—— (1995) 'The theoretical and practical bases for empowerment', in Carolyn Medel-Anonuevo (ed.) *Women, Education, and Empowerment: Paths towards Autonomy*, Hamburg: UNESCO Institute for Education.

Valdés, Alejandra (2000) 'Formación de liderazgos: Transformaciones y transgresiones', in R. Cortina and N. P. Stromquist (eds) *Distant Alliances*, New York: RoutledgeFalmer.

Ware, Cellestine (1970) *Woman Power. The Movement for Women's Liberation*, New York: Tower Publications.

Winfield, Linda (1994) *Developing Resilience in Urban Youth*, Urban Monograph Series, Oak Brook, IL: North Central Regional Educational Laboratory.

World Education (*c.* 1999) *Girls' Access to Education (GATE) in Nepal: Reaching Adolescents with Literacy, Health Knowledge and Skills*, Boston and Kathmandu: World Education.

Yudelman, Sally (1993) *Hopeful Openings*, Arlington, VA: Fundación Interamericana.

Zúñiga, Miryan (1999) 'From development as a social motherhood project to development as a prospective for new gender relations in the coming century: Some thoughts from the experience of the women from El Tambo, Colombia', paper presented at the International Seminar on Literacy for Women's Empowerment in the 21st Century, 10–14 December, Bangkok: UNESCO.

Part II

Women's empowerment in a global world

3 Envisaging power in Philippine migration

The Janus effect

Pauline Gardiner Barber

Migrants, time and local spaces

The people who are social subjects (recipients, clients, targets) for empowerment interventions typically live in a home base described as a 'community'. While empowerment is usually associated with a bedrock of 'community' and is thought about in localizing terms, threats to local empowerment are often seen as originating in processes of modernity and globalization. This chapter investigates empowerment through migration scenarios where community and a sense of what is local take on different connotations. It questions how migration scenarios can enhance our understanding of empowerment in a context of local–global processes. Migration engages local and global spaces, and produces multiple and mobile attachments to place, thereby detaching empowerment scenarios from one locale. The Philippine migrants described here traverse and negotiate mutually entangled local and global spaces and power structures. For them, globalization processes at the macro-level are rendered concrete in the micro-politics of daily routines that entail attachments to various people in the local spaces of communities far flung from the place where daily life is being lived. This applies to Philippine migrants living in the Philippines who desire to re-migrate as much as it does to migrants living overseas and longing to be back in the Philippines. The migrant narratives presented here extend over different configurations of community and nation. They express the spatially mobile yet contingent qualities of agency and empowerment. Their example provides a challenge to localized and community-based understandings of empowerment and how the articulation of the local with global processes is represented in development writing.

The shifting vistas of empowerment and migration invite further critical unpacking of how community development scenarios and their social dynamics are discursively located in time, not just in space. Migration reveals the ways in which development writing can over-represent the temporal continuity of social and cultural rhythms in the local, for example the expectation that communities are bearers of indigenous knowledge. Because of migration and other interruptions in communities, local continuities such as knowledge cannot be assumed and should be a matter for research. Where this is not done, empowerment discourses continue a 'tradition' of romanticizing notions of community in development writing (Li 1996; Agrawal 1997) where uncritical and untheorized reference to 'community' as a site for empowerment assumes social cohesion and avoids questions of social power differentials and divisions. In communities that experience migration, social power differentials are likely to be altered in obvious and less obvious ways. Migrants typically bring new perspectives and resources to their communities of origin. Thus, even when absent, migrants contribute to local empowerment dynamics.

For migrants, inasmuch as empowerment is a subjective matter, their sense of personal power is seen as relative to the various contexts they have lived and worked in over time. For migrants, personal power is fluid and subject to constant reworking. As time passes and they reflect on their experiences, migrants' assessments of the positive and negative aspects of migration are subject to contradiction and shifts in meaning. In other words, empowerment for migrants is time and context sensitive – it is contingent. This is also true for the kin of migrants. Migration and its circular temporal qualities thus eclipse the linear formulation of time for those who travel and those who remain behind. This has implications for assessments of empowerment both for migrants and for their communities.

In effect, migration exposes an ambiguous relationship between empowerment and development. It also invites a different critical purchase for empowerment discourse, one that embraces the ambiguities of power and subject agency, how these are contingently processed in contexts that extend beyond the local. When thinking about migration and/as empowerment, it becomes difficult to isolate empowerment as a clear-cut condition. Rather, empowerment occurs within a process of ongoing micro-political negotiation – it is not a state or condition that once arrived at is achieved and moved on from. Empowerment is an ever-present possibility. However, Philippine migrants also reveal the interconnections between empowerment and disempowerment, especially when we consider the structural conditions that compel migration.

Empowerment and 'the local'

Communities are not as neatly configured socially, spatially and temporally as many who use the concept suggest. They are shot through with different sets of social interests, minimally those of social class, gender and age, plus other various local sub-sets based on identity-related differences in power and powerlessness. Moreover, communities and those who 'belong' to them are not contained in local named places (Appadurai 1991; Basch *et al.* 1994; Clifford 1994; Rouse 1995). Migrants, because they are out of sight locally, do not figure significantly in mainstream development imaginings of community, and their concerns are off the page in writing about empowerment in local communities. This is curious because migrants play a significant role in the livelihood practices of their families and their 'home' communities, and traces of their presence are evident (for example, migrants often contribute to housing upgrades, from wood to concrete). Disclosure of the 'true value' of such contributions by the 'disempowered' is an important stage in becoming 'empowered' (all too often the only stage). In many instances of empowerment 'training' for women, group discussion reveals the economic significance of their routine maternal and wifely duties, which are often double- and triple-tracked with various forms of household production, subsistence agriculture, community work and so on. How often do such activities include discussion of migration and local power flows? Migrants are important 'behind the scene' actors in shifts in livelihood and class and cultural practices in their Philippine and overseas communities. This chapter can be regarded as an invitation to write migrants into empowerment scenarios, albeit in a manner that challenges ideas about local continuities and definitions of empowerment. Philippine migration reveals local and global processes to be in ever-present tension, as are stability and flux. Time, space and places migrants call 'home' – 'communities' in our texts – are also reworked through migration. Class and cultural practices lie at the centre of migration and empowerment scenarios.

As this volume demonstrates, some feminist writers link empowerment to forms of collective political action explicitly and consciously concerned with social transformation. Some even dismiss the usefulness of attributing empowerment to individuated action and knowledge. In concluding the chapter, I caution against those theoretical models that insist upon collective political action as evidence that empowerment has occurred. This limitation is particularly germane to Western-based models that cast labour migrants as victims. As the migrants described here illustrate, agency and related empowerment dynamics can be interpreted in the light of culturally infused discourses of migrant sacrifice, suffering and romanticized notions of community, a reading that suggests all migrants are disempowered. The cultural 'surface' of such discourses, however, does not necessarily negate individual assessments of empowerment (see Chang and Groves 2000). Some migrants see migration as an opportunity; others express ambivalence. Nonetheless, the discourses of suffering and tragedy are often called upon to highlight the structural inequities that underlie Philippine migration generally. Thus, the cultural and positional politics associated with attributing agency and empowerment in migration scenarios are especially challenging and push beyond simple binary explanations about individual and collective politics and the matter of social transformation. In insisting that claims about social transformation and empowerment involve a dialogue between theoretical and socially located knowledge, this chapter navigates between structural understandings of migration and its classed aspects, and post-structural insights about the contingencies of migrant experience. Examples are drawn from my own fieldwork in the Philippines and Canada, and from other studies.

Gender in Philippine labour migration

Migration has long been a feature of Philippine society. International labour migration and its diaspora have become the cornerstone of Philippine 'development', and a primary means for servicing national indebtedness. In 1995, the

Philippine Overseas Workers' Welfare Administration estimated the number of legal and undocumented Philippine workers abroad to be 4.2 million persons, some 43 per cent of whom were probably working illegally (Go 1997). International migration is but one of the legacies of colonial domination, first by Spain and then the USA (from 1898 until nominal independence in 1946). Underscoring the relatively recent escalation in migration is widespread poverty, caused in part by limited access to resources such as land and secure employment for many Filipinos.[1]

Historically, US colonial policies precipitated several waves of Philippine migration, namely, contract labourers in the agricultural industries of Hawaii and California, and professional and skilled workers in the USA and its regions in the Asian-Pacific. By the 1960s Philippine men were also becoming prominent in international seafaring labour markets (Go 1997). However, the scale and nature of Philippine international migration shifted dramatically during the 1970s as demand for male construction workers in the Middle East accelerated, and increasing numbers of Filipinos responded to economic disadvantage by taking on overseas contract work (Pertierra 1994; Margold 1995). As the economy worsened in the mid-1980s, Filipinos turned to Asian labour markets, encouraged by official policies that saw labour export as a means of generating revenue and easing local unemployment (CIIR 1987; Chant and McIlwaine 1995). Also during the 1980s, Philippine women who had long migrated domestically in search of employment (Koo and Smith 1983; Trager 1984, 1988; Findlay 1987; Eviota 1992), increased their employment overseas. At this time, there were well over one and a half million Filipinos employed as contract workers in over one hundred and twenty countries (CIIR 1987; Arao 1991). Even more remarkable than the overall size of the Philippine migrant labour force is the relatively recent, rapid change in its gender structure. In the early 1980s, men comprised the majority of land-based Filipino labour migrants – by 1994 women made up 60 per cent of neophyte migrant workers leaving the Philippines (Go 1997).

While Philippine colonial history clearly created many of the preconditions for Filipino mobility, shifts in the gender, class and racialized configurations of globalized labour markets are also important. Typically, male labour migrants continue to seek employment in shipping and construction trades while women work in all tiers of service sectors in Southeast Asian, North American, European and Middle Eastern labour markets. The majority of Philippine women labour migrants – 92 per cent of them in 1992 (Beltran and Rodriguez 1996) – work in domestic service, so much so that the word 'Filipina' has undergone a shift in meaning. Once proudly (and sometimes controversially) mobilized discursively by Philippine feminists and others who wished to distinguish Philippine women from the generic Filipino, 'Filipina' is becoming negatively coloured by the demeaned class and status connotations accorded paid domestic labour.[2] To speak of Filipina now, particularly from outside of the Philippines, is to conjure up the idea of domestic service. For example, 'Filipina' has become synonymous with maid in Hong Kong (Constable 1997) and with nanny in some affluent urban neighbourhoods in Canada. To be a 'maid' overseas, however, does not have the same meaning in the Philippines that it does in Hong Kong and Canada.[3]

Sometimes Philippine women's migration produces im/migrants elsewhere, as in Canada where the majority of Filipino migrants are women who have entered Canada with employment visas under the 'Live-in Caregiver Programme'. This programme provides visas that allow women to apply for Canadian landed immigrant status as a prerequisite to permanent citizenship after a set period of time and various conditions have been met (Daenzer 1997). Bakan and Stasiulis's (1997) investigation of foreign domestic workers in Canada found that women from the Philippines comprise the largest group of entrants under the Caregiver Programme, for example, 61 per cent in 1992 and 75 per cent in 1995.[4] The number of visas awarded to domestic workers under this programme fluctuates dramatically (down from 10,739 in 1990 to around 2,000 in 1996) with shifting state assessments of economic priorities and desirable citizenship subjects. Put differently, visa allocations are based on state practices infused with class, gender and race concerns, both internal to Canada and in international relations.

As with other migrant destinations, estimates of Philippine women working illegally in major Canadian cities such as Toronto are high (Bakan and Stasiulis 1997: 50). Advocates for foreign domestic workers routinely protest declines in the numbers of legally issued visas on the grounds that this simply increases the number of illegal workers because the demand remains high. Moreover, the flow of workers continues because the transnational 'infrastructure' of recruitment agencies includes some who operate outside the reaches of official policy. The nannies in Toronto and other Canadian cities are, however, only one contour of the Philippine labour diaspora.

Reading power in migration

The strikingly gendered character of Philippine migration and its classed qualities suggest a need to dislodge homogenizing discourses about migration and diaspora.[5] Many critiques can be and have been made about the disruptive effects of national reliance upon women's migration (Heyzer *et al.* 1994; Chant and McIlwaine 1995; Hernandez and Tigno 1995) and the subordinated character of their service sector employment, for example in Canada (Macklin 1994; Bakan and Stasiulis 1997) and in Hong Kong (Constable 1997). However, as Tyner (1994) has noted, much theoretical work remains to be done, particularly with regard to the gendered quality of Philippine migration. This is because migrant experience tends to be used strategically in writing that calls for political action and policy review. Understandably, the priorities have been to secure equitable employment through bilateral agreements and to hold Philippine and other states accountable, as when, for example, Philippine migrants are subjected to legal regimes Filipinos regard as unjust. As I have argued elsewhere (Barber 1996, 1997), one discursive outcome of these political interventions is that

Philippine women migrants are alternatively construed as heroines (mostly in state-derived discourses) and/or victims (in advocacy discourses, including those from feminist perspectives). Such binary representations downplay migrant agency, the differences between migrants and the possibility that migration can lead to personal empowerment. They also obscure the class dynamics that migration engages. Here, I want to suggest the interrelationship between personal empowerment and its infusion into class and cultural politics. I also hope to make clear that disempowerment and empowerment can be different renderings of the same sets of experiences viewed from separate angles for different audiences. Political economy, however, frames relations of power that remain intransigent.

My research spans eight years of routine visits to several Philippine Visayan communities where I have tracked migration in conversations with migrants and their kin, including social networks extending to Canada.[6] This work demonstrates how migration creates new conditions and spaces for the reworking of Philippine class, gender and cultural identities. On the one hand, daily life in many Philippine communities is now punctuated by the comings and goings of migration, the receipt of gifts and remittances, or the unrealized longings generated by these possibilities. On the other hand, the migrants themselves are inserted into various foreign contexts and the intimate environments of their workplaces, some stark and hostile, others more welcoming and alluring. Conditions and feelings can shift register. For example, migrant voices can be stoic for Philippine relatives, despondent with other migrants and social activists, but more positively animated about the class and cultural capital acquired through migration when a deeper temporality is invoked, such as occurred in Hong Kong in 1997 when Philippine migrants fretted over the effects of China's impending governance (Constable 1999). Regardless of the character of the host country, its policies and employers, migrants strive to exert control over their lives as they negotiate their various local and global 'homes' and workplaces; they do so through mobilizing, reflectively, various social, cultural, political and economic resources.

In my conversations and review of media accounts, none of these women see themselves as disempowered, although they have experienced disempowering conditions. Neither are they victims. They are, however, exposed to serious risk; the nature of their migration and work makes them vulnerable to various forms of exploitation, harassment and even violence. Yet, the manner in which they seek control over such conditions, their strategic negotiation with such odds, is not often discussed. Exceptions include Hong Kong-based research by Constable (1997) and Groves and Chang (1999). The former explores agency and its relationship to collective political action addressing longer-term migration policy and its political and economic structural preconditions. The latter, in an interesting dialogical framework, explore different interpretive possibilities for understanding Philippine migrants' agency and cultural politics, and the subtleties of this interplay. Both projects point, although not explicitly, to the Janus (double-faced) aspects of agency; how migrants' actions to assert control and dignity in the personal nooks and crannies of their constrained living spaces and long working hours can be recast against them. Both studies reveal self-disciplining regimes for personal conduct.

Constable's study examines the contradictions associated with *Tinig Filipino*, a migrant newsletter that includes correspondence extolling maids to be better, more polite (subservient) employees and more publicly demure, civic-minded Filipinos. This advice responds to negative commentaries in local media about the unreliability of Filipino maids and their purportedly raucous social demeanour when they congregate in public squares on their days off. Similarly construed racist challenges to Philippine maids are also present in Malaysia (Chin 1997) and Singapore (Yeoh *et al.* 1999). In Constable's reading, *Tinig Filipino* articles represent a Foucauldian self-disciplining subversion of political potential. Similarly, Chang and Groves (2000) identify an 'ethic of service' among some Hong Kong-based Philippine women. Paradoxically, the ethic, they suggest, constitutes one expression of resistance from this structurally disempowered group (migrant Filipino women) to counter racialized public challenges to their sexuality and the lingering effects of their historical (colonial) association with prostitution (see also Groves and Chang 1999). Some women practise lesbian sexuality, others monitor the sexual expression of their peers, yet others experience overseas work as a respite from their sexually demanding partners. As Tacoli (1999) suggests in research on Philippine migrants in Italy, overseas work represents one avenue for women to escape an unhappy marriage, or to avoid the social stigma of marital breakdown. It also enables women who are mothers to practise self-interest (in travel and personal savings) disguised as maternal effort. None of these researchers explicitly engage with debates over empowerment but their work lends itself to my argument about the double-faced nature of power.

Most Philippine women migrants who exit their country legally are over-educated for the forms of employment they take on overseas. We would expect them, therefore, to hold strong images, empowering yet shifting imaginaries (in Anderson's 1983 sense) of new lives – for themselves and their family members – beyond their tenuous location in the Philippine economy and their overseas underemployment. This is particularly true for the women who enter Canada where their predominance in the Live-in Caregiver's Programme suggests both their desirability as employees and their longer-term im/migration strategies (Macklin 1994). As one Canadian newspaper editorial tellingly suggested, the normative middle-class Canadian family in the late 1990s includes a Philippine nanny and a four-wheel drive vehicle (*Globe and Mail*, 18 September 1997). The following sections present four different narratives, three from my own research, one from media voices. They reveal the shifting terrain of class processes, cultural politics and personal agency in the complexly articulated identities of the women who migrate. Empowerment issues for women like Christina, Maria and Portia (all pseudonyms) and Leticia Cables are influenced by events in the lives of other people they care about or feel obligated to in Philippine communities. Their decisions are affected by notions of femininity in Philippine culture politics, particularly with regard to mothers (Maria and Leticia) and daughters (Christina), but also aunts (Portia, Christina and Maria). The personally empowering aspects of migration for these and other migrant women are thus in flux, tied to contingencies and power flows in two (or more) locations. This would also be true for empowerment scenarios in any local community where ideas of community common interest can disguise the contingencies of micro-power.

Note the dynamic spatial-temporal perspectives at play in the narratives. Through the process of ordering their memories, the women reflect on their pre-migration and post-migration experiences, in effect their *past* personal histories. Because they are citizens of Canada, Maria and Portia, and potentially Leticia, represent most directly the contingencies of empowerment. In their *present* circumstances they are concerned about a *future* that is cast in terms of different scenarios of 'community', where should they live, with whom, how to determine this? Also informing this research are conversations with other women in Philippine communities about an imagined *future* migration. These women articulate the reworking of gendered cultural and class understandings of migration and diaspora. They show how 'local' cultural knowledge (the sub-text in empowerment processes) is constantly being infused with novel understandings of migration both from returning migrants, communications from friends and kin overseas, and media pronouncements about the pitfalls and opportunities posed by overseas work.

Agency, class and the cultural politics of leaving

During a research trip to the Philippines in 1997, I met Christina, a 30-year-old woman who had just returned to her home in Iloilo city after completing a two-year employment contract with a five-star hotel in Dubai. She carried with her an array of expensive consumer goods, such as leather products and gold jewellery, to distribute to family and friends in the customary gift exchange of homecoming Filipinos, or *balikbayans* (Basch *et al.* 1994: 257). After a respite of several months in Iloilo, Christina returned to Dubai for a further contract with the same employer. In several meetings she told me her overseas experience has been relatively successful from her point of view. Of course, the work has been tedious at times but she has felt relatively safe given the misfortunes of some fellow travellers she knows about (particularly illegal Russian women migrants and Philippine women who have risked sexual liaisons and become pregnant). As she put it 'there have been no major surprises for me'. Most importantly, she feels she has done well through the 'help' she has provided to her parents and younger siblings.

As all migrants desire, Christina's efforts interrupt class and gender certainties in Philippine society. Her remittances to family members contribute to the education of younger siblings, and she expects her savings to afford a more secure, personally independent future than seemed possible given her family background. There have been costs, however, and overseas employment is the culmination of years of hard struggle, first to complete university education and then to earn sufficient wages that, as she puts it: 'I would not be working just for myself, but also for my family.' For single women in Christina's position, negotiating these obstacles represents a personally satisfying process of class transition, especially in terms of cultural norms. However, the experience is also contradictory. This is especially so when read against gender and class geopolitics. Her work (in a gendered job in an overseas tourist sector) contributes to Philippine national foreign debt repayments even as it represents her underemployment and the loss of benefit from her skills and education in her 'home' community. On the other hand, for a woman to contribute to the well-being of her family fulfils one of the dictates of Philippine femininity. Morally, she is a good and dutiful daughter both in terms of the family and the Philippine state that calculates the export of gendered labour into its development policies. And this is what Christina finds personally rewarding, empowering even, however constrained it might seem through 'Western eyes'.

Christina's agency in class and cultural processes is of wider significance. After graduating from a local university with a Bachelor of Science, she travelled to Manila where she took secretarial work for 4,000 pesos per month (approximately US$160), barely sufficient to meet her living expenses. Frustrated with her underemployment, she investigated overseas employment opportunities before settling on the Dubai contract. It appeared less risky than some of the more exploitative and degrading scenarios she had heard about from the media and first hand from friends. For example, she knew lesser-ranked hotels often called upon staff to provide sexual services to hotel guests. Recruitment fees and charges for travel documents amounted to three months wages and were paid for with money loaned from kin. Since her salary increased by 1,000 pesos and the hotel provided her with accommodation and meals, the loan seemed manageable. Friends working in Dubai hotels and official state-sponsored seminars provided information about Philippine and Dubai regulatory regimes and prepared her for periodic pregnancy testing and state-enforced celibacy when in Dubai. Because of the commonplace nature of the comings and goings of overseas workers in Philippine communities, these invasions of personal privacy – embodied discipline in Foucault's sense (cf. Constable 1997; Ong 1995; Margold 1994) – are seen as 'normal' to migration time–space.

Christina is the seventh daughter in a family of twelve children, four of whom have become overseas workers. A brother works in shipping, one older sister is in Malaysia and a younger sister, her confidence bolstered by the apparent success of the others, moved to Hong Kong early in 1998. Before retirement, both parents worked in domestic service in a Philippine middle-class professional household, her mother as a housekeeper, her father as a driver and gardener. Members of the employer's family continue to provide economic support to the elderly parents and one of Christina's other sisters works in the household of one of the children of her parents' employers, such is the mutually negotiated imbrication of domestic service employment in middle-class Philippine society. Indeed, it continues to be common for middle-class families to 'take-in' a young person from a poor household, usually a female but sometimes a male. In return for domestic service, what Filipinos term 'helping', the youth is typically provided with the resources, social and economic, necessary to complete high school and sometimes university. On university campuses, this relationship may be mirrored in arrangements that place students in faculty housing and allow them to pay for their accommodation and food with labour.

Such arrangements challenge class boundaries as young women from rural and working-class urban households obtain education not otherwise possible. As a result of their engagement with the norms of middle-class culture in the households they work in, they acquire what Bourdieu (1984) calls 'cultural capital' in their exposure to otherwise unfamiliar class practices. This kind of shift, as Christina's example indicates, helps some to achieve their personal goals. But most importantly, the class practices Christina's case exposes are foundational to the scale and form of gendered Philippine labour migration. Many of the well-qualified women who migrate overseas originate from households defined by economic hardship, yet they present middle-class cultural capital confidently, just as they are the bearers of the highly regarded conventions of Philippine cultural femininity in overseas labour markets. Again, this reveals that migration can be construed as personally empowering in economic and class terms, at least subjectively, even when the results suggest otherwise.

Christina is but one of many women I have encountered who has benefited from the migration of female kin and gone on to reproduce that same relationship for younger relatives. This process of generationally gendered class negotiation remains invisible in many accounts of Philippine migration, particularly those emphasizing victimization. In Christina's case and for her friends contemplating overseas work, the contingencies of migration are set aside through reference to the Filipino cultural idiom of *bahala na*, which communicates something equivalent to 'so be it', the rest lies 'in God's hands.' By the same token, fate is negotiated with agency and agency has links, however tenuous, to empowerment. Of course, not all plans will flow as smoothly as those recounted here. Eventually, Christina hopes to settle in the Philippines and develop a pig farming business. Many return migrants want to start businesses with the financial capital from overseas wages but few achieve these goals (see also Cruz and Paganoni 1989; Lane 1992; Osteria 1994). Instead, capital is exhausted through debt repayment, emergency expenses and requests for consumer goods from kin – often leading to sequential labour. Indeed, Christina has taken a further contract.

Contingent sojourns

For migrants who travel to Canada where wage rates are minimal by Canadian standards, but relatively high for overseas domestic labour markets, migration trajectories differ from those in Asia and the Middle East. As mentioned, Philippine women entering Canada are eligible for more permanent immigration status, which many take up, thus diasporic possibilities for long-term resettlement are more likely. In Asian and Middle Eastern states, repressive migrant labour regulations proscribe citizenship claims. In Canada, however, resettlement remains conditional upon familial and community relations in Canadian and Philippine locales. Such conditionality tempers feelings of personal empowerment.

This is true for Maria, now a Canadian living in Ottawa. Like Christina, her migration history began with underemployment in Manila. Maria is from Negros Oriental. She is ten years older than Christina and has less formal education. Her experiences, however, also include her negotiation of different class practices and locales, the successes from which rebound in her Philippine home community where I first met her in 1993 on one of her periodic visits with family. Maria's path to Canada included a sojourn in Hong Kong, a popular destination for Visayan women seeking overseas employment and a means to migrate to Canada. In Hong Kong, she worked for employers of different nationalities in the sizeable expatriate community before moving to Canada with her Canadian employers. As for Christina, Maria's many siblings have benefited from having female kin dispersed through Southeast Asian countries and in Canada. The remittances provide housing and education for younger relatives.

Maria's migration, paradoxically, originated in her need to provide for her son after her separation from his father. When I first met her, she was trying to bring her son to Canada where she is employed as a community care nurse and holds citizenship. It had been ten years of struggle to arrive at that point and while there had been some challenging moments, such as her *de facto* detention by one Hong Kong employer, she has accomplished much and has few regrets. As is common for women who came to Canada under the Live-in Caregiver Programme, her Canadian employers hired her sister.

Maria's migration goal has always been to secure her son's future and to provide for her parents. She has succeeded in the latter: her parents live with Maria's son (in his late teens when I first met her), in one of the few two-level concrete houses in their coastal *barangay* (the smallest political unit in the Philippines). There has been, however, a glitch in Maria's plans. Apparently, her son is reluctant to relocate to Canada. He visited Maria in Ottawa during the winter of 1997 where he experienced severe 'homesickness'. After three months, the draw of his Philippine 'home', kin and friendships proved too strong and his mother's dreams of their better life too remote from his own experience. He returned to his grandparents' household in the Philippines. Maria's Canadian 'home base' thus remains provisional. She returns regularly to her Philippine 'home' fearing that her son could be 'entrapped' by a local family keen to tap into her remittances. An accidental pregnancy of a daughter would be one vehicle for entrapment. Maria's concerns are such that 'she would drop everything and go there to try to stop this'. In Canada, however, she enjoys her work, maintains an active social life with other Filipino migrants, mostly through church-based Philippine networks (Nagata 1987) and is politically active around issues of justice for Philippine migrants.

In contrast, Portia, who travelled from a Visayan community to Halifax some twelve years ago, migrated mainly out of curiosity and a desire for travel. The support she has extended to Philippine kin has been elective, not obligatory. Friends and kin also preceded and followed her as domestic service workers, and they provide an important Philippine social community for her in Canada. She is a member of a church-based group of Filipinos, mostly from the Visayas, who hold monthly suppers and evenings of entertainment where Philippine news and cultural experiences are exchanged. In this diasporic niche, Philippine cultural affinities take precedence over the class loyalties that otherwise mark Halifax society socially and spatially. Were it not for the cultural politics set in motion by diaspora and the class distortions of Philippine development, prominent members of the Halifax medical establishment – once themselves migrants from the Philippines – might not so readily mingle socially with care-giving service providers and, on occasion, Philippine crew members from the busy Halifax container port. However, class differences are muddied by the vagaries of Philippine development and muted by the draw of sharing Filipino culture with fellow travellers. Cultural differentness thus serves to diminish the usual social lines drawn by Halifax's medical hierarchies and Philippine cultural loyalties remain strong, even as they are reworked within this particular configuration of class and community.

When I first met Portia she was 'content' with her life in Halifax 'for the time being at least'. She said, 'It is my choice to stay here or go there.' Unlike Maria, familial disruption does not draw Portia to an imagined future return 'home'. Rather, it is memories of familial continuity and its absence in her Halifax home that fuel her somewhat romantic vision of a Philippine-based retirement. She sees it as a place where she could enjoy the company of her nieces' and nephews' children, some of whom she has helped to educate. This image is particularly acute because her employment entails care-giving to an elderly woman whose children reside outside of Canada. On bad days, she finds her responsibilities daunting, and cannot see herself remaining in Canada in her old age, despite her Canadian citizenship, pension and health benefits. Portia's elderly employer has recently passed away. Portia's contract was extended to prepare the employer's house for sale. Subsequently she moved to a rented apartment and is supporting herself doing housekeeping for members of her parish. She would prefer to work for a single employer and to maintain her own residence. The fact that she returned despite the fact that her employer died while she was on 'vacation' in the Philippines suggests Canada's draw continues despite future uncertainties.

This is also true for Leticia Cables who is arguably the most well-known Philippine woman working in Canada. Unlike other Philippine women migrants such as Flor Contemplacion and Sarah Balabagan,[7] whose criminal prosecution and severe sentencing in foreign states (Singapore and the United Arab Emirates respectively) received widespread international coverage in 1995, Leticia Cables's reputation is localized in Canada. I include her as a final 'reading' of the complexities of agency and empowerment for individual migrants.

On 17 February 2000, the *Globe and Mail* headline read, 'Filipina nanny agrees to leave Canada.' So begins the penultimate article in a series of commentaries about Leticia Cables, all of which seemed calculated to encourage support for her claim to remain in Canada. She is described in this particular piece as 'The popular Edmonton nanny who ran afoul of immigration authorities because she worked too hard.' Leticia Cables violated the terms of her visa that restricted her to one employer for an initial two-year period. She took additional part-time work, we are told, because her employer, a lawyer, agreed her wages were too low. Apparently, she was highly valued by her employer and members of the parish in which she twice sought sanctuary. Some months earlier, after the first threat of deportation, Leticia had fled to her church where she remained for four months while attempting to overturn the deportation order. She was partially successful in November when the Immigration Minister allowed the case to undergo review by the Federal Court. On 24 December she was granted a temporary work visa while she awaited the court's decision.

Globe and Mail readers were introduced to Leticia Cables in a series of articles extending back to the beginning of her church 'exile' and intensifying in December 1999. For example, on 24 December, the banner was '"Let me work again", the Christmas wish of Filipina nanny: The threat of deportation has ended but she still cannot provide for children back home.' At this moment, with her deportation order under appeal, Leticia joined her employer's household which in February publicly noted their distress about the possible loss of their new but beloved nanny. Despite the publicity, the court declined to review the case, and Leticia returned to her church while calling for a reprieve from the minister. 'Why are they being so mean to me?', she is reported to have said. Nonetheless, by mid-February, she agreed to leave Canada and was escorted to Manila by two immigration officers on 29 February 2000.

Six days later, the paper provided an update: 'Philippine nanny wants to return to Canada. Leticia Cables is praying that she'll soon be back in Canada' begins the account. We are told that she considers Canada 'the best country in the world' and, despite her extreme fatigue, soon after her arrival in Manila she visited the Canadian embassy to begin the process of filing papers, obtaining policy and medical clearances to apply for a second Canadian live-in care-giver's visa. One has to ask here how her medical circumstances and her relationship to criminality in the Philippines might have shifted over the forty-eight hour period since her arrival. On the other hand, the Philippine (and Canadian) state's bureaucratic processing of im/migration generates significant revenue. In order for her reapplication to be successful, it was necessary for Leticia to receive special written ministerial consent. Such consent is a condition of re-entry for a deportee and was verbally promised in the negotiations over deportation. The article concludes with a pronouncement by Leticia on the generosity of the Canadian people and the mainly fair treatment she feels compelled to report, although she declared the Federal Court of Appeal's dismissal of her case to be unfair.

On 28 June 2000, maintaining the same tone, the headline was 'Industrious nanny can return to Canada.' On 6 July, the paper carried a picture of her thoughtfully studying her *Filipinas* passport. The caption read: 'Back to work.

Filipina Leticia Cables checks her passport and her new Canadian work visa during a stopover at Vancouver Airport yesterday, on her way to Edmonton … she was deported from Canada for working more than federal rules allow so she could supplement her nanny wages.' This may be the last Canadians learn about Leticia Cables but my research suggests she will continue to negotiate the policy and personal environments she deems vital to her own and her family's future. Media reports suggest remittances supported her husband and two adolescent children in the Philippines.

Prior to her arrival in Canada, Leticia, like Maria, had worked for ten years as a 'maid' in Hong Kong. Her work history suggests she has not lived with her Philippine family during most of her children's childhood, some eleven years. What is quite striking in the Canadian media coverage is the insistence that being deported from Canada constitutes the deprivation, that hard-hearted 'mean' officials victimized her. Interestingly, unlike many discussions of Philippine women overseas workers, both academic and popular, the *Globe and Mail* reports said little about any familial or maternal deprivation arising from her overseas employment. This silence may be partially explained by Leticia's agency in directing the public discourse dissecting her life; that for her to express some measure of joy in deportation would be an easing of her seemingly tight control of the media storyline about her Canadian future. But more than this, the media accounts reveal how Philippine migrants transcend their victimizing representation. Leticia Cables's struggles acquired a public profile that she and her supporters (described in one report as her 'adoptive' group) skilfully employed to advantage. However, all migrants contend with migration legalities, the vagaries of official policy, unfounded 'friendly' advice (Leticia's downfall, she claimed) and unreliable employers. Here it is useful to consider Leticia Cable's negotiation of her Canadian visa in terms of empowerment discourse.

Researchers on Philippine women working in regional labour markets have only recently begun to explore the cultural politics surrounding Philippine women's migration and to discuss forms of ambivalence about returning 'home' to the Philippines. As noted, Constable (1999) and Chang and Groves (2000) explore the possibility that migration may free some women from their husband's sexual demands and control. Both studies describe Philippine women's economic entrepreneurialism on their days off, where they generate income through selling goods and services to each other as one means to counter their exploitative work environments. Similarly, they maintain Filipino social networks in church settings and in other organizations where activist politics are expressed. This research demonstrates some women's commitment to living and working outside of the Philippines, just as others struggle with a pull toward home in the face of certain repeat labour contracts. Other studies of domestic service workers (for example, in the USA, Romero 1994) demonstrate that, and as Portia and Maria make clear, live-out employment is preferable because it allows time for personal pursuits beyond the scrutiny of employers.

Empowerment dialectics

For Maria, Portia, Leticia and many other Philippine women living in diaspora space (Brah 1996), their imagined futures are constantly reworked, in part because their form of labour migration requires that they travel and live alone. Their family relations are maintained around the edges of employment and state dictates in home and host locations. Some women find freedom from the cultural constraints of marriage liberating (Parrenas 1997). This is quite likely true for Leticia Cables and for some women interviewed by Constable (1999) in Hong Kong who expressed their ambivalence about returning to Philippine cultural and familial constraints. Others, such as Maria, worry that their economic gains occur at the expense of a more personally fulfilling life, 'what might have been' as she puts it in a darker moment. All of the women I have met negotiate confining and liberating tendencies in Philippine culture as they live it. For them and other diasporic Filipinos, their culture is both mobile and gendered. Likewise, the structural and personal dynamics of their particular form of employment pose many challenges because the work is transacted in intimate spaces where exploitation is emotionally loaded and abuse more readily disguised (Barber 2000). These conditions can be read simultaneously as empowering and disempowering.

To conclude, the frames (temporal and spatial) and the social realities within which power is negotiated are not locally bounded; that is they can only be minimally construed as community centred. Here I think of the changing class and gender connotations of the 'Filipina' as a result of negative 'feedback' from international migration experiences and other contingent processes of identity construction and interpretation. Also relevant here is Maria's struggle to be a good 'mother' to her son, *in absentia*, understood through a filter of Philippine and Canadian cultural politics. Normatively, Philippine families are emotionally 'close' and supposed to live together, as Portia suggests, in layers of generations when this is not interrupted through migration. This makes Maria's distance from her son emotionally difficult. Alternatively, by Canadian middle-class standards, she is a 'good mother' in her concern over his education and future. Yet he remains disaffected from his mother's ambition. Maria's situation guides my earlier reference to the silence surrounding Leticia Cables's family. In both cases, ambivalence and contradiction attend any attribution of dis/empowerment.

Further translocal dynamics arise from the national and international policies that circumscribe Philippine labour migration – for example, Christina's need to finance her overseas work with funds borrowed from relatives. And in terms of micro-politics and disciplined subjects, there are the ways in which migrants adapt to controlling state and employer practices; for example, the manner in which Christina uncritically subjected herself to state scrutiny and employer surveillance. However, despite the fact that domestic service is demeaning, low-waged and often risky, it is constructed as a viable livelihood strategy by many of the women university students I have talked to (with emergent middle-class orientations) and in the working-class environs of coastal Visayan communities.

Migration thus sustains its draw in contemporary Philippine cultural politics – by class and gender – with plenty of encouragement from the Philippine state. For all that is known about the reasons not to migrate, women still leave encouraged by their kin. Their acts fall within a regime of power and discipline from an engendered global political economy that manages to capture their future vision. Does this structural disempowerment preclude individual agency and its empowering possibilities? I think not.

Migration inflects local class practices in ways that tempt visions of empowerment. Ethnographically this is revealed through the quotidian character of Philippine migration, seen in the comings and goings of people, the cash and commodities they carry, and the ideas exchanged about these flows in the migrant-sending communities. Global processes are 'localized' through the anticipation of departures and the enthusiasm created by returning migrants. At such moments it is possible to overlook that the Philippine state orchestrates and depends economically upon labour migration and the funds it generates. Also set aside are remonstrations that many others profit from labour migration both in smaller and larger ways, by providing financial and employment placement services, often with exorbitant fees (Bakan and Stasiulis 1995). Most remarkably, Philippine women's migration encompasses complex shifts in gender and class, and these include the assumption of cultural capital by women during their tenure as domestic workers in better-off households. The shifts seem modest when placed alongside the patterns of cyclical contracts, the risks that the work entails and the fact that women beneficiaries of migration remittances may well end up in the same circuits of labour migration, even in Canada – as we saw in the case of Maria's sister and Portia's nieces. Nonetheless, the desires compelling migration remain strong in Philippine communities and can withstand the test of the realities of structural, actual and symbolic violence in Bourdieu's (1977) sense of emotional indebtedness (Barber 2000).

Given the contradictions and contingencies, both cultural and strategically personal in migrant narratives, it is striking that migrant Philippine women are unwilling to construe their lives as disempowered in ways that match up with international discourses of victimized domestic workers. Most media coverage of migrant Philippine women that I have read in Philippine and Canadian papers discusses their abuse. This is why the media examination of Leticia Cables, her inspirational courage and strength is remarkable. Nonetheless, her story holds some parallels to the portrayal in the media of Sara Balabagan's story (see note 7). Both accounts embody central contradictions with respect to Philippine gendered cultural politics. As with Cables, Balabagan's status as a contemporary heroine arises in part because, initially, she took desperate measures to defend herself against injustice. Balabagan also had moral appeal because she acted in defence of her honour, a gendered example of Filipino triumph against adversity. In Catholic Philippines, different actors can read the Balabagan story strategically to extract different sorts of meanings. For the state, it is a story about its care-taking role in assisting distressed migrants. For potential migrants it provides a narrative of hope about fateful suffering as well as survival against great odds. For non-governmental organizations it becomes a cautionary tale about the pitfalls of migration and the need to address domestic and international policies. However, as I hope I have demonstrated here, migration experiences are more varied and complexly articulated (historically, culturally, socially) than is suggested through the telling and retelling of the Contemplacion tragedy and the Balabagan travesty. The reading of empowerment into these scenarios is politically fraught, not the least because the attribution of empowerment to individual acts of agency invites a liberal view of empowerment that seems untenable given the structural disadvantage of Philippine women.

Taking a longer view, however, the class environments that migration engages – both working class and middle class – provide sites for new personal and collective empowerment politics. In keeping with Margold's (1999) compelling argument about Philippine working-class political activism, it seems premature to discount the links between acts of self-disciplining resistance (those which refuse collective mobilization) and change-oriented (transformative?) actions expressing empowerment. I leave the last Janus vision to two Hong Kong contributors to *Tinig Filipino* (cited in Chang and Groves 2000). Where do their voices position development as empowerment discourse? I suggest their personally empowering narrative coincides with Philippine development priorities even as it suggests class shifts in their own lives and their vision for a different Philippines that they contribute to.

> Through your good works in those places where you are temporarily working, you will become instruments in the economic improvement or progress of your 'sick nation' through the dollars you send back home. In the future, through your perseverance and hard work, your children and your children's children will be the ones to benefit from your nation's progress.
>
> (Layosa 1994: 6)

> With this very inspiring title 'hero', I could walk straight with my head up high in the busy streets of the hot city of Manila. It is indeed very flattering. Whew! I'm a hero. In my little peaceful town of Sanchez, Mia, I'm improving my life and most of all, I'm a dollar earner – much more than other people in higher ranks.
>
> (Estabillo 1994: 10)

Notes

1   Official estimates of the number of Filipinos who live below the poverty line vary from slightly over 50 to 70 per cent. In the Visayan communities I am familiar with in Negros Oriental, poverty hovers around 60 per cent. Here, the poorest communities reside in the uplands, along the coast and on sugar hacienda lands they are unable to cultivate. In urban areas, poverty is typically associated with districts where people live in makeshift forms of accommodation. It is also disguised, however, through the living arrangements of migrants who are employed as poorly paid domestic and

service sector workers residing with their employers, or who squeeze into sub-standard shared accommodation to extend their modest incomes.

2   My understanding of the current cultural politics surrounding usages of 'Filipina' is based on personal correspondence with feminist friends and colleagues in an area where women's migration rates are particularly high.

3   In their 'home' communities in the Philippines these women are often referred to as 'domestic helpers' (DHs for short), or as in official discourse 'OCWs' (overseas contract workers).

4   During the 1940s and 1950s, most foreign domestic workers in Canada were British or European. By 1989, 50 per cent came from the Philippines (Daenzer 1997).

5   See Brah (1996) and Ong and Nonini (1997) for further discussion on this point.

6   This research is funded by the Social Sciences and Humanities Research Council of Canada (SSHRC). Other Philippine research has been supported by two Dalhousie University projects with the University of the Philippines (UPV) at Los Banos and Iloilo, and Silliman University, funded by the Canadian International Development Agency (CIDA). Andrea Alviola and Maria Bueros worked with me under the Environmental Resource Management Project (ERMP) on gender and household livelihood – Andrea continues her generous support. Betty Abregana (Silliman) and Rosaria Asong and Meloy Mabunay (UPV, Iloilo) continue collaboration and friendship. I am forever grateful to all of them and others too numerous to mention here.

7   In September 1995, in the United Arab Emirates, 16-year-old Sara Balabagan was found guilty of stabbing her male employer whom she claimed had attempted to rape her soon after she arrived. In response to Philippine domestic protests and with widespread international support, the Philippine state managed to have her death sentence reduced to public flogging plus one year in jail. Earlier that same year, in Singapore, Flor Contemplacion had been tried for murder, ostensibly the outcome of a quarrel between friends. She was executed, despite much public agitation in the Philippines. Since Balabagan's case, official Philippine reactions to migrant misfortune are now more assertive and proactive. Philippine overseas workers are now proclaimed as 'hero/ines' and 2000 was officially dedicated to their honour – the 'Year of OFWs'. Sara Balabagan returned home to a heroine's welcome in 1996 and has become associated with celebrity, even in Canada. While Balabagan and Contemplacion are emblematic of the darker, 'victimized' side of migration, Sara Balabagan might equally serve as an empowerment example over time and through subsequent experience.

References

Agrawal, A. (1997) *Community in Conservation: Beyond Enchantment and Disenchantment*, Gainesville: Conservation and Development Forum.

Anderson, B. (1983) *Imagined Communities: Reflections on the Origin and Spread of Nationalism*, London: Verso.

Appadurai, A. (1991) 'Global ethnoscapes: Notes and queries for a transnational anthro-pology', in R. Fox (ed.) *Recapturing Anthropology: Working in the Present*, Santa Fe: School of American Research, pp. 101–210.

Arao, D.A. (1991) 'Migrant workers: The export of labour', *Kabalikat* 12 (September): 3–7.

Bakan, A.B. and D. Stasiulis (eds) (1997) *Not One of the Family: Foreign Domestic Workers in Canada*, Toronto: University of Toronto Press.

—— (1995. 'Making the match: Domestic placement agencies and the racialization of women's household work', *Signs: Journal of Women in Culture and Society* 20(2): 303–35.

Barber, P.G. (2000) 'Agency in Philippine women's migration and provisional diaspora', *Women's Studies International Forum* 23(4): 399–411.

—— (1997) 'Transnationalism and the politics of "home" for Philippine domestic workers', *Anthropologica* 39: 39–52.

—— (1996) 'Modes of resistance: Gendered responses to global impositions in coastal Philippines', *Asia Pacific Viewpoint* 37(2): 181–94.

Basch, L., N.G. Schiller and C.S. Blanc (1994) *Nations Unbound: Transnational Projects, Post-colonial Predicaments and Deterritorialized Nation-states*, Langhorne: Gordon & Breach Science Publishers.

Beltran, R.P. and G.F. Rodriguez (eds) (1996) *Filipino Women Migrant Workers: At the Cross-roads and beyond Beijing*, Quezon City: Giraffe Books.

Bourdieu, P. (1984) *Distinction: A Social Critique of the Judgement of Taste*, Cambridge, MA: Harvard University Press.

—— (1977) *Outline of a Theory of Practice*, Cambridge: Cambridge University Press.

Brah, A. (1996) *Cartographies of Diaspora: Contesting Identities*, London: Routledge.

Chang, K.A. and J.M. Groves (2000) 'Neither "saints" nor "prostitutes": Sexual discourse in the Filipina domestic worker community in Hong Kong', *Women's Studies International Forum* 23(1): 73–87.

Chant, S. and C. McIlwaine (1995) *Women of a Lesser Cost: Female Labour, Foreign Exchange and Philippine Development*, London: Pluto Press.

Chin, C.B.N. (1997) 'Walls of silence and late twentieth century representations of the foreign female domestic worker: The case of Filipina and Indonesian female servants in Malaysia', *The International Migration Review* 31(2): 353–85.

Catholic Institute for International Relations (CIIR) (1987) *The Labour Trade: Filipino Migrant Workers around the World*, London: Catholic Institute for International Relations.

Clifford, J. (1994) 'Diasporas', *Cultural Anthropology* 9(3): 302–38.

Constable, N. (1999) 'At home but not at home: Filipina narratives of ambivalent returns', *Cultural Anthropology* 14(2): 203–28.

—— (1997) *Maid to Order in Hong Kong: Stories of Filipina Workers*, Ithaca: Cornell University Press.

Cruz, V.P. and A. Paganoni (1989) *Filipinas in Migration: Big Bills and Small Change*, Quezon City: Scalabrini Migration Center.

Daenzer, P. (1997) 'An affair between nations: International relations and the movement of household service workers', in B. Bakan and D. Stasiulis (eds) *Not One of the Family: Foreign Domestic Workers in Canada*, Toronto: University of Toronto Press, pp. 81–118.

Estabillo, Gloria (1994) 'Where do I stand?', *Tinig Filipino* (March): 10.

Eviota, E. (1992) *The Political Economy of Gender: Women and the Sexual Division of Labour in the Philippines*, London: Zed Books.

Findlay, S. (1987) *Rural Development and Migration: A Study of Family Choices in the Philippines*, Boulder: Westview.

Go, S.P. (1997) *The Changing International Migration Landscape: A View from the Philippines*, Hong Kong: Workshop on Travelling Cultures, the University of Hong Kong.

Groves, J.M. and K.A. Chang (1999) 'Romancing resistance and resisting romance', *Journal of Contemporary Ethnography* 28(3): 235–65.

Hernandez, C.G. and J.V. Tigno (1995) 'ASEAN labour migration: Implications for regional stability', *The Pacific Review* 8(3): 554–7.

Heyzer, N., G. Lycklama a Nijeholt and N. Weerakoon (eds) (1994) *The Trade in Domestic Workers: Causes, Mechanisms and Consequences of International Migration*, Kuala Lumpur: Asian and Pacific Development Centre and London: Zed Books.

Koo, H. and P.C. Smith (1983) 'Migration, the urban informal sector, and earnings in the Philippines', *The Sociological Quarterly* 24 (Spring): 219–32.

Lane, B. (1992) 'Filipino domestic workers in Hong Kong', *Asian Migrant* 5(1): 24–32.

Layosa, Linda R. (1994) 'Into their hands', *Tinig Filipino* (March): 6.

Li, T.M. (1996) 'Images of community: Discourse and strategy in property relations', *Development and Change* 27(3): 501–27.

Macklin, A. (1994) 'On the inside looking in: Foreign domestic workers in Canada', in W. Giles and S. Arat-Koc (eds) *Maid in the Market: Women's Paid Domestic Labour*, Halifax: Fernwood Publishing, pp. 13–39.

Margold, J. (1999) 'Reformulating the compliant image: Filipina activists in the global factory', *Urban Anthropology* 28(1): 1–35.

—— (1995) 'Narratives of masculinity and transnational migration: Filipino workers in the Middle East', in A. Ong and G. Peletz (eds) *Bewitching Women, Pious Men: Gender and Body Politics in Southeast Asia*, Berkeley: University of California Press, pp. 274–98.

—— (1994) 'Global disassembly: Migrant masculinity in the transnational workplace', *Masculinities* 2(3): 18–36.

Nagata, J. (1987) 'The role of Christian churches in the integration of Southeast Asian immigrants in Toronto', *Studies in Urban Anthropology* 6 (December): 41–60.

Ong, A. (1995) 'State versus Islam: Malay families, women's bodies, and the body politic', in A. Ong and M.G. Peletz (eds) *Bewitching Women, Pious Men: Gender and Body Politics in Southeast Asia*, Berkeley: University of California Press.

Ong, A. and D. Nonini (1997) *Ungrounded Empires: The Cultural Politics of Modern Chinese Transnationalism*, New York: Routledge.

Osteria, T.S. (1994) *Filipino Female Labour Migration to Japan: Economic Causes and Consequences*, Manila: De la Salle University Press.

Parrenas, R. (1997) 'Patriarchy, Filipina domestic workers, and the international transference of mothering', paper presented at the International Conference on Mothers and Daughters, York University, Toronto.

Pertierra, R. (1994) 'Lured abroad: The case of Ilocano workers', *Sojourn* 9(1): 54–80.

Romero, M. (1994) 'Chicanas and the changing work experience in domestic work', in W. Giles and S. Arat-Koc (eds) *Maid in the Market: Women's Paid Domestic Labour*, Halifax: Fernwood Publishing, pp. 40–55.

Rouse, R. (1995) 'Thinking through transnationalism: Notes on the cultural politics of class relations in the contemporary United States', *Public Culture* 7: 353–402.

Tacoli, C. (1999) 'International migration and the restructuring of gender asymmetries: Continuity and change among Filipino labor migrants in Rome', *The International Migration Review* 33(3): 658–82.

Trager, L. (1988) *The City Connection: Migration and Family Interdependence in the Philippines*, Ann Arbor: The University of Michigan Press.

—— (1984) 'Family strategies and the migration of women: Migrants to Dagupan City, Philippines', *International Migration Review* 18 (winter): 1264–77.

Tyner, J. 1994. 'The social construction of gendered migration from the Philippines', *Asian and Pacific Migration Journal* 3(4): 589–617.

Yeoh, B. S. A., S. Huang, *et al.* (1999) 'Migrant female domestic workers: Debating the economic, social and political impacts in Singapore', *The International Migration Review* 33(1): 114–36.

4 Women's rights, CEDAW and international human rights debates

Toward empowerment?

Shaheen Sardar Ali

In this chapter I seek to analyse the potential of human rights law as an effective tool for women's empowerment. Starting from a brief overview of the international norm of non-discrimination and equality culminating in the adoption of the United Nations Convention on the Elimination of All Forms of Discrimination Against Women (CEDAW), the chapter explores the difficulties arising from employing notions of formal equality to seek empowerment for women in a diverse world. I do so by examining the alternative 'Islamic' discourse of human rights and instruments presented from Muslim forums.

Modern theories of human rights and women's rights have historically developed in two separate theoretical strains (Eisler 1987). Leading philosophers, such as John Locke in the seventeenth century and Jean Jacques Rousseau in the eighteenth century, defined men as individuals innately possessed of certain 'natural rights' (Rousseau 1947). Women, on the other hand, were defined not as individuals, but as members of men's households and thus, along with their offspring, under male control (Eisler 1987).

The UN has been key in acknowledging that women's rights have been marginalized both institutionally and conceptually from national and international human rights movements.[1] Starting from the UN Charter, a wide array of human rights instruments promulgated by the UN and regional organizations included provisions for the protection of women's rights and non-discrimination on the basis of sex (see Brownlie 1992; Ghandhi 1995). These include the UN Charter (1945), the Universal Declaration of Human Rights (UDHR 1948), the International Covenant on Civil and Political Rights (ICCPR 1966), the International Covenant on Economic, Social and Cultural Rights (ICESCR 1966), the Declaration on the Elimination of All Forms of Intolerance and of Discrimination Based on Religion or Belief (the Religious Declaration 1981), the European Convention on Human Rights and Fundamental Freedoms (ECHR 1950), the American Convention on Human Rights (ACHR 1969) and the African Charter on Human and People's Rights (African Charter 1987). All these documents prohibit discrimination on grounds of sex (article 2, UDHR; article 2, ICCPR; article 2, ICESCR; Preamble, the Religious Declaration).

Statements of formal equality and non-discrimination in general human rights instruments were considered inadequate, however, and, since 1945, more than two dozen international legal instruments have been drafted that deal specifically with women. Each of these instruments reflects an international consensus on particular problems relating to women and provides a unique insight into the apparent international consensus on the rights of women in society (see Hevener 1983). However, because of their restricted scope and lack of provisions for enforcement, these instruments have had little impact on the condition of women worldwide. Neither did they succeed in integrating women's human rights into the mainstream human rights framework. From the mid-1960s, the impact of existing instruments has inspired efforts to develop international instruments that would conceptualize the human rights of women globally and contain concrete measures for implementation and supervision. These efforts led to the adoption of the Declaration on the Elimination of All Forms of Discrimination Against Women (United Nations 1967) and culminated in the Convention on the Elimination of All Forms of Discrimination Against Women (CEDAW) in 1979. CEDAW thus recast concepts of 'women's rights' in a global perspective and established a supervisory machinery with terms of reference similar to those of existing human rights organs.

CEDAW: a tool for women's empowerment?

CEDAW highlights the inequities faced by women and affirms non-discrimination and equality as an overarching human right for women. The treaty has been hailed as a major breakthrough in international human rights law since it adopts a holistic approach toward human rights law as an effective tool for women's empowerment. It recognizes the need to go beyond legal documents to address factors that will help to eradicate *de facto* inequality between men and women (CEDAW 1979: Preamble). The establishment of a New International Economic Order, the eradication of apartheid, racism, foreign occupation and domination, and the strengthening of international peace and security, including nuclear disarmament, are all viewed as being essential to the equality of men and women.

In adopting CEDAW, the UN sought to lay the foundation for an international women's law of human rights that transcends the borders of national, religious and customary laws (Hellum 1999). CEDAW was to provide 'a socio-legal tool which within a single and unified framework is intended to help women fit into social, economic and political modernization processes in all parts of the world' (Hellum 1999).

Rebecca Cook sees CEDAW as the third stage of overlapping and interactive developments within women's human rights law (1994: 4–7). During the first phase of development, states focused on the promotion of specific legal rights of particular concern to women in regard to employment. During the second stage, states included sex as a prohibited ground for discrimination in instruments such as the UDHR, the ICCPR, the ICESCR and regional human rights conventions. CEDAW, as the third stage of this development, addresses the structural nature of violating women's human rights. As such, Hellum argues that CEDAW is informed by various theories that address women's roles in development processes (1999: 23).

The provisions of equality

The definition of discrimination against women put forward in CEDAW is important as it transcends the traditional public/private dichotomy by calling for the international recognition of women's human rights both inside and outside the familial sphere (article 1). The framers of this Convention realized that customs and practices as well as formal legislation often perpetuate discrimination against women (article 2). Article 5 of the Convention, for example, addresses this issue by committing state parties (i.e. signatory states to the Convention) to modify 'the social and cultural patterns of conduct of men and women' in order to eliminate prejudices and practices based on notions of inferiority and superiority of either sex. Other substantive provisions demand that state parties grant women complete equality in every field of life, be it nationality, family matters, contracts, right to property, etc. (articles 9, 13, 15 and 16).

The four parts of the Convention cover the major areas of women's rights within the rubric of the human rights discourse. As overlapping areas, addressing historical/cultural exclusion through affirmative action (Part 1) sits well with endorsing women's participation in public political life (Part 2) and is substantiated through covering in Part 3 the arena of socio-economic rights, including of education and employment. These rights are stabilized within a legal regime of equal rights in civil law (Part 4).

The implications for states are potentially far-reaching. Not only must they abolish all existing discriminatory legislation and practices, they are also obliged to eliminate stereotyped concepts of male and female roles in society. Hiding behind 'traditional customs and practices' will not do. The Convention's language is essentially universalist and non-discriminatory, and emphasizes a rights-based framework, representing a significant difference from previous legislation that was usually welfarist and 'protective' in tone.

While obliging state parties to provide the socio-legal framework for women's equality, CEDAW also provides local struggles with a possibility of speaking a global legal language. It creates the possibility for local groups and movements to bypass national institutional constraints and structures, and appeal to the international legal institutions for redress. However, as the study of the monitoring processes of CEDAW show below, nation states and cultural norms can place considerable limitations on a universal rights discourse that women seek to employ as part of their strategy for empowerment.

Part 5 (articles 17–22) of the Convention outlines the monitoring rules for CEDAW. Pursuant to these provisions, the Convention established the Committee on the Elimination of All Forms of Discrimination Against Women, a body of twenty-three experts, elected by the state parties to serve in their personal capacity (see Byrnes 1988, 1989–90). The Committee was established 'for the purpose of considering the progress made in the implementation of the Convention' (article 17(1)), to be carried out by examining reports submitted by state parties – to be submitted every four years or whenever the Committee requests them.

However, unlike the Convention on the Elimination of All Forms of Racial Discrimination (on which CEDAW is closely modelled), no provision was made for one state to complain about a violation by another state. Neither was there any provision for an individual who claims to have suffered a violation of the Convention to submit a complaint against a state party.[2] The approach taken toward the enforcement of the Convention is one of 'progressive implementation' rather than a requirement of immediate action. 'Constructive dialogue' rather than formal censure has been the preferred practice. The result has been that, while countries remain party to the Convention, and are not alienated within that system, there is little immediate pressure to implement and conform to the requirements of the Convention.

Until June 1999, the reporting procedure was the only enforcement mechanism established under the Convention.[3] This is perhaps the least effective method devised by international law to enforce human rights standards. Its success or failure depends heavily on the goodwill of state parties. The Committee's ability to assess the accuracy of state reports and comment upon them has been hampered by the lack of information on the status of women in state parties. This problem has been compounded by the lack of any formal procedures to ensure effective consultation between non-governmental organizations (NGOs) and members of the Committee. Such consultation is essential to ensure that Committee members have access to independent information that enables them to assess the accuracy of state reports.[4]

Law, cultural norms and women's rights

Women's human rights, as set out in CEDAW, are based on a predominantly Western liberal feminist discourse that insists on individual rights of woman to the exclusion of the multiplicity of her identities. Several writers argue that this approach is premised on a combination of law, modernization theory and Western liberal feminist jurisprudence (Charlesworth *et al.* 1991; Hellum 1999: 412). It assumes an identifiable human nature is at the heart of recognizing appropriate rights to develop, protect and contain elements of this core human identity. Further, it assumes that underdevelopment and gender inequality in the Third World are caused by traditional values and social structures. The prescription for attaining equality for women is therefore to address the human rights of women without reference to the cultural embeddedness of these rights in Western liberal states. However, the question that is being posed by women around the world is: to what extent are the concepts of equality and non-discrimination cast within the Western liberal framework equally beneficial for all women? For example, in the African and Asian contexts most women rely on entitlements embodied in family and community relationships that do not relate to 'equal rights' language. Similarly, religion forms an important part of many women's identity. They are not comfortable with being asked to frame their identities within a discourse that is avowedly secular. Is the monolithic and individualistic concept of abstract equality able to meet the everyday needs of such women?

Critiques of CEDAW point to the presence of conflicting human rights principles such as gender equality on the one hand and the right to freedom of religion, culture and custom on the other. Indeed, it may be argued that the Religious Declaration of 1981, in conjunction with article 18 of the Universal Declaration of Human Rights and articles 18, 26 and 27 of the International Convention of Civil and Political Rights (ICCPR) create an invisible hierarchy of human rights by placing freedom of religion at a higher level than right to equality irrespective of sex and gender. It follows therefore that if the freedom to manifest and practise one's religion or belief led to discrimination against women, such discrimination could be upheld on the basis of these conventions. Thus, despite its holistic approach toward questions of women's empowerment through human rights, CEDAW fails to provide a clear methodology to resolve these conflicting rights.

'Complementarity' of rights: a 'Muslim' view of the norm of non-discrimination and equality

Initially, CEDAW received little support from Muslim states.[5] This situation has improved considerably, and presently forty-one Muslim jurisdictions are party to the treaty (Afghanistan has signed but not ratified).[6] For the most part, Muslim states today accept and participate in the UN system in order to contribute to the development of universally acceptable principles of international law. Since the inception of the UN, they have actively collaborated in drafting and ratifying human rights instruments, including the UDHR (see Kelsay 1988), the Convention on Rights of the Child and the CEDAW (see Rehof 1993; Connors 1996). Furthermore, the principle of *pacta sunt servanda* is entrenched as a religiously sanctioned norm in the *Quran* – the primary source of Islamic law. Hence, if a Muslim state has given its consent to human rights treaties, it incurs the strict legal obligation to honour it in international law as well as to ensure enforcement at home (Schacht 1959).

Reservations to CEDAW by Muslim states

Muslim states have addressed the issue of CEDAW's implementation by making 'reservations' to the Convention. These reservations are based on the legal supremacy of the Islamic religion, the country's constitution, cultural practices and other laws related to the substantive rights protected in CEDAW. Complementarity of rights has been used to explain the need for reservations. For example, the Egyptian state presents the following argument in favour of its reservation to article 16 of the UDHR:

Reservation to the text of article 16 concerning the equality of men and women in all matters relating to marriage and family relations during marriage and upon its dissolution, without prejudice to the Islamic Sharia's provisions whereby women are accorded rights equivalent to those of their spouses so as to ensure a just balance between them. This is out of respect for the sacrosanct nature of the firm religious beliefs which govern marital relations in Egypt and which may not be called into question and in view of the fact that one of the most important bases of these relations is an equivalency of rights and duties so as to ensure complementarity which guarantees true equality between the spouses.

(United Nations 1997: 172–3)

Reservations to CEDAW formulated by Muslim states demonstrate the disparate positions on the subject of women's human rights. The signature and ratification of some, such as Algeria, Egypt, Malaysia, Pakistan, Tunisia and Turkey, are subject to substantial reservations. Others, such as Albania, Bosnia and Herzegovina, Burkina Faso, Cameroon, Guinea, Nigeria, Sierra Leone, Tajikistan and Uzbekistan, have ratified CEDAW without reservations. The reservations of Indonesia and Yemen are confined to article 29(1), relating to the settlement of disputes that may arise concerning the application or interpretation of CEDAW (United Nations 1999). Muslim states are not the only parties hedging their positions on important aspects of women's human rights. What sets them apart is that these qualifications are often based on Islamic traditions. Women's rights as enunciated in CEDAW are seen as valid only to the extent that they conform to principles of Islamic law in a particular state. This is another way of adopting a relativist stance toward human rights and declaring the divergence between women's human rights in international human rights laws and those acknowledged within the Islamic tradition. The fact that there is no monolithic view of women's human rights in Islam, and that religion combines with culture, economic and political conditions, is reflected in the various reservations by Muslim countries to CEDAW. Thus, of the forty-one Muslim countries that are party to CEDAW, eight countries (Bangladesh, Egypt, Iraq, Kuwait, Libya, Malaysia, Maldives and Morocco) make their reservations to the Convention on the basis of conflict with Sharia, while the others (Algeria, Indonesia, Jordan, Pakistan, Turkey, Tunisia and Yemen) do not expressly mention it. It is also important that the most reserved articles relate to rights of women in the area of family law, which has always been jealously guarded by Muslim states as being regulated by Islamic law. Other fields of life, including the running of governments and financial institutions, are not so guarded against 'infiltration' of 'secular' laws.

Evolution of an Islamic state perspective on human and women's rights

Alongside the UN and regional political systems, Muslim states have in the past few decades aligned themselves at the international level in a loose association known as the Organization of Islamic Conference (OIC). In recent years, OIC has convened several conferences and meetings focusing on human rights (both in general terms and specifically on women's human rights). Some of these human rights documents suggest there is a Muslim view of women's rights. What I wish to highlight here is that while the starting points of the human rights instruments emanating from the UN and the OIC were quite different, in recent years we see a growing convergence between the two, particularly in the way the language of human rights has been adopted by the Islamic human rights discourse.

Since the adoption of the UDHR as the foundational human rights document emanating from the UN, Islamic scholars and politicians, as well as official statements of Muslim states, have declared human rights a basic norm of the Islamic tradition. Over the years, and in response to international human rights instruments, politico-legal discourses offering the Islamic contribution and perspective to human rights have emerged. While some Western scholars regard these debates as evidence of neglect of women's rights within Islamic human rights discourse (Mayer 1995), I would argue that this view is hardly plausible considering that even the harshest critics of the Islamic tradition have conceded that Islam does accord several fundamental human rights to women.

On 19 September 1981, a Universal Islamic Declaration of Human Rights (UIDHR) (see http://www.alhewar.com/ISLAMDECL.html) was adopted by the Islamic Council. In the foreword, Salem Azzam, the Secretary-General of the Council, states that the Declaration 'is based on the *Quran* and *Sunnah* and has been compiled by eminent Muslim scholars, jurists, and representatives of Islamic movements and thought'. The UIDHR does not take note of any international human rights document, treaty or convention, recalling in its preambular statements only the Islamic tradition. For example, article 3 is entitled 'Right to Equality and Prohibition against Impermissible Discrimination'. The phrase 'impermissible discrimination' gives the impression that, where permissible, discrimination will be permitted. The inference is that on literal, traditional readings of the religious text in Islam, women may be discriminated against (Mayer 1995: 102–9). Similarly, article 19 of the UIDHR outlines the 'Right to Found a Family and Related Matters', within which, under the Islamic legal tradition, a Muslim woman may found a family only by marrying a Muslim male whereas a Muslim male may marry a Muslim woman or a woman professing one of the revealed religions (*kitabia*)[7] and under the husband as head of the household by obligating him to maintain his wife and children (article 19(c)).[8] Despite the divergence outlined above, article 19(i) of UIDHR appears in line with UN human rights provisions in stating that 'No person may be married against his or her will, or lose or suffer diminution of legal personality on account of marriage.'[9]

Since the publication of the UIDHR, various Muslim states have agreed on three other declarations: the Cairo Declaration of Human Rights in Islam (August 1990), and the Tehran and the Islamabad Declarations (both in 1995). The latter are distinctive in that women debated, drafted and adopted the issues relating to the rights of Muslim women in conferences where these rights were the focus of discussion. These declarations are also important statements of Muslim women's perspectives regarding their human rights prior to the Beijing Conference held in September 1995.

The first of these conferences, the Organization of Islamic Conference Symposium of Experts on the Role of Women in the Development of Islamic Society, was held in Tehran.[10] The recommendations of the Symposium to the Twenty-third Conference of Islamic Foreign Ministers present several interesting points of departure from other documents coming from Muslim forums, including the UIDHR and the Cairo Declaration. The most prominent of these, the Preamble, reiterates the commitment of member states of the OIC to the principles and objectives of the UN Charter. Second, it clearly acknowledges and upholds the interdependence and indivisibility between civil and political, and economic, social and cultural rights, and underscores recognition of 'cultural' Islam and the manner in which it adversely affects the rights and status of women in Muslim countries. However, adverse cultural encroachments that are detrimental to the identity and personality of Muslim women are rejected (para. 1.4). This commitment is further elucidated by demanding the:

> eradication of all forms of violence and exploitation of women, including domestic violence, sexual exploitation, pornography, prostitution, trafficking in women, sexual harassment, genital mutilation and other negative traditional and cultural practices.
>
> (para. 1.6)

The fact that women's roles are not confined to motherhood is also made clear by the need for:

> facilities to effectively meet the requirements of women and encourage their participation in public life thus enabling them to reconcile their family and professional responsibilities with their political rights and participation in decision making.
>
> (para 1.8)

A particularly ground-breaking provision of the recommendations is one that accepts that women may be heads of households, thus moving away from the traditional statement that men alone are, or can be, providers and maintainers of households.[11] The recommendations also demand the facilitation and enhancement of women's full access to appropriate, readily available and free, quality healthcare and related services and facilities, including family planning, and reproductive, maternal and infant health in the context of Islamic principles. This contradicts the position held by some that Islam prohibits family planning (para. 1.18). The importance of education as an effective tool of empowerment is underscored, as is the recognition of women's roles as *Mujtahid* (one who can make *Ijtihad*).[12]

The Islamabad Declaration was adopted at the first Muslim Women Parliamentarians' Conference in Islamabad, 1–3 August 1995, prior to the Beijing Conference.[13] The main objective of the conference was to allow women parliamentarians from Muslim countries to meet in order to forge closer links and to develop a deeper understanding of the problems facing Muslim women. The conference adopted the Islamabad Declaration on the Role of Muslim Women Parliamentarians in the Promotion of Peace, Progress and Development of Islamic Societies (Islamabad Declaration).

Like the Tehran Declaration, the striking feature of the Islamabad Declaration is its recognition of and commitment to international human rights instruments affecting women. It resolves to 'promote the implementation, as appropriate, of the provisions of international conventions on the rights of women and urge all countries to adhere to these conventions' (Shirkatgah 1995: 4). It may be argued that by specifically taking note of human rights conventions affecting women's rights, the Islamabad Declaration appears to be formulating an 'operative' Islamic international law norm of non-discrimination on the basis of sex, evidence of which was barely visible in either the UIDHR or the Cairo Declaration. A further outstanding feature of the Islamabad Declaration is its recognition of Muslim women's rights to participate in public and political life and decision-making, including the right to become head of state and government.[14] This pronouncement, I would argue, indicates an emerging 'operative' Islamic law regarding women's right to public life. Building upon the Tehran Declaration (although the two documents had no official connection), the Islamabad Declaration seeks to establish the interdependence and indivisibility of all three generations of rights, and also echoes the linkage and interdependence now being sought within the UN system between the United Nations Convention on Rights of the Child (CRC) (1989) and CEDAW (p. 3, para. (a)). Furthermore, the provisions of the Tehran and Islamabad Declarations, and those of human rights documents adopted at the UN, emphasize women's central role within the family, which is seen as the basic unit of society.[15]

As compared to the UIDHR and the Cairo Declaration, the Islamabad and Tehran Declarations present a tone and terminology that is closer to the women's rights language of the UN. However, some differences are also discernible, the most pronounced being the fact that interdependence of rights and obligations is highlighted in the Muslim declarations. That is not to argue, however, that UN human rights documents lack the element of corresponding obligations; the distinction appears to be one of emphasis.

Further, obligations of state parties, as opposed to individuals as key participants in the fulfilment of rights, has been the norm in UN human rights instruments. This lack of emphasis on private actors has been critiqued on the basis that, beyond state institutions, it is in the private sphere and at the level of society and community that human rights are denied to women. In contrast, 'Islamic' human rights documents place responsibility both on the shoulders of recipients of these rights, i.e. individuals within the state, and on state structures and institutions.

However, the question arises: how representative of Muslim thought, belief and views are these forums and writings? This question does not lend itself to an easy response. It is a very complex problem indeed, and no straightforward answer is possible. It is evident, however, that male interpretations of the Islamic tradition with regard to women's rights are invariably more restrictive than the formulations of women's forums. For instance, the Tehran Symposium, despite being hosted by Iran, a regime widely known for its strong religious conviction and inhibiting laws for women, sought to present the more positive side of rights for Muslim women (OIC 1995).

It has to be conceded that the documents reviewed fail to adequately spell out and address the problematic areas relating to women's rights in Islam. The areas awaiting deliberation include evidence rights of women, polygamy, divorce, inheritance rights and custody and guardianship of children. However, the Tehran and Islamabad Declarations have drawn attention to these difficult areas by subsuming them under the heading of 'problems' to be resolved by Muslim women or through progressive 'women-friendly' interpretations of religious texts considered as legitimate grounds for the human rights of Muslim women.

Beyond equality and rights: toward a (re)definition of empowerment?

This chapter has explored the potential of women's human rights, emanating from two streams of legal tradition, i.e. international human rights law and human rights in Islam as an effective tool for women's empowerment. In this section I analyse the similarities and differences between these two legal traditions in order to present a clearer understanding of how commonalities of human rights concepts may be used to advance the position of women in diverse societies.

The first inference that may be drawn from developments outlined above is that, at the level of international law, a hierarchy of rights has been created in existing human rights discourse. Of the human rights that form *jus cogens*, i.e. a peremptory norm of international law from which no derogation is permissible, genocide, slavery, torture and racial discrimination appear on the list with a certain degree of consistency. Non-discrimination on the basis of sex fails to find the same level of acceptance, leading to the view that *jus cogens* is gendered and male-biased. Gender discrimination has also been omitted from the identified categories of what constitutes the contemporary customary international law of human rights (Section 702 of the *Restatement (Third), Foreign Relations Law of the United States*). Likewise, in describing peremptory norms of international law, General Comment 24(52) of the Human Rights Committee does not include non-discrimination on the basis of sex in its list (General Comment 1995).

On the other hand, some writers have also pointed out that the norm of non-discrimination on the basis of sex constitutes a non-derogable right under major human rights instruments, including the ICCPR, the ICESCR, CEDAW and the CRC (Bayefsky 1994: 352). Practice however points toward a different direction. For example, some European countries, such as the United Kingdom, reserve the right to give the throne to a male over a first-born female child. How might we argue then that the norm of non-discrimination on the basis of sex has become a part of *jus cogens*? This argument is particularly important with regard to the UDHR, considered by many as constituting a norm of customary international law. The problem arises due to the gulf between standards and enforcements as this reflects a virtual non-recognition of these rights (Bayefsky 1994). If this was not the case, then the question of the extent of legal obligations incurred on the part of states that have not ratified the above mentioned human rights instruments would become essentially a non-issue, as states are bound by norms of customary international law.

A similar analysis of women's human rights in Islam also points towards a hierarchy of rights. Esposito classifies women's rights in the Islamic legal tradition of *muamalaat* and *ibadaat* categories of rights. The *ibadaat* set of rights in the Islamic tradition denotes entitlements with spiritual, moral and ethical dimensions, and these rights are accorded to men and women equally. For example, the concept of equality in human dignity and worth, crime and punishment rewards in the hereafter, and responsibility for performing religious obligations fall within this category of rights. In contrast, adult male Muslims are accorded a higher degree of responsibility and rights in the *muamalaat* or socio-economic sphere of life. Thus, share of a female heir is half that of a male; the husband has the superior right of *talaq* (divorce) over his wife; the father is the legal guardian of his children; the Muslim husband can marry more than one wife, and so on. It may therefore be argued that both international human rights law and the Islamic tradition create and indeed lend support to a hierarchy of rights, relegating women's human rights to the lower rungs of the rights ladder.

A particularly striking contradiction is manifested in the various human rights instruments affecting women's right to equality and non-discrimination. CEDAW proclaims complete equality to all women in all areas of life. Thus, article 16 demands equal rights to women within the family including equal rights to inheritance, entrance into marriage, the right to dissolve a marriage and so on. On the other hand, the Religious Declaration affords everyone the right to manifest his/her religion as he/she understands it. As indicated above, traditional interpretation of Islamic law clearly provides women with fewer rights than men within the sphere of family life. If one were to respect the right to religious freedom of an individual or a group to practise this version of their religion, then arguably this right to religious belief would negate article 16 of CEDAW.

Closely linked to the hierarchy of norms, *jus cogens* and the generational concept of rights is the public/private dichotomy. One of the main areas of focus within human rights is the division drawn in most Western legal systems between the public and private spheres of society. Moreover, this distinction is central to Western legal thought and the philosophical traditions from which it grows. A defining feature of liberal political theory has been commitment to spheres of individual autonomy free from state intrusion. Thus, the law, it has been argued, operates in the public sector of the legal, economic and political spheres, leaving the private sector of home and family, in which most women operate, unregulated (see Charlesworth 1989–90). The reality, however, is more nuanced than this supposedly straightforward division. In the present day, it is difficult to believe that the private or domestic spheres go unregulated. What actually transpires is that in the so-called private sphere of life, which is purportedly immune from law, there is always a selective application of law (Schneider 1992).

Human rights discourse, especially its practice, continues to focus primarily on the public and political spheres. The result is that abuses of women's human rights, many of which occur in the private or familial sphere, are excluded from the human rights agenda and are perceived as a private, cultural or individual issue, not a political matter justifying state action. Thus, beating a 'disobedient' wife has societal sanction in some cultures. Likewise, the practice of female circumcision has only recently been exposed to public attention and to date international human rights organizations have failed to adopt a firm position on the issue (see Boulware-Miller 1985; Slack 1988; Abdul Haleem 1992). Charlesworth *et al.* (1991) argue that the marginalization of women by domestic legal systems is exacerbated not only by the structure of international law, which emphasizes the abstract entity of the state, but also by the almost total exclusion of women from its processes (see Halliday 1991; Clapham 1993). This, for example, accords precedence to the state as the sovereign political actor. The UN Charter states:

> Nothing contained in the present Charter shall authorise the United Nations to intervene in matters which are essentially within the domestic jurisdiction of any State or shall require the Members to submit such matters to settlement under the present Charter.
>
> (article 2(7))

The UN has watered down this provision on several occasions. For instance, CEDAW, the CRC and the UN Declaration on Elimination of Violence against Women address this problem and demand that the state, in accepting the legal obligation for protecting the human rights of its citizens, move beyond the public sphere and take cognizance of any violations of these rights taking place within the private sphere and by private actors. However, state primacy enshrined in the UN Charter continues to weaken the human rights documents affecting women that emanate from the UN (Coomaraswamy 1994: 15–16, para. 70).

On the other hand, the Islamic view of the state mitigates against a public/private dichotomy as each and every sphere and aspect of life is regulated by Islamic law, principles and norms. The concept of autonomy, either at an individual level or for the state, is alien to the Islamic tradition (Moinuddin 1987: 16). Each person is accountable to God for his or her actions. At present, however, the practice of Muslim states does not reflect this Islamic concept and women's human rights are violated with impunity in most Muslim jurisdictions in the name of Islam. It may be argued that the 'Western' concept of state sovereignty and an autonomous private sphere of life beyond state regulation present major obstacles toward enforcement and implementation of women's human rights.

Finally, in assessing the reality of equal rights for women in international human rights law, we must question the meaning, adequacy and efficacy of the term 'equality' for empowering women. It may be argued that interpretations and manifestations of the concept remain flawed on several counts. Equality continues to be perceived and is defined as 'being like a man' except where women's difference is emphasized, largely attached to the biological and private/social spheres. Further, international human rights as well as domestic legal systems appear to function on the premise that formal equality translates into substantive equality. Nothing could be further from the truth. People, whether men or women, starting from an inherently unequal position resulting from weak economic, social, health or other factors, will end up being unequal, despite the equality provisions in laws. Several questions flow from this statement. For instance, why and how has the UN human rights movement marginalized women's rights? Is it because the political and public face of rights so crucial to men is replicated and placed at a higher level on the hierarchy of rights at the international level? Coupled with this issue, is the lack of similar value placed on rights that are crucial to making women's rights a reality? Thus economic, social and cultural rights, including the right to education, health and employment, which can make the difference to women's lives, fail to make an impact in international human rights instruments. Men and women therefore start the race for equal rights from totally different starting points. Having the legal right to education rings hollow if there are no schools for girls and custom requires segregation of male and female children. The legal right to employment is even more far-fetched where basic education and skills necessary for that employment are unavailable to women. Hilary Charlesworth therefore raises a very fundamental question in relation to the human rights of women when she asks: 'Do legal rights really offer anything to women? Women's disadvantages are often based on structural injustice and winning a case in court will not change this' (cited in Cook 1994: 4).

The 'equality' concept in various human rights instruments also fails to take account of the special needs of women. Thus, women's needs as pregnant and nursing mothers or as basic carers of family members are obscured in the equality debate. Within the Islamic tradition, child bearing and rearing are considered a joint parental as well as social responsibility, and the need to provide help and support to women in child bearing and rearing situations is emphasized (Ali and Jamil 1994). Further, although the point is controversial in feminist discussions, mothers are under no obligation to breastfeed or look after their children should they so choose. The father is legally obliged to provide financial and other support to a woman who decides to nurse their child (Ali and Jamil 1994). Likewise, household work must be remunerated and taken account of in the event of dissolution of the marriage contract. The latest legislation in Iran provides an example of this Islamic norm. However, these rights are undermined by social norms that continue to assume the nurturing role of the mother and emphasize the male role of breadwinner, even though this places him under contract to provide for the wife and family.

Conclusion

In summing up this analysis of the limits of the international norm of non-discrimination on the basis of sex, it has to be admitted that the journey on the road to equal human rights for men and women within the UN system has indeed come a long way from 1945. From modest beginnings in the UN Charter and the UDHR, the ICCPR and the ICESCR expanded the concept. The decades of the 1970s, 1980s and 1980s lent tremendous impetus to these initiatives, and women's human rights can no longer be ignored. The UN efforts were greatly facilitated by the international NGO community, particularly at the four world conferences on women. Each conference expanded the content of women's human rights to a point where virtually every aspect of women's lives are touched by the rights discourse. Although many problems persist, the major ones relating to state sovereignty and weak and ineffective enforcement mechanisms, a beginning has been made.

Judgements using the rights language in general and CEDAW in particular are mushrooming in non-Western jurisdictions. These include the *Unity Dow* case from Botswana where Unity was not allowed by the law to pass on her nationality to her husband and children; the *Shrin Munir vs. Government of Punjab* (PLD 1990 SC 295) case from Pakistan where applicants to medical schools won their right to admission to these schools on the basis of the equal rights arguments; and *Naseem Firdous vs. Punjab Small Industries Corporation* (PLD 1995 Lah. 584) from Pakistan who won the right to apply for a job on a basis of equality with her male colleagues. However, these judgements also portray in their formulation the centuries-old customs, culture and (male-defined) religious traditions that cling tenaciously to the laws and institutions from which equal rights and equality flow. Although the plurality of norms compete to undermine whatever empowerment women might achieve through formal laws, this factor may also be perceived as a strength of CEDAW. Article 5 of CEDAW provides the space for women to challenge custom, culture and traditions by asking whose custom, as defined by whom, when and under what circumstances. By deconstructing customs and religious tradition from a woman's standpoint and reconstructing it on the basis of their own experiential norms and lived realities, CEDAW may emerge as an effective tool in the empowerment strategy for women.

In the context of non-Western women including Muslim women, complete equality as the term has come to be understood in modern-day usage is difficult to infer from any of the human rights schemes available to them. Women in these societies are considered a 'protected' section of the community. It might therefore be strategically opportune to seek a rigorous implementation of all the protective/corrective categories of rights before embarking upon the 'equality' and non-discrimination path. A move toward substantive as opposed to mere formal equality for all may be possible if we apply the Islamic paradigm of equality of human dignity and worth, and require 'those in authority' (i.e. men and the state) to accept responsibility for fulfilling the material needs of women, children and other disadvantaged sections of society in their charge and for providing them with access and control over resources.

Notes

1   For a detailed discussion of how the human rights of women have been split off from the mainstream of the international human rights movement, see Hosken 1981.

2   In June 1993, the World Human Rights Conference in Vienna emphasized the need for 'the adoption of new procedures to strengthen implementation of the commitment to women's equality and the human rights of women'. It called upon the CSW and CEDAW to examine the possibility of introducing the right of petition through the preparation of an optional protocol to the Women's Convention. Since January 1994, efforts have been underway toward the achievement of this goal, including discussions on a draft optional protocol, but these have not yet reached fruition. See A. Byrnes, 'Highlights in the Development of an Optional Protocol to the Women's Convention and Selected Background Materials', circulated at a consultation meeting organized by the International Women's Rights Action Watch (IWRAW) in New York in January 1998.

3   An optional protocol adopted recently has enabled the right of individual petition to women.

4   In this regard, the International Women's Rights Action Watch (IWRAW), based at the University of Minnesota, regularly monitors the implementation of CEDAW through annual parallel meetings with CEDAW. IWRAW has brought together thousands of women from around the world to participate in these meetings, as well as for lobbying members of CEDAW.

5   The identifying criteria for Muslim countries are many and varied. One criterion is to consider those countries where Muslims constitute over 70 per cent of the total population as Muslim countries. Weeks (1984: 882–911) uses member states of the Organization of Islamic Countries (OIC) as the determining criteria for identifying states with large numbers of Muslim populations.

6   Afghanistan, Albania, Algeria, Azerbaijan, Bangladesh, Benin, Bosnia and Herzegovina, Burkina Faso, Cameroon, Chad, Comoros, Egypt, Gabon, Gambia, Guinea, Guinea-Bissau, Indonesia, Iraq, Jordan, Kuwait, Kyrgyzstan, Lebanon, Libyan Arab Jamahiriya, Malaysia, Maldives, Mali, Morocco, Mozambique, Nigeria, Pakistan, Senegal, Sierra Leone, Suriname, Tajikistan, Togo, Tunisia, Turkey, Turkmenistan, Uganda, Uzbekistan and Yemen. Muslim countries that have so far refrained from signature/ratification of the Women's Convention include Bahrain, Brunei, Djibouti, Mauritania, Niger, Oman, Qatar, Iran, Kazakhstan, Saudi Arabia, Somalia, Sudan, Syria and the United Arab Emirates. Updated information on signatures, ratifications and accessions is available on the Internet. A useful website is gopher://gopher.un.org:70/00/ga/cedaw/RATIFICA.

7   Cf. article 16(1) of the UDHR, which provides: 'Men and women of full age, without any limitation due to race, nationality or religion, have the right to marry and found a family'. Article 16 of the Women's Convention provides: 'States Parties shall take appropriate measures to eliminate discrimination against women in all matters relating to marriage and family relations and in particular shall ensure, on a basis of equality of men and women: a) the same rights to enter into marriage.'

8   Cf. discussion in the *Quran*, verse 4:34, stating that men are providers and maintainers of women since they are obligated to provide for them out of their earnings.
9   Cf. article 16(2) of the UDHR which provides: 'Marriage shall be entered into only with the free and full consent of the intending spouses'. Article 16(b) of the Women's Convention makes a similar statement: 'The same right freely to choose a spouse and to enter into marriage only with their free and full consent.'
10 This Symposium was organized in accordance with Resolution 10/7-C (IS), adopted by the Seventh Islamic Summit Conference. Delegates from thirty-four Islamic countries participated in the deliberations. Three documents were submitted to the Seminar: Recommendations of the Seminar to the Twenty-third Islamic Conference of Foreign Ministers; Principles Presented as Guidelines to the Fourth World Conference on Women in Beijing; and the Tehran Declaration on the Role of Women in the Development of Islamic Society.
11 Paragraph 1.15 provides for 'provision of necessary financial and social support and protection and empowerment of women heads of household'.
12 A person with the capacity to engage in independent legal reasoning. Paragraph 1.3 of the Tehran Declaration calls this process *Ijtihad*.
13 Thirty-five high-level delegations from Muslim countries participated, including representatives from Pakistan, Libya, Chad, Malaysia, Oman, Azerbaijan, Morocco, Syria, Yemen, Albania, Algeria, Kyrgyzstan, Iraq, Bangladesh, Egypt, Palestine, Jordan, Senegal, Iran, Indonesia, Sudan, Turkish Republic of Northern Cyprus, Turkey and a representative of the International Parliamentary Union.
14 Cf. Tabandeh's view that women are not allowed in public life. Also note the *Hadith* where it is stated that 'Those who entrust their affairs to a woman will never know prosperity.'
15 See Preamble of the Islamabad Declaration, which states: 'Recognising that woman, as enshrined in the *Quran* and *Sunnah*, is the centre of the family which is the basic unit of society and hence the cornerstone of the edifice of a stable, peaceful and prosperous polity.' UN human rights instruments articulate similar formulations. See, for example, article 23 of the ICCPR and article 10 of the ICESCR.

References

Abdul Haleem, A.M. (1992) 'Claiming our bodies and our rights: Exploring female circumcision as an act of violence', in M. Schuler (ed.) *Freedom from Violence*, Washington, DC: OEF International.

Ali, S.S. and B. Jamil (1994) *The United Nations Convention on Rights of the Child, Islamic Law and Pakistan Legislation*, Peshawar: Shaheen Printing Press.

Bayefsky, A.F. (1994) 'General approaches to the domestic application of women's international human rights law', in R.J. Cook (ed.) *Human Rights of Women: National and International Perspectives*, Philadelphia: University of Pennsylvania Press; http://www.law-lib.utoronto.ca/diana/fulltext/byr2.htm.

Boulware-Miller, K. (1985) 'Female circumcision: Challenges to the practice, as a human rights violation', *Harvard Women's Law Journal* 8: 155.

Brownlie, I. (1992) *Basic Documents on Human Rights*, 3rd edition. Oxford: Oxford University Press.

Byrnes, A. (1989–90) 'Women, feminism and international human rights law: Methodological myopia, fundamental flaws or meaningful marginalisation', *American Yearbook of International Law* 12: 207.

—— (1988) 'The other human rights committee', *Yale Journal of International Law* 14.

Charlesworth, H. (1989–90) 'The public/private distinction and the right to development in international law', *American Yearbook of International Law* 12: 190.

Charlesworth, Hilary, Christine Chinkin and Wright (1991) 'Feminist approaches to international law', *American Journal of International Law* 85: 613–45.

Clapham, A. (1993) *Human Rights in the Private Sphere*, Oxford: Clarendon Press.

Connors, J. (1996) 'The Women's Convention in the Muslim world', in M. Yamani (ed.) *Feminism and Islam. Legal and Literary Perspectives*, Reading: Ithaca Press, pp. 351–76.

Cook, R. (1994) 'Introduction: The way forward', in R. Cook (ed.) *Human Rights of Women: National and International Perspectives*, Philadelphia: University of Pennsylvania Press.

Coomaraswamy, R. (1994) *Preliminary Report Submitted by the Special Rapporteur on Violence against Women, its Causes and Consequences*, presented to the UN Human Rights Commission: UN Doc. E/CN.4/195/42, 15–16 November, para. 70.

Eisler, R. (1987) 'Human rights: Toward an integrated theory for action', *Human Rights Quarterly* 9: 287–308.

General Comment on issues relating to reservations made upon ratification or accession to the Covenant or the Optional Protocol thereto, or in relation to declarations under article 41 of the Covenant, CCPR/C/21/Rev.1/Add.6, Paragraph 8. Reproduced in *Human Rights Law Journal* 15 (1995): 464–7.

Ghandhi, P.R. (1995) *International Human Rights Documents*, 1st edition, London: Blackstone.

Halliday, F. (1991) 'Hidden from international relations: Women and the international arena', in R. Grant and K. Newland (eds) *Gender and International Relations*, Buckingham: Open University Press, pp. 158–69.

Hellum, A. (1999) *Women's Human Rights and Legal Pluralism in Africa*, Aschehoug, Tano: Mond Books.

Hevener, N. (1983) *International Law and Status of Women*, Boulder, CO: Westview Press.

Hosken, F.P. (ed.) (1981) 'Symposium: Women and international human rights', *Human Rights Quarterly* 3.

Kelsay, J. (1988) 'Saudi Arabia, Pakistan, and the Universal Declaration of Human Rights', in D. Little, J. Kelsay and A.A. Sachedina (eds) *Human Rights and the Conflict of Cultures: Western and Islamic Perspectives on Religious Liberty*, Columbia: University of South Carolina Press, pp. 33–52.

Mayer, Ann Elizabeth (1995) *Islam and Human Rights: Tradition and Politics*, Boulder, CO: Westview, pp. 102–9.

Moinuddin, H. (1987) *The Charter of the Islamic Conference and Legal Framework of Economic Cooperation Among its Member States*, Oxford: Clarendon Press.

Nasir, J. (1986) *The Islamic Law of Personal Status*, London: Graham & Trotman.

Organisation of Islamic Conference (OIC) (1995) *Recommendation of the Seminar to the Twenty-third Islamic Conference of Foreign Ministers*, Tehran.

Rehof, L.A. (1993) *Guide to the Travaux Preparatoires of the United Nations Convention on the Elimination of All Forms of Discrimination against Women*, Dordrecht: Martinus Nijhoff.

Restatement (Third), Foreign Relations Law of the United States, sec. 702, p. 145.

Rousseau, J.J. (1947) 'From the social contract', in S. Commins and R. Linscott (eds) *The World's Great Thinkers: Man and the State*, New York: Random House.

Schacht, J. (1959) 'Islamic law in contemporary states', *American Journal of Comparative Law* 8: 133–47.

Schneider, E. (1992) 'The violence of privacy', *Connecticut Law Review* 23: 973–99.

Shirkatgah (1995) 'Official report prepared by the Conference Secretariat', *Newsheet* 7.

Slack, A. (1988) 'Female circumcision: A critical appraisal', *Human Rights Quarterly* 10: 437.

United Nations, General Assembly (1967) *Declaration on the Elimination of All Forms of Discrimination against Women*, General Assembly Resolution 2263 (XXII), UN Doc. A/6717 (1967).

United Nations, Secretary General (1999) *Multilateral Treaties Deposited with the Secretary General*, New York: United Nations.

—— (1997) *Multilateral Treaties Deposited with the Secretary General*, New York: United Nations.

Weeks, R.V. (ed.) (1984) *Muslim Peoples: A World Ethnographic Survey*, 2nd edition, Westport, CT: Greenwood Press.

5 Feminizing cyberspace
Rethinking technoagency

Gillian Youngs

Introduction

The Internet (Net) is the new space of empowerment and it is adding to, and transforming, the diverse contexts for economic, political, cultural and social transactions. In many ways it is the first truly potential global space because access to it is absolutely possible for all, although only a concrete reality for the few right now. Those few are concentrated in the North where the communications infrastructure and technological hardware and software are widely available and accessible. With 19 per cent of the world's population, the rich Organization for Economic Co-operation and Development (OECD) countries had 91 per cent of Internet users as we moved into the new millennium (UNDP 1999). However, the Internet is reaching and being reached by an increasing number of people across the world every day, including those in the South, and the networking and activist work undertaken through it is forging new communities and collective strategies (Escobar 1999). These developments increasingly cross North/South boundaries. The Internet is facilitating an international grassroots communications revolution where more and more individuals and groups, including women and women's groups, are communicating, campaigning and community building through websites, e-mail networks and discussion groups.

One does not have to be a cyberfanatic or a naïve futurist to recognize that, while such activities do not automatically and immediately overturn the state- and corporate-based power that holds sway at the global level, they are contributing to changes in its operation. We should therefore consider the Internet as a potential means for democratization of the international arena through its facilitation of a growing number of voices and collective strategies. The possibilities for long-term change are well worth recognizing. The impact of cyberactivism and its part in mobilizing real-time protests, and the derailing of the WTO meeting in Seattle toward the end of 1999, was one of the first high-profile events demonstrating the concrete effects of international virtual political activity (see Protest.Net, http://www.protest.net, and ZNet, http://www.lbbs.org/Activism/actst.htm).

This event signalled the degree to which the Net is aiding 'active' participation in international processes by a growing number of individuals and groups.

The day-by-day and minute-by-minute realities of Internet exchange incorporate the development and operation of 'interactive networks' (Escobar 1999: 34) around all kinds of interests and shared concerns. Through such networks, the Net is expanding 'horizontal' forms of communication that associate citizens and interest groups to some extent outside of, or alongside and at times interacting with, the traditional 'vertical' structures of political and economic (including media) power, involving state and international institutions and corporations. The following discussion examines how attention to the nature of the Internet as a communications medium and the kinds of interactions it facilitates emphasizes an approach to empowerment as 'process' (Rowlands 1998: 28).

The chapter pays particular attention to the Internet's potential for women in this regard and demonstrates how it is being harnessed, including across North/South divides. The Internet increases the visibility of women's issues at the international level, develops new communities based on common interests, and works explicitly to pursue the possibilities offered to women by cyberspace. I will draw on my experience in the UNESCO-Society for International Development (SID) Women on the Net (WoN) project (see http://www.waw.be/sid/won/won.htm and Harcourt 1999), which was launched in 1997 and brought together a group of technicians, researchers, activists and development practitioners from Africa, the USA, Canada, Europe and Asia.

The project focused directly on women, empowerment and the Internet. As one of its originators Lourdes Arizpe (1999: xiii) explained: 'The main thing is that women must now be active agents in experimenting and interpreting the new forms of communication that the new technologies offer us.' The aims of WoN included examining the implications of the social contexts of information and communication technologies (ICTs) and the particular challenges women confronted in participating as fully as possible in their development and application, including at the policy level, locally and globally.

> ICTs are developed and configured in social realities in which men and women have differential access to power, economic opportunities and resources. How to fulfil the potential of the Internet depends very much on opening up the vertical power structures for women and women creating horizontal power structures through networks which could serve their varied needs within and across regions.
>
> (Harcourt 1997: 4)

The following discussion will begin with an assessment of cyberspace and its implications for thinking about boundaries and agency. This section emphasizes the importance of understanding cyberspace in socially contextualized ways: as a space within, connected to and interacting with other social spaces. I explain how cyberspace problematizes traditional senses of boundaries (physical, social, political, cultural) and actively encourages fresh thinking about different kinds of potential for transcending them. I argue that the Internet highlights the importance of technoagency: technological access and know-how. It expands perspectives on campaigns for global equality, drawing attention to the growing role of technological needs and capacities in definitions of it. The current communications revolution has raised the development stakes, as it were, adding modems and computers to the more familiar basic needs of water, food, shelter and healthcare.

The next section focuses on women and cyberpolitics, and explores the specific meanings of cyberspace for women's lives and development. I assess the particular impact of Internet access for women who have been too much a missing force in male-dominated international politics, and, importantly, who have had limited means of reaching each other across national boundaries (Enloe 1990; Peterson 1992; Pettman 1996; Youngs 1999a and b). I illustrate the ways in which the Internet offers radical collective opportunities in this context, arguing that the relationship of women to ICTs and thus the gendered implications of the so-called information age are essential considerations.

The third section discusses cyber possibilities and development. It considers how the whole notion of development is being reframed to take account of the influential role of ICTs in transforming societies. The ICT revolution is pervasive, incorporating (actually and potentially) economic, political, social and cultural activities. As Fatma Alloo, founder of the Tanzania Women's Media Association (TAWMA) has explained: 'We must recognize that this information technology is here to stay …. What we have to decide is we either play the game … and turn it to our advantage or lose out completely' (*Women in the Digital Age* 1998: 14). I believe 'playing the game' offers opportunities for women to build new alliances across North/South divides and to actively address the problems of access to ICTs and their use, including their gendered characteristics. With respect to the latter, there are many challenges to share related to the traditionally male-dominated history of science and technology. And, as Sandra Harding has recently argued, these should be addressed with feminist and postcolonial sensitivities that move away from rigid and hegemonically informed North/ South technology-transfer paradigms to more open dialogues that validate local contexts, knowledges and cultural capacities.

> [T]his postcolonial science theory organizes its concerns and conceptual frameworks from outside the familiar eurocentric ones and, in that sense, its 'subject' or 'author' is not the familiar enthusiastic European beneficiary of northern sciences and technologies. Such a strategy enables postcolonial theory to detect features of different cultures' scientific and technological thought and practices that are not visible from within the familiar western accounts of science.
>
> (Harding 1998: 8; see also Pillai 1996)

The communicative power of the Internet is both part of the problem and part of the solution in this context. While it is an expression of the triumph of Western technology it is also a means of engaging critically with the nature of that technology, of opening up lines of interrogation and transformation.

Cyberspace, boundaries and agency

Cyberspace undoubtedly brings a new era of social interaction. *Online* it is possible to be in touch with audiences across the globe, offering them extensive information on individual concerns or group campaigns, and soliciting responses, even from strangers in distant locations, within minutes. The distinctive technological advance that the Internet symbolizes for the information society is the fusion of information *and* communication technologies to combine the power to communicate in depth and at speed. There simply is no comparison, for example, between the capacity of the fax machine to transmit information through cumbersome hard copies page after page and the megabytes of data that can be uploaded and downloaded via the Internet in minutes. ICTs mean that it is possible to have cyberneighbours/friends/colleagues with whom one chats/works daily or hourly by e-mail, and in this sense they truly give meaning to the now familiar cliché of the global village (McLuhan *et al.* 1997).

It is helpful to think of the Internet as a man-made environment because that prompts us to focus on the kind of 'village' that it permits: one that facilitates communication and even intimacy without physical presence. This is quite a different sense of village to traditional notions that are highly dependent on a defined and usually small geographical location with close physical proximity of people and buildings. In contemporary times we need to work with different senses of proximity, some of which are totally dependent on communication via ICTs and some of which involve usual notions of social interaction through physical presence (Tomlinson 1999). Closer contact, both professional and personal, may well be generated by one or both means.

So how does cyberspace change the social world we live in? It clearly expands the scope of communication geographically. It also speeds up the potential for communication and makes a greater density or intensity of communication over shorter periods of time possible. It also allows larger amounts of information, faster than ever before, to be posted (as on websites) or transmitted from one address to another. So the ways in which it helps to shrink the world are equally about the amounts and the nature of information as about the actual process of communication of it. One of the key starting points of the WoN project – culture – is interesting in this context because it identifies the social potential of ICTs with informational content that is explicitly about peoples, their ways of life, their histories and practices. It has meaning at the collective and the individual levels, and this is essential since ICTs link both.

> Access to information and facilitation of communication provide new and enhanced opportunities for expression and perpetuation of the cultural life of communities and peoples, with the potential to accelerate political, economic, social, educational and cultural advancement beyond the scope of traditional institutions and forms of communication. Regional and global information networks expand the voices of cultures and peoples via elec-

tronic fora to raise awareness and focus international attention and support on specific cultural issues and efforts. The ability to transcend present boundaries and create what would be an even finer web of information systems is the key to taking cyberculture to its next level.

(Bray-Crawford 1999: 162)

This and many other exchanges within the project have emphasized the challenges and opportunities offered by cyberspace for *expanding* what we understand to be the global informational sphere. It is increasing the number of new voices and new knowledges, and, crucially, enhancing the ability to campaign for the interests and concerns of a growing number of people around the world. By focusing on culture, the WoN project has explored the *located* nature of cyberspace in several complex ways. It has linked the potential of cyberspace to people, their lives, their problems and their aspirations. It has recognized the potential informational power of cyberspace to inform, educate and combat ignorance in such areas. Perhaps even more importantly, it has considered cyberspace as just one of the interacting media through which social communication and action takes place. In this way it highlights the need for critical thinking about the social relevance and potential of cyberspace and the ways in which it can *connect* people and communities, and begin work toward *transcending* traditional barriers that have divided and limited people's knowledge about one another. 'Cyberspace offers the possibility to move from segmenting knowledge to integrating and sharing it across traditional academic categories, expertise, technical skill, scientific know-how, political weight and cultural hierarchies' (Harcourt 1997: 4).

Cyberspace has the potential to cross many traditional boundaries. The degree to which it ultimately does so is dependent only on the ways in which societies and individuals use and develop it. Part of its potential is to reach across social and geographical contexts, breaching public and private, national, political and economic divides (Youngs 1999c). It brings the local and the global into much closer relation and thus the most powerful possibilities for transcendence it offers relate to the most influential of boundaries dividing nations and cultures. This presents a conceptual as well as practical challenge because international theories and political practices, and the common sense resulting from them, have to date been dominated by billiard-ball state-centred frameworks, which define collective and individual political identities through the boundaries that *separate* states and peoples from one another (Walker 1993; Youngs 1999b). This helps to lock 'political imagination' as well as political identity into state-bound orientations (Walker 1993: ix–x) and this is highly problematic when thinking about the possibilities for expanded cross-boundary political activity and experience offered by the Net. Imagination beyond traditional political realms, participation and identities is an integral part of such processes and, crucially, the motivation for them. This situation is further complicated by the technical boundaries that ICTs present, which have implications for all those who are down the technological hierarchies for one reason or another. Two great divides lie between the so-called developed and developing worlds, and between men and women. One of the strengths of the WoN project has been its deliberate decision to work across these boundaries.

This picture implies that cyberspace is expanding the scope and nature of political agency. In certain respects it is linking, and is likely to increasingly link, such agency to varying forms of technological agency. Questions of techno-agency are central to the transformations defining the move to information societies. The pursuit of human goals is being increasingly integrated with the capacities of various forms of advanced technologies, including ICTs. The current genetic debate, for example, touches on many aspects of human repro-duction, health, food and the environment. It relates to other forms of technological developments based on the most sophisticated of scientific infor-mational techniques. Technological syntaxes are beginning to saturate our social and communicative environments.

> The computer is by all odds the most extraordinary of all the technological clothing ever devised by man, since it is the extension of our central nervous system .... The important thing is to realize that electric information systems are live environments in the full organic sense.
>
> (McLuhan *et al.* 1997: 35–6)

There are processes of recognition, familiarization and adjustment to be taken account of here as well as the influential hierarchical barriers concerning access to technology and technological knowledge, basic education and literacy, and English (American) as the dominant language of the ICT age. The WoN project has stressed that the challenges we share cross all these areas. It has recognized, along with other Net-oriented global projects, the contemporary importance of technoagency, and has focused on the specific issues faced by women across cultural contexts.

Women and cyberpolitics

ICTs carry the gendered legacy of historically established male domination in the realms of science and technology. Women's relationship to modern technolo-gies has been largely defined and mediated by men. Donna Haraway's provocative discussion of the contemporary era of 'technoscience' draws us directly into the realms of subjectivity and agency: 'I want feminists to be enrolled more tightly in the meaning-making processes of technoscientific world-building' (1997: 127). At issue is women's fundamental relationship to technology and any politics associated with it. Feminist perspectives draw attention to the need for critical thought about both: the implications of women's historical alienation or separation from key technological processes by masculinist science, and the subject/object separations common to scientific traditions of thought (see Youngs 2000a). Haraway's sense of the woman/computer ('cyborg') rela-tionship is embodied, or at least one that attempts to interestingly blur the distinction between person, machine, purpose and political imagination (see also Haraway 1991).

> Communication and articulation disconnected from yearning toward possible worlds does not make enough sense. And explicit purposes – politics, rationality, ethics, or technics in a reductive sense – do not say much about the furnace that is personal and collective yearning for just barely possible worlds.
>
> (Haraway 1997: 127)

Haraway embraces and articulates the virtual possibilities of cyberspace and the political purport of the tracks we follow and connections we build within it. She prompts us to probe the 'knot[s] of knowledge-making practices' (1997: 129). Women's relationship to and use of ICTs cannot be taken for granted. It has to be worked through with critical regard to the gendered social constructions of technological capacities and tools, and this is not just a practical matter but one that has implications for the alternative world visions that women can weave together. Use of ICTs goes hand in hand with questions about purpose. As Lourdes Arizpe has argued:

> Cyberspace will greatly accelerate our capacity to create and build. This will have important effects in encouraging women to participate in designing and implementing models of economic development, constructing stable democracies, ensuring that different cultures can exist side by side without violent conflict and providing the sense of trust, partnership and solidarity that are necessary to any society in which people co-operate for mutual well-being. Such a vision calls for women cyber-citizens who are rooted in their local cultures yet have a stake in national and global civil society.
>
> (*Women in the Digital Age* 1998: 2)

This sense of women as *located* yet globally *connected* through cyberspace reveals the complex spatial politics of technoagency. It also signals the importance of an awareness of cyber-citizens as embodied (Youngs 2000b) and technoagency as something which connects virtual space with the more conventional and overtly concrete spaces of political, economic, social and cultural activities and processes. ICTs are multidimensional tools whose power rests largely in their capacities to link places and people, and we already have strong evidence that women can harness and exploit that power to their own purposes. This has particular importance at the international level where the scope for women's political activity has been most severely restricted (compared to men) and where, subsequently, political and personal linkages with one another have been limited.

At this point it is useful to remember that the arrival of the ICT age accompanied a growing international focus on women's issues and women's movements with the United Nations conferences on women and its decade for women (1976–85) playing key roles. The ICT dimension in women's activism came to the fore in a major way at the fourth world conference in Beijing in 1995 as well as earlier in the preparations for it (Gittler 1999). Those involved in the process, however, have stressed that 'networking' by no means arrived with the Internet. Rather, this new medium expanded the established practices and networking possibilities that had already been contributing to building different strands of international women's movements (Gittler 1999: 92). The numbers of newsletters had been expanding and fax networks had been 'instrumental in multiplying messages and mobilizing action in campaigns' internationally (Gittler 1999: 93). The Beijing process was a profound example of the potential of the Internet to deepen women's global connectivity and transform their collective sense of political action.

> [W]omen accessed draft versions of the *Platform for Action*, regional action plans and caucus documents. They downloaded them, disseminated them, analyzed them, drafted additions and deletions, reached consensus on issues, circulated statements and mobilized support. NGOs in some countries found themselves better informed than their national delegations. The public electronic spaces for discussion and information sharing also helped demystify the UN proceedings. Discussions previously reserved for a few government delegates and observers at the United Nations were now open to anyone able to access the medium.
>   Electronic communications promoted a feeling of being part of a larger process …. Women who met on-line found an immediate network in Beijing. Electronic conferences and mailing lists sprang up on issues ranging from violence against women to spirituality, gender, science and technology.
>
> (Gittler 1999: 95)

Relevant to our considerations of technoagency is the interactive influence of *collective* political work and association in this context and *collective* learning about ICTs and the problems and potential they present. The pull of the possibilities for political involvement was coupled with the pull to get *online*, to work together to make ICTs meaningfully accessible and usable for growing numbers of women and women's organizations in larger numbers of locations. Training and technical assistance was a large part of the empowerment picture in this process, with notable networks specifically designed for this purpose such as the Association for Progressive Communications (APC) Women's Outreach Program (Gittler 1999: 96 and Gittler 1996; Farwell *et al.* 1999). The Global Knowledge '97 conference hosted by the World Bank and the Canadian government with other private and public organizations was another focal point for the women's ICT movement, to use the term loosely, as was its follow-up in 2000 (Sreberny 1998; Huyer 1999).

   As explained below, the WoN project is one among many around the world that are continuing and developing the efforts that have surrounded these major global events. Such work indicates shared commitment to use ICTs to work toward creating forms of global spheres for women's politics. They are a manifestation of the kinds of local–global connections mooted in debates about globalization and, as I have argued, they are transformative not only in respect to women's politics but also women's evolving relationship to new technologies and both are equally influential in defining the future global potential of women.

Cyber possibilities and development

Technology, and ICTs in particular, have become central to development debates, with technological capacities and access taking up a growing part in considerations of equality and rights (World Bank 1999, 2000; UNDP 1999). The various economic, political and cultural functions of ICTs contribute directly to processes of globalization, and major international reports of recent times have focused on the implications of these developments. In major respects ICTs as definers of the knowledge age help to shape the characteristics of inequities within it. These cover a whole range of communications and technological infrastructure, knowledge, education and training issues. The USA stands out at the top of these league tables in the industrialized world with significant combined concentrations in areas such as e-commerce spending, home Internet use and numbers of personal, including networked, computers (UNDP 1999: 66; see also Youngs 2000c).

Technology gaps are coming to represent one of the most serious concerns in the assessment of what it means to lose in the game of globalization. The 'new rules of globalization – privatization, liberalization and tighter intellectual property rights – are shaping the path of technology, creating new risks of marginalization and vulnerability' (UNDP 1999: 68). With the knowledge sector growing fast in the global economy, market and major corporate power are increasingly driving the agenda for control over innovation and technology transfer (UNDP 1999: 67–8). Developing countries figure little in the intellectual property rights scenario, with industrialized countries holding 97 per cent of all the patents in the world (UNDP 1999: 68). ICTs, as the huge profile of the likes of Bill Gates and Microsoft indicates, are among the key moneymakers of the high-technology sector. A small but growing number of developing countries have become players in the software market, but the industrialized OECD countries took the lion's share – 94 per cent – of the 1994 global total of $79 billion for final, packaged software (UNDP 1999: 69). Despite the rapid growth in areas such as mobile telephone use, most of the figures for the global ICT picture at the end of the twentieth century looked depressingly daunting.

There are more Internet hosts in Bulgaria than in sub-Saharan Africa (excluding South Africa). The USA has more computers than the rest of the world combined, and more computers per capita than any other country. Just fifty-five countries account for 99 per cent of global spending on information technology. Most telephones in developing countries are in the capital city, although most people live in rural areas. Connections are often poor in the rainy season, and the costs of calls are very high. In several African countries average monthly Internet connection and use costs run as high as $100 – compared with $10 in the USA (UNDP 1999: 62).

Perhaps the elitist nature of the Internet revolution at this point is its most worrying aspect, particularly in relation to the optimistic claims made for its potential to bring new expanded forms of democracy in relation to information and society. Critical debates in this context focus on the dominance of English (American) on the Internet and the requirement of basic literacy as well as general and technological education. Only 2 per cent of the world's people are part of the Net, with nearly 80 per cent of websites in English. Thirty per cent of users possess at least one university degree (UNDP 1999: 62). Women represent 38 per cent of users in the USA, 25 per cent in Brazil, 17 per cent in Japan and South Africa, 16 per cent in Russia, 7 per cent in China and 4 per cent in the Arab States (UNDP 1999: 62).

The Internet clearly brings long-established concerns about the gendered character of technology use into fresh perspective. In the information age these divides inform the politics of empowerment. One of the major features of global restructuring has been feminization of the labour force and this has undoubtedly increased the number of women having access to ICTs. However, there are influential contrasts in the possibilities this opens up. While certain professions, such as business, academia and non-governmental organizations (NGOs), provide access to a wide range of facilities and opportunities, we must not forget that a substantial number of women work in secretarial and clerical roles. Their *relationships* to these technologies tend to be much more rigidly defined, including time to experiment and explore (Runyan 1996; Walby 1997; see also Marchand and Runyan 2000). However, overall, the increased access of women to ICTs across such different circumstances remains a key factor in their potential (as well as actual) empowerment through the use of these new technologies. As one respondent from Peru to the APC's Women's Networking Survey of 1996 commented:

> After six years of being dedicated to administration tasks I was given the opportunity to combine my work with information and communication tasks and this has allowed me to discover within myself unknown areas and a great inclination for the area of information and telecommunications.
>
> (APC 1997)

The increased double burden for women of work inside and outside of the home has also eaten further into the time available to pursue independent non-work and care-based activities (UNDP 1999: 80–1; Walby 1997: 53–5). As one respondent to the APC Survey explained, 'in some ways the Internet is a tool for those with lives of leisure' (APC 1997; see also Youngs 2001).

One of the functions of projects like WoN is to help disrupt the historically and economically created relationships (or lack thereof) of women to high technology. It encourages collective spaces where women can think creatively and independently about what ICTs have to offer and how they would like to capture, utilize and influence these possibilities. In line with other similar projects, most of the work has been done through face-to-face workshops and online debate, development of website material and publications. This includes an accessible introductory digital age handbook to introduce the Internet and to offer practical advice to individuals and groups about getting online (Harcourt 1997, 1999; *Women in the Digital Age* 1998).

All aspects of WoN's work have emphasized partnership and collaborative discovery about the actual nature and potential of the Internet. As a project, it has been rooted in the local and the global in different contexts, focusing on the ways in which the Internet brings one to the other and makes linkages within and across them. Fundamental questions underpinning the work have been along these lines: What do we want the Internet to do? How can it help us in our local goals, in education and health? How can we be present there? What kinds of global networks do we want to form and to what ends? What do we want to say about ourselves, our communities, our cultures and our lives? What kinds of technological skills do we need to do this effectively? How easily can such skills be accessed and shared? The list is of course endless. The workshops, which have been both ideas-based and practical, have all been conducted in a participatory manner. The exchanges demonstrate the potential for sharing across national boundaries, for information and for priorities for learning as well as for imagining what is and might be possible.

In trendy terminology we can think in terms of WoN being a small part of women's Internet learning curve in a global context, or as Jo Rowlands powerfully and simply puts it: 'The central issue of empowerment is one of *process*' (1998: 28). The role of the Internet as part of the overall development process has distinctive qualities in this respect. Among other things, it facilitates ongoing shared connection and learning, and even the development of communities of empowerment over extended periods of time. The communications and information links that it provides enable deep exchange and connection. Of course, these cannot be taken for granted and they don't just happen. They have to be built by individuals and groups, but, as I have indicated, this is already being done successfully across the North and the South.

Because the Net is both an information *and* a communication technology, it has a complex role in the area of empowerment. If it can be accessed actively it can be used to gain and communicate information, to work toward building new transnational communities and to obtain and share technical and other forms of knowledge. WoN, in common with other empowerment-oriented Net projects, has been focused on the potential of this medium for generating and sharing *new* information, including about women's lives, interests and activities, as well as their communities. Therein lies part of the transformative potential of the Net in Northern and Southern, as well as North–South, communicative contexts.

The collective focus of WoN has tapped into important practical priorities that are driving Net development projects aimed at tackling the global inequalities in technical knowledge and equipment. These priorities disrupt the highly individualistic model of the personal computer at work and at home that tends to be the received view of the information society in the North. Clearly the priority for the majority of the world is how to get access at all to the Net and, apart from the fundamental issues of telecommunications infrastructure, this directs attention to community/collective rather than individual links (UNDP 1999: 63–5). Some of the most innovative work relating to the Internet is centred on the establishment of telecentres and village information hubs. They integrate various communications and computer technologies with energy sources such as solar power, thus providing local, including rural, communities with different forms of access to the Net (UNDP 1999: 64). One example is Canada's International Development Research Centre's Acacia project in Africa that is establishing telecentres in four countries: Mozambique, Senegal, South Africa and Uganda (*http://www.idrc.ca/acacia*).

Expanding access to the Internet is partly about expanding the *sources* of information on it, and this has been one of WoN's primary activities. Two Internet workshops for women, women's NGOs and community group representatives, in partnership with local NGOs in Tanzania (Zanzibar) and Kenya (Nairobi) in 1999, decided that they wanted to establish websites and enhance those which already existed on local groups and organizations. Information on Africa *by* Africans, the participants argued, had been a major goal along with access to the Net's wealth of information for local purposes and interests, including the commercial. WoN's work has emphasized how the Internet, for all its virtual and boundary-crossing qualities, actually facilitates new awareness of and emphasis on the local, or more specifically 'place' (see *Development* 1998). As Arturo Escobar has put it: ' a reassertion of place, non-capitalism and local culture should result in theories that make visible possibilities for reconceiving and reconstructing the world from the perspective of place-based practices' (1999: 46).

The Net is a mechanism for disseminating the hidden stories of globalization. Information about happenings in particular places at particular times can be shared and thus drawn on to increase understanding and to contribute to various local and global political (and other) processes. However, the potential for social transformation, as Escobar stresses, rests partly on the determination to 'build bridges between place and cyberspace' with political effect (1999: 52). In this sense it is important that cyberspace and its potential is evaluated within the context of broader social structures and processes.

Hence the new focus on ICTs in development and empowerment debates should be seen as an extension of their more established preoccupations rather than, as in any way, a substitute for them. In certain ways it can be argued that ICTs have made these debates even more complex and challenging. The World Bank's (1999) key *World Development Report: Knowledge for Development* highlights the capacity of the new information and communication technologies to fulfil one of the more positive promises of globalization to bring North and South closer together.

> This new technology greatly facilitates the acquisition and absorption of
> knowledge, offering developing countries unprecedented opportunities to

enhance educational systems, improve policy formation and execution, and widen the range of opportunities for business and the poor. One of the great hardships endured by the poor, and by many others who live in the poorest countries, is their sense of isolation. The new communications technologies promise to reduce that sense of isolation, and to open access to knowledge in ways unimaginable not long ago.

(World Bank 1999: 9)

We are only talking about *promise* at this point, as the profound global inequalities in ICT access discussed here make clear, but the WoN project, among others, has taken seriously aspects of the challenges contained within such promise and the possibilities for working collectively and actively to address them. WoN has also, with others, addressed the critical issues associated with the predominantly male- and Western-centred tendencies of these new mainstream development policy debates.

Cyberspace cannot remain the domain of the powerful telecommunication companies and markets which profit from its use, nor the child of the (mostly male) technicians which have created the software and language that goes with it. Rather local groups have to become confident with the medium and to negotiate and to help shape the direction the Internet will take through incisive strategizing. The global communication culture would presumably then take on a much more diverse perspective, responding and interacting to the margins which recognise the politics and power of communications and its potential which is currently only glimpsed.

(Harcourt 1997: 3)

Conclusion

It is hard to be optimistic about global access to the Internet or to ICTs more generally, as it is no more than a distant dream right now. The arrival of the information age has been accompanied by profound and, to some extent, deepening inequalities across the world. By the late 1990s, the fifth of the world's people living in the highest income countries had 86 per cent of world gross domestic product, 82 per cent of world export markets, 68 per cent of foreign direct investment and 74 per cent of telephone lines. The bottom fifth of the world's population had just 1 per cent in the first three categories and one and a half per cent in the fourth. The assets of the top three billionaires amounted to more than the combined gross national product of all least developed countries and their 600 million people (UNDP 1999: 3).

The concentration of Internet access in the rich North reflects the dramatic knowledge divides between the developed and developing worlds in the expanding high technology sectors. As more and more activities across the political, commercial and cultural realms intensify on the Internet, concern will continue to grow about those who are left out of this expanding global communications sphere. The discussion in this chapter has illustrated different ways in which women's movements have launched diverse strategies to tackle this problem, however overwhelming it might seem.

Globally, women's organizations and campaigns have been actively addressing the challenges of getting *online*, embracing the empowerment opportunities of the Internet revolution. My arguments have stressed that these opportunities are far from restricted to issues of technology. They incorporate new possibilities for building global networks of, and strategies for, women. Their *collective* modes, in bringing growing numbers of women together across national boundaries to exchange views and work for shared ends, represent the quiet dawning of what might be considered a new era in international politics. While these developments do not sweep away the historical weight of male dominance in the international sphere, they do potentially disrupt some of its seamless qualities.

Therein lie some of the central messages of the achievements on the Internet by women to date and the orientations of projects like WoN. A starting point is the recognition of the Internet as a tool to be used. Thus, a priority must be gaining access to that tool and to working to overcome historically entrenched gendered technological barriers. Equally important is the creative work to establish precisely what role the Internet can play in building new transnational communities that incorporate 'place-based knowledge and action' (Arizpe 1999: xvi). These can only be processes of empowerment because they take time and collective effort. They include the ongoing building and strengthening of horizontal links – some based on established networks and others generating entirely new ones. From these can come strategies to continue both engaging critically with the vertical structures of political and economic power, and pressing for policies and conditions that will expand ICT access and counter the trends toward a global society divided along the lines of the information rich and poor.

References

Arizpe, L. (1999) 'Freedom to create: Women's agenda for cyberspace', in W. Harcourt, (ed.) *Women*, London: Zed Books, pp. xii–xvi.

Association for Progressive Communication (APC) (May 1997) *APC Women's Networking Survey: Summary of Findings*, London: APC Women's Networking Support Program, GreenNet Ltd/GreenNet Educational Trust.

Bray-Crawford, K.P. (1999) 'The Ho'okele netwarriors in the liquid continent', in W. Harcourt (ed.) *Women* Zed Books, pp. 162–72.

Development (1998) 'Globalism and the politics of place', 41(2) (June).

Enloe, C. (1990) *Bananas, Beaches and Bases: Making Feminist Sense of International Politics*, London: Pandora.

Escobar, A. (1999) 'Gender, place and networks: A political ecology of cyberculture', in W. Harcourt (ed.) *Women*, London: Zed Books, pp. 31–54.

Farwell, Edie, Peregrine Wood, Maureen James and Karen Banks (1999) 'Global networking for change: Experiences from the APC women's programme', in W. Harcourt (ed.) *Women*, London: Zed Books, pp. 102–13.

Gittler, A.M. (1999) 'Mapping women's global communications and networking', in W. Harcourt (ed.) *Women*, London: Zed Books, pp. 91–101.

—— (1996) 'Taking hold of electronic communications: Women making a difference', *The Journal of International Communication* 3 (1): 85–101.

Haraway, D.J. (1997) *Modest_Witness@Second_Millennium. FemaleMan©_meets_OncoMouse™: Feminism and technoscience.* London: Routledge.

—— (1991) *Simians, Cyborgs and Women: The Reinvention of Nature*, New York: Routledge.

Harcourt, W. (1999) *Women*, London: Zed Books.

—— (1997) *An International Annotated Guide to Women Working on the Net*, revised version, Rome: UNESCO/Society for International Development.

Harding, S. (1998) *Is Science Multicultural: Postcolonialisms, Feminisms, and Epistemologies*, Bloomington, IN: Indiana University Press.

Huyer, S. (1999) 'Shifting agendas at GK97: Women and international policy on information and communication technologies', in W. Harcourt (ed.) *Women*, London: Zed Books, pp. 114–30.

McLuhan, M. and Q. Fiore (produced by J. Agel) (1997) [1968] *War and Peace in the Global Village*, San Francisco: HardWired.

Marchand, M.H. and A.S. Runyan (eds) (2000) *Gender and Global Restructuring: Sightings, Sites and Resistances*, London: Routledge.

Peterson, V.S. (ed.) (1992) *Gendered States: (Re)Visions of International Relations Theory*, Boulder, CO.: Lynne Rienner.

Pettman, J.J. (1996) *Worlding Women: A Feminist International Politics*, London: Routledge.

Pillai, P. (1996) 'Postmodern feminism and postcolonial criticism: A paradigm for transational feminist media studies', *The Journal of International Communication* 3(1): 42–65.

Rowlands, J. (1998) 'A word of the times, but what does it mean? Empowerment in the discourse and practice of development', in H. Afshar (ed.) *Women and Empowerment: Illustrations from the Third World*, London: Macmillan, pp. 11–34.

Runyan, A.S. (1996) 'The places of women in trading places: Gendered global/regional regimes and inter-nationalized feminist resistance', in E. Kofman and G. Youngs (ed.) *Globalization: Theory and Practice*, London: Pinter, pp. 238–52.

Sreberny, A. (1998) 'Feminist internationalism: Imagining and building global civil society', in D.K. Thussu (ed.) *Electronic Empires: Global Media and Local Resistance*, London: Arnold, pp. 208–22.

Tomlinson, J. (1999) *Globalization and Culture*, Cambridge: Polity.

United Nations Development Programme (UNDP) (1999) *Human Development Report*, New York: Oxford University Press.

Walby, S. (1997) *Gender Transformations*, London: Routledge.

Walker, R.B.J. (1993) *Inside/outside: International Relations as Political Theory*, Cambridge: Cambridge University Press.

Women in the Digital Age (1998) Rome: A Society for International Development and UNESCO Publication.

World Bank (2000) *World Development Report: Entering the 21st Century*, New York: Oxford University Press.

—— (1999) *World Development Report: Knowledge for Development*, New York: Oxford University Press.

Youngs, G. (2001) 'The political economy of time in the internet era: Feminist perspectives and challenges', *Information, Communication and Society* 4(1): 14–33.

—— (ed.) (2000a) *Political Economy, Power and the Body: Global Perspectives*, London: Macmillan.

—— (2000b) 'Embodied political economy or an escape from disembodied knowledge', in G. Youngs (ed.) *Political Economy, Power and the Body: Global Perspectives*, London: Macmillan, pp. 11–30.

—— (2000c) 'Globalization, technology and consumption', in G. Youngs (ed.) *Political Economy, Power and the Body: Global Perspectives*, London: Macmillan, pp. 75–93.

—— (1999a) 'Boundary breaking and cyberspace', paper presented at the International Studies Association Annual Convention, Washington, DC, February 16–20.

—— 1999b. *International Relations in a Global Age: A Conceptual Challenge*, Cambridge: Polity.

—— 1999c. 'Virtual voices: Real lives', in W. Harcourt (ed.) *Women*, London: Zed Books, pp. 55–68.

Websites

Canadian International Development Research Centre Acacia project. http://www.idrc.ca/acacia.

Protest.Net. http://www.protest.net.

Women on the Net. http://www.waw.be/sid/won/won.htm.

ZNet. http://www.lbbs.org/Activism/actst.htm.

Part III

The nation state, politics and women's empowerment

6 Engaging politics

Beyond official empowerment discourse

Kathleen Staudt

Women winners. Empowered, encouraged, enriched – 'e-[m]n' words.

Replace the word women above with another phrase about the disempowered or dispossessed, and you tap late twentieth-century political formulaic rhetoric for new initiatives with the promise to facilitate and accomplish transformations. Whether discussing women, displaced workers, ghetto dwellers or youth, the language is the same. Large-scale, macro-level structures have set the stage that disempowers people, and yet staff from some of those same structures revisit the stage with empowerment language. In this process, do women and other marginalized people acquire power to shift power relations?

In this chapter, I discuss the origins and meanings of the term women's empowerment, arguing that it must be viewed in both process and outcome terms. Women's empowerment involves a *process* of shifting the (gender) power imbalance within public and private society. Public society is the focus of this chapter, although I recognize that the two cannot be entirely separated. Necessarily, this shift involves power with others in *politics*: people organized to engage official state and international agencies *and/or* other organizations. Women's empowerment is also an *outcome* that can be documented with economic, budgetary and concrete achievements. In this discussion, I thread examples of official international and bilateral technical assistance agencies, examining what they say they do (rhetoric that must be examined critically) versus what they do, with whatever exists as evidence in documents and trans-parent indicators. Finally, I discuss official empowerment language in the late twentieth-century USA, bipartisan rhetoric that belies an overall context of economic, budgetary and spatial outcomes that have not transformed unequal relations. In so doing, I aim to bridge the global to local of the US–Mexico borderlands, making the bottom-line argument that women's organized and crit-ical political voices and justice agendas empower women. Top-down institutional rhetoric can translate into resources, commitments, legitimacy and policy/legal principles that foster justice outcomes.

By official institutions, I refer to public agencies that generate financial support from tax-paying citizens and residents (including immigrants) in (multiple) states. I focus especially on those agencies that claim to foster 'development' through loans, grants and experts, a.k.a. 'technical assistance' (as the agencies call themselves, though sometimes the word 'donor' is used instead). Development is a hotly contested term (see discussion in Staudt 1998a: 15–18; Ch. 2) that usually privileges economic growth, but sometimes fosters poverty alleviation, economic redistribution and access to health and education among other crucial social services. Bilateral institutions refer to government-to-government relationships, such as 'foreign aid', while multilateral institutions refer to multiple governments' relationships through international or global agencies. In this chapter, I focus on those multilateral institutions that are loosely or closely affiliated with the United Nations (UN). Readers, beware! If I am to avoid wordiness, my analyses of these institutions will involve acronyms. The sources for this chapter come from interview and document data from the United Nations Research Institute for Social Development (UNRISD), analysed in Staudt (1998a: Ch. 8–9); from secondary studies and updates provided through web searches (the UN agencies publicly present themselves with rich narrative); and from observations/interviews I have conducted over the last two decades (see especially Staudt 1985, 1997; UN/DAW 1994).

Empowerment terminology

The language of empowerment emerged in the last third of the twentieth century from outside and inside official institutions, perhaps visualized as poles on a continuum. On one side of a continuum, we hear social movements call for 'power to the people' to confront systemic domination based on race, class, gender, spatial location and age. Movement activists made such calls in the face of repressive or resistant official agencies and corporations in which power was concentrated, centralized and distant from ordinary people. They recognized that the relations of power must shift to accomplish real change in the established status quo. Those with less power must amass more power within and with others to redistribute resources and values, utilizing leverage obtained with voice, expertise, money, protests and force among other tools.

States and official agencies rarely used empowerment language (unless they claimed revolutionary mantles), preferring instead the language of reform. Reform, often appearing behind the adjective 'incremental', rarely addressed problems at their roots. Minor tweaks in policy may go unnoticed, perpetuating problems and inducing cynicism.

Meanwhile, economic crises in the early 1980s led to calls for dismantling and downsizing the state. Power shifts, in the name of structural adjustment, redistributed state budgetary priorities and reduced commitments to social spending, especially in education and health (Cornia *et al.* 1987). Simultaneously, adjustment language gave new leverage to marketplace solutions. Official agencies began to formulate development strategies that legitimized people's own use of power resources (money, collective strength, knowledge, work, political representation and constituencies) to exercise choice and self-sufficiency. Rhetorical responsibility shifted to individuals. The critical language of activists outside the state was co-opted by those inside the state along with other official international agencies. Official rhetoric like this can induce cynicism in the *contexts* wherein those same institutional policies disempowered people and places.

Empowerment can hardly occur in contexts lacking democratic account-ability relationships among those who make decisions and constituencies affected by such decisions. As Robert Reich has written about the global economy, national-level governance is the only real accountability relationship that exists for people (1992). Yet in national accountability relations, to whom and to how many are governments accountable? In democracies, people can organize, vote and use other means to influence representatives. No such accountability exists globally, even in the kinds of international non-government organizations that depend on agencies for contracts. The anxiety over regional regimes like the NAFTA (North American Free Trade Agreement), the World Trade Organization at its Seattle meeting in 1999 and the World Bank International Monetary Fund (IMF) meeting in Washington illustrate the distant, even non-existent, accountability that ordinary people lack with non-elected, appointed and/or technical decision-makers. People resort to street or electronic struggle (see Youngs chapter) to publicize decision-making behind closed doors, to demand accountability and to exercise leverage on decision-makers in national governance.

International organizations, like those affiliated with the United Nations, illus-trate the same distant accountability relationships. As Rounaq Jahan has persuasively argued, bilateral donors are frequently more responsive to gender than multilateral donors precisely because of the nationally concentrated (bilat-eral) rather than diffused and fragmented (multilateral) accountability relationships (1995). Of course, the accountability in bilateral donor organiza-tions occurs *within* the national boundaries of the donor and not across boundaries to 'recipient' nations. As we see in later sections, nations like Norway and the Netherlands, with well-organized women, create greater gender balance in their countries' international technical assistance. Thus, a hierarchy of respon-siveness and accountability (which may or may not exist) privileges constituencies organized around in the North (the donor nations) rather than the South.

The challenge to empowerment in both process and outcome terms is a chal-lenge of political engagement in accountability relationships within and across national boundaries. With this framing, we now move to international organiza-tions (the 'global') and, subsequently, to local organizations within nations.

A multilateral case

Consider this example. The World Bank president authorizes reprints of his addresses, viewed on its website's (http://www.worldbank.org) gender section, in which he occasionally uses (or repeats, depending on the audience for the speech) the phrase 'women's empowerment'. On the up side, there is a feel-good quality to these words, and the language provides legitimacy and leverage for ever-vigilant inside and outside change advocates. Yet we must understand these words in historic context of how 'the' Bank (as it is reverently known by some) distributes and redistributes funds within given national contexts.

The virulent pursuit of the Bank's structural adjustment policies and dismantling of the state since the early 1980s (Staudt 1990) has had real outcome consequences for gender relations. One can look far beyond critical scholars (i.e. Benería and Feldman 1992; Elson 1991) or non-government organization (NGO) critiques (i.e. DAWN 1985) to find mainstream articulation of the damages done to people in poverty, the majority of whom are women. UNICEF's (the UN Children's Fund) plea for *Structural Adjustment with a Human Face* (Cornia *et al.* 1987) and various UNDP (UN Development Programme) *Human Development Reports*, published annually since 1990, discuss outcome damages and increasing global and gender inequalities. The exception to damage involves increased literacy and longevity, for the gender gap in education is diminishing and maternal/girl mortality is declining, resulting in extended female longevity. While acknowledging some developmental successes, the Bank also documents damage in its own internal studies, analysing women's difficult survival strategies in 'households' (Moser 1997). International lending agencies force national budget cuts to health and education. Women are the shock absorbers, increasing their paid and unpaid labour with meagre returns. This looks 'efficient' to economists.

Who controls these nation states undergoing challenge from international lenders? The 1995 *Human Development Report* contains an elaborate analysis of men's gross over-representation as presidents/prime ministers, legislators/parliamentarians and cabinet officials. Historically, states have been the organized bastions of men pursuing strategic men's interests (Charlton *et al.* 1989; Parpart and Staudt 1989; Rai and Lievesley 1996). Thus, if states are dismantled, will institutionalized *male* privilege also be dismantled? As the excellent UNRISD study, *States in Disarray* (1995), elaborates, most states claim to act on behalf of their citizens, male and female alike. Within states, residents and citizens are authorized to hold their states accountable, however weak their political voices and weapons may be. Outside the state, neither leaders nor international institutions are directly accountable to women (or men) within national boundaries.

How, then, do we understand the Bank's impact on power relations? In *process* terms, the Bank is the quintessential mainstream economists' agency that justifies actions in terms of efficiency, cost–benefit (profit) and loan-repayment terms (Kardam 1991). It prides itself as 'technical' rather than political, even as realities belie those labels. The Bank initially had minimal 'Women in Development' (WID) advocates (1.5 staff in the mid-1970s), but now considerable numbers of 'gender' technicians (the Bank was a pioneer on renaming this pocket in 1992) are at work. Gender technicians pursue policy analyses compatible with Bank language and design gender plans in the project documents that 'move money' through the Bank bureaucracy. Project language in design papers may never connect with actual implementation or outcomes. Project language is the language of promise, and even this process is cause for scepticism given that less than half of projects make gender promises, as internal and external reports show (Razavi and Miller 1995).

Gender analysts have called upon two bureaucratic functions to make institutionalized male privilege more visible in *outcome* terms: evaluations and budgets. In development institutions, evaluation units are subordinate to rather than independent of the executive and the money-moving priority mission (Staudt 1985, 1998a). Even when the most superficial of gender-disaggregated data emerge, gaps are rarely used to halt or redirect funding and future investments. More recently, Diane Elson has called for a gendered approach to budgeting, to understanding investments and expenditures (including women's unpaid contributions and burdens), and to concentrating powerholders in decision-making (1996). Budget control is typically centralized and secret, but if the process and figures were transparent, one would likely document minimal funds to women amid the gendered power relations in the states to which the Bank lends money.

To their credit, the Bank gender staff members (unlike the President) do NOT use empowerment terms to label the Bank's work on their website: rather, they call their principles 'efficiency' and 'equity', two of five now-famous principles that Moser analysed for women/gender activities (1989, 1993). (The other principles are welfare, anti-poverty and empowerment.) The major contributions to altering gender outcomes have occurred in family planning, education and rhetoric surrounding micro-enterprise credit. It almost goes without saying that the Bank would not justify funding to engage women in the political process or to strengthen women or gender-equality NGOs. Remember, the Bank views itself as technical, rather than political (Ferguson 1990); technical solutions stand apart from politics in the economists' dream world.

The Bank case illustrates the problems associated with many official agencies. Like other multilateral agencies, it works with states and reproduces gendered legacies and practices therein. It prizes planning to move money, rather than using outcomes to hold planners responsible or push them to change their ways. It acts as if it is cleansed from politics, prioritizing efficiency, repayment and profit over public accountability. On paper, its gender thinking seems to have come a long way over the last third of a century, but incremental improvements in 'human capital' (education) investment are its major claims to altering gendered outcomes. (See Stromquist in this volume on formal education.)

Empowerment *is* political

As Vina Mazumdar once said, 'My only request is that we do not treat politics as a dirty word; but rather recognize the inherently political aspects involved in any process of change' (1989). Official agencies are embedded in a political process, whether in the national fund-raising contexts or the so-called 'host-country' governments in which funds are spent. These are politics of the budgetary process. The voices that challenge existing, unequal power relations are often muted in the political processes that involve budgetary allocations for and expenditures by technical assistance institutions. Voices are organized within collectivities known as non-government organizations, some of which engage with and/or lobby government and others that aim to remain autonomous and self-sufficient.

And are there reformer and transformer NGOs among them? Some NGOs are part of establishment politics, tapping bilateral and multilateral institutions for contracts and grants, and becoming dependent upon them. Others avoid engagement with establishment politics that are considered corrupt and/or hopeless. Progressive organizations in the last quarter-century have wavered between organizing outside official politics, often mired in authoritarian or partisan co-optation, and engaging with those politics, hoping to change laws, enforce existing policies/laws and transform power relations through legitimization, systemic changes and extensive public funding. In various edited collections, readers learn the diverse strategies pursued (Basu 1995; Nelson and Chowdhury 1994). NGOs are not, by definition, agents of empowerment, but they have the potential to become such agents in democratic, and even some not so democratic, contexts if and when they are accountable to members and members' interests.

Some bilateral technical assistance organizations recognize politics in their funding strategies and the importance of supporting autonomous, non-governmental organizations in 'recipient' countries, especially those NGOs that historically lacked a public voice. But one must ask – which NGOs get support, and whose interests do they represent? Unless funders know their national contexts and women's class politics therein, such support can reinforce or aggravate women in poverty, or facilitate cross-class coalitions to change gender structures (see various selections in Staudt 1997, especially Alvarez on Brazil, Lewis on Cameroon). Or support can get snarled in partisan politics, virtually intrinsic to development funding generally (but see chapters in this volume on Chile, Turkey and India). Yet women sometimes coalesce around strategic policy reforms across party lines, as occasionally occurs in Mexico over domestic violence and rape (Rodríguez 1998).

Among those bilateral institutions that acknowledge politics, NORAD (Norwegian Agency for Development Co-operation) and DGIS (Directorate General of International Co-operation in the Netherlands) stand out for their support of women's NGOs determined to tackle changes in gender relations. NORAD also consistently presses multilateral institutions (as do other Nordic countries) to implement their women/gender policies. The Netherlands even speaks of women's 'political poverty', a discourse unknown to the other development institutions. Those national contexts appear to offer a deeper democratic process that includes women's voices in structured, proportional ways. Both Norway and the Netherlands have been at the lead in female representation in parliaments and cabinets, with more than a third women. Their multiparty democracies offer a wider range of ideological policy agendas to voters, including a process agenda with minimal quotas of women representatives. NORAD and DGIS seek public consultation on development assistance policies, tying funding strategies less to foreign and trade policy than other 'donor' countries. And the Netherlands, historically, has supported higher educational institutions with WID/Gender research and training (Staudt 1998a: Ch. 9). Both the Netherlands and Norway target and earmark larger budgets for women/gender than other bilateral institutions (Jahan 1995).

Policy priorities: little dent on gender relations

The UNDP, like the Bank, is a mammoth multilateral organization, but it is far more decentralized than the Washington, DC-focused Bank. Only 15 per cent of its staff work in headquarters, versus 82 per cent of staff in the Bank (Razavi and Miller 1995: 72). Like the Bank, the UNDP had a WID unit that turned into a 'gender' (GAD) unit in 1992. Gender promises have the potential to become outcomes when UNDP Regional Representatives and country-level staff connect host-country agencies and NGOs with the progressive policies in country planning documents (Kardam 1991). However, countries vary in the extent to which they are accountable to women. The UNDP respects sovereignty, including non-democratic male-privileged sovereignty. Under previous leadership, the UNDP proclaimed itself pro-poor, pro-environment, pro-women and pro-jobs, the rhetoric for which emerged in speeches on the elaborate UNDP website (http://www.undp.org).

The annual UNDP *Human Development Reports* (HDRs) consistently highlight gender, reprinting year after year that human development can only occur when it is 'engendered' (beautifully phrased, but as another 'en' word, the meaning is potentially cloudy). The HDR features a Human Development Index (HDI), based on income, education and life expectancy, to rank order countries. In recent years, the HDI has disaggregated data by gender, an adjustment that usually reduces country rank. Expert knowledge like this can provide organized women with data to strengthen advocacy claims for change. Analyses like these make gender inequality visible, which has brought criticism from UN member states. As a result, the 'UNDP has been forced to distance itself organizationally from the report'. This is one more illustration of the reality that the 'UNDP speaks with many voices' (Razavi and Miller 1995: 23, 26).

The United Nations hosts three units that are small, but cutting-edge analysts and advocates of women's advancement and empowerment (two words prominent on the UN's 'womenwatch' link to the home page (http://www.un.org/womenwatch)). All shrink in staff and budget size compared to the Bank and UNDP. The UNDP claims a partnership with UNIFEM, the UN Voluntary Fund for Women, which moved toward 'mainstreaming' initiatives soon after the 1985 women's conference on women. UNIFEM makes prominent its interest in funding activities with the potential to transform power relations and mainstream gender in public policy. Other units include INSTRAW (the International Research and Training Institute for the Advancement of Women), with its focus on training, and DAW (Division for the Advancement of Women), a high-level policy unit that supports the UN's longstanding Committee on the Status of Women with its appointees from member states.

Thus, we see some tentative steps toward acknowledging politics and power in progressive spaces of official assistance institutions. The HDR provides extensive data, publicly available with language that would buttress gender claims by those seeking accountable outcomes. The HDR's Gender Empowerment Measure (GEM) enshrines the word power in its quantitative equations. GEM, however, draws from the mere superficial, establishment figures of gender in high-level political and economic decision-making positions, thus contesting nothing about economic class and poverty or cultural practices (see volume chapters by Parpart and by Rai). However, these progressive tentative steps are fraught with contradictions and setbacks, including a meeker HDR, which in 1999 curtailed its usually sharp critique of the global economy, replacing it with a naturalistic acceptance of globalism as something inevitable and potentially beneficial to people with proper management.

Political dents on policy priorities will hardly occur unless women's organizations connect with potentially tainted establishment politics. Engagement has begun and borne fruit, at the international and national levels. Baden and Goetz (1997) analyse the 1995 world conference in women in Beijing and post-Beijing global women's movement that gained much ground over its two-decade history, forming alliances and coalitions. Issue by issue, the decades count achievements at the national level as well. Many women's anti-violence organizations once considered the state and establishment politics beyond hope. They organized self-help clinics, shelters and rape crisis centres in various countries around the world. Radical and Marxist feminists considered the lawyers, democracy activists and legal reformers to be deluded and misguided. Without public funding, however, it was difficult to sustain feminist outreach activities over time and address the large-scale, society-wide problems. Over the years, some convergence has occurred between more radical and reformer feminists who share common ground and build political coalitions for change. See Staudt (1998a: Ch. 1) for a comparison of different feminist ideologies and organizational strategies and how some, like radical and liberal feminisms, converged on anti-violence efforts.

Democratic spaces: contexts of democracy, peace and/or redistribution?

Thus far, the discussion has assumed some semblance of democracy, by which I mean freedom to organize, to speak and to utilize electoral and other strategies to hold officials accountable for decisions. A single, rather than plural system of legalisms also bears on women's ability to draw on legal leverage to establish and maintain rights and entitlements, much less transform gender relations. In many African and Asian countries, multiple religions and traditions sit side by side with a so-called 'modern' law; women lack precedents that offer power and authority in them all. In the 1990s, much hope has been expressed about a so-called 'transition to democracy', a transition with implications for gender relations. (See also Ali and Patel.) Yet as cross-regional comparative studies sometimes show, democracy can diminish female voice as occurred in parts of Latin America and

Eastern Europe (Jaquette and Wolchik 1998; see also Bodur and Franceschet, this volume). In authoritarian regimes, civic leaders confront multiple negative trade-offs about decisions whether to engage in or to avoid the establishment political process.

Of course, many countries' so-called democracies offer little voice and leverage to women, and/or pursue policy outcomes that transform gender relations. In the worst or mediocre democracies, external funds often support existing power relations and the institutionalization of male interests in the state. Many bilateral institutions fund without regard to the kind of democracy in which funds get spent, for foreign policy or trade interests prevail in decisions about countries to support. Economic criteria are prominent in banking institutions. Other countries are isolated for their redistributive agendas or revolutionary politics. Cuba, for example, continues its excommunication from the US recognition, trade and bilateral assistance. Rich countries use the leverage of their proportional funding decisions to coalesce with other like-minded countries to exclude regimes that defy the existing economic order. The fates of Sandinista Nicaragua and Chile under Allende were sealed in part by these boycotts.

Most multilateral and bilateral technical assistance agencies fund governments whether they are semi-democratic or not. In so doing, they strengthen established power relations, including relations that privilege men and the dominant economic class. And in the world of ironies and contradictions, they represent projects as 'women's empowerment'.' In the best-case scenario, some women acquire economic resources perhaps to purchase and compensate for social services in the downsized state. In the worst-case scenario, the value of women's work and voice is undermined even as the rhetoric seems threatening and creates male backlash against women.

International technical assistance and 'democracies'

Occasionally, bilateral institutions support those countries with policy agendas compatible with poverty reduction. While some bilateral institutions support former 'colonies', for better or worse, others focus on countries with redistributive agendas. SIDA (Swedish International Development Authority) sought what it called 'partners' who shared the focus on structural change. In so doing, 1970s Tanzania and Mozambique, once excluded from mainstream assistance, found external support.

UNICEF's non-threatening historic mission to focus on children, maternal and infant health has increasingly drawn on stark language to confront gender power inequality. 'Gender apartheid' is one example of language in its portfolio. UNICEF claims an empowerment strategy, and it works with national agencies and NGOs, though this is not developed on its website. The annual *State of the World's Children* allows UNICEF to talk about peace and conflict resolution in ways from which other agencies shrink. The discourse involves child conscripts, refugees, orphans and victims of war. In 1999, UNICEF parted ways with most other mainstream agencies in analysis that argued 'free markets hurt women' (Bellamy 1999). In an HDR comparison of human development spending (health and education), UNICEF ranked highest in comparison to other UN organizations (UNDP 1994).

Bring politics in *with* women and gender equality agendas

Advocates within official institutions have been very busy developing language and levers for change that are compatible with and/or transform institutional missions. However, those missions have long histories, other agendas and numerous competing interests for priority and budgetary support. This language uses women and gender, along with various principles from equality to poverty reduction and empowerment. Ultimately though, these advocates operate within the constraints of their institutions, institutional missions and orientations. Those missions offer little space and power to women and gender agendas, with several notable exceptions such as UNIFEM. The orientations are either top-down (the Bank), which privilege efficiency principles and men, or they depend on host countries that tend to privilege men's voices in their governance structures (UNDP).

In countries, from national to local levels, women are gaining ground in the spaces of political power. However, their voices are still muted, as discussed previously. Silenced even more are social justice and gender equality agendas, even in countries that claim the democratic label for themselves. Global and transnational NGOs exercise voice and power but toward and connected with national-level political decisions *in* democratic spaces and places where women must engage with and gain power in civil associations, NGOs, labour unions and government itself. In this engagement, they can draw on whatever leverage, tools, legitimacy and resources that global NGOs and international agencies can supply.

To emphasize the centrality of national political engagement, the theme of this chapter, let me utilize one more multilateral institution illustration. The International Labour Organization (ILO), born in 1919 before the UN but affiliated with it, is one of the few institutions that claim a social justice mission and institutionalize a tripartite place for trade unions, governments and business to negotiate labour conventions. Thus, its mission is far different than that of UNICEF or the Bank; it offers far more focus than the UNDP. The ILO is also more permeable and thus democratic than most multilateral institutions (Razavi and Miller 1995). Its budget is minuscule, compared to the UNDP and Bank, but its merger of ILO headquarters and national levels of political and public policy processes fosters democratic possibility.

Despite these possibilities, the ILO record on gender equality and the national enforcement of gender-relevant conventions is modest. The ILO website presents WOMEMP as equality and empowerment principles, but the 'emp' stands for employment, not empowerment. The focus is on 'more jobs' and 'better jobs' for women. Given women's structural position in the global economic market, one might question what more jobs would mean for their increasing power (or powerlessness). Why have ILO accomplishments been so modest? Women's voices are muted in trade and labour union organizations, and feminist organizations' effective alliances with unions are rare. As compelling a problem, though, is the fact that many women workers are unorganized, and either unpaid or working in informal economies (Razavi and Miller 1995; Prugl 1999; Staudt 1998b). The ILO has supported critical analyses of economies that do not value or count women, to its credit, but these analyses do not inform the technical core of the ILO mission. Unless women are organized, engaged and allied with other social justice organizations, their interests will be muted and labour conventions unenforced.

The terrain in which to gain and share power is in the political process. Once active, policy and budgetary levers from that process can be evoked and accessed to negotiate gender equality outcomes. Those outcomes are part of the lived, everyday reality that connects global to national and local. The connections are outlined below in the US–Mexico borderlands, along with some dreadful prospects for rapid change.

Empowerment in US bipartisan discourse: from global to local

The word empowerment resonates well in the peculiar democratic capitalism of the USA. Take Republican Jack Kemp, elected to the Congress in 1970, with his libertarian ideology (called supply-side economics in the 1980s) that government 'get off people's backs'. People figure prominently in this discourse with its reassuring populist flair. In the Bush administration, Kemp was named Cabinet Secretary for Housing and Urban Development (HUD) in 1989. He pioneered the use of empowerment language to discuss tax incentives for businesses to set up shops in depressed urban areas that would be known as 'Enterprise Zones'.

In the clever co-optation of Republican Party language, conservative Democrats in the 1992 election and beyond elaborated on these concepts to foster two fundable initiatives for tax incentives, private partnerships, job creation and a (fledgling) community-voice component: Enterprise Zones and Empowerment Zones. In the border city where I live, new HUD leadership awarded Empowerment Zone (EZ, as it's called) money support to the 'El Corazon de El Paso' ('the heart of the city'), a warm-sounding project that holds promise for poverty neighbourhoods, 90 per cent of the residents therein being people of Mexican heritage ('Hispanic' citizens as well as immigrants). Originally, the award was to be $10 million each year for ten years, but in the interests of wider award distribution (in the ever-important geography of power) and in recognition of the presidential election of 2000, this was reduced to $3 million each year for two years (but then increased to expectations in year three). As important though, only 10 per cent of the $3 million will trickle down to the Community Resource Councils, where the 'voices' (politics? leadership?) decide how to use resources to meet their needs. For the remaining 90 per cent, an EZ Board of Hispanic and Anglo professional men and women will decide how to spend the money in ways that leverage public and private commitments. This is a structure with obvious flaws, but it is politically realistic and even typical in the sort of 'democracies' that exist in our global political economy

In subsequent years, the EZ obtained its promised level of funding and a progressive-majority board began to allocate funds in ways that could result in power-relational shifts. For example, one funded project proposed not only to fund allied community organizations in an alliance, but also to develop plans that would build assets among this alliance through property acquisition and investments. Interestingly, though, the assets would deepen community organizations' stakes in capitalist economic growth. Empowerment strategies in the USA are connected with risk-taking, material acquisition and competitive investments. Other federally funded efforts also use market rhetoric in the labels former community organizations adopt – Community Development *Corporations* (CDCs) – in their pursuit of better housing for their constituents.

El Paso, the seventeenth largest city in the USA, has a dubious distinction: it leads the country with its more than 10,000 NAFTA-displaced workers. A foundation (whose name is associated with garment manufacturing) awarded a grant to educational institutions with which I work for 'youth empowerment'. The project is and will spread leadership and skill building to middle- and high-school students in the fine arts and humanities, so this is no total sham. Gender equality pervades the project in these public schools. However, the foundation represents part of an industry that moved plants and sub-contracting outside the USA, not only since NAFTA, but long before as the global division of labour in the world trade regime was consolidated. Thus, a trickle of money perhaps emPOWERs those young people whose parents, however, still struggle (some from the same institutional source) to find jobs that pay decent wages. Can school-based leadership and everyday oral history collections drawing on the struggles of low-income, mostly immigrant workers really compensate for unemployment and cheap wages?

In the larger borderlands, neither public nor private 'empowerment' projects address larger policy incentives that encourage capital movement, job loss and cheapened wages. This is clearly in the interests of (disempowered) US working people. Nor do the projects address the lack of accountability of US corporations in Mexican space to provide decent wages in environmentally safe contexts. This is clearly in the interests of Mexican workers. The differences between *national* wage rates far exceed those of *gender* differences with*in* each nation. The accountability of the Mexican government is just as minimal in this fledgling democracy, for it sets the artificially low minimal wage and permits environmental policies to go unenforced (see Staudt 1998b on free trade at the border). To draw on that stark UNICEF language, nation-based *apartheids* are perpetuated in a global economy of free trade, even amid various local, but relatively small-scale, empowerment activities.

The local policy incentives to stimulate local business, human capital (as the economists call it) and job creation are found in the discourse of official and foundation-funded empowerment efforts. Meanwhile political engagement has occurred over the colonization of the region by national banks, unresponsive and unaccountable to local needs. Although neither labelled empowerment nor officially funded by charitable or government agencies, bankers and community activists have polarized over the limited capital available to local businesses (see http://www.communityscholars.org). Challenge and confrontation have entered the local public domain, as local hospital, county and city boards now consider whether and where to invest public funds and the criteria over investment. In autumn 1999, one of these three local boards decided to use 'social' criteria in decisions over where to place its considerable financial deposits. Through political engagement like this, empowerment occurs in both process and outcome terms: people actively engage in building new relationships with public officials, and some of these officials alter the policies used to make financial deposit decisions. Those decision outcomes will redistribute the placement of capital in institutions that use lending decisions to strengthen local investments.

Concluding implications

The flaws of both public and private (foundation) initiatives to empower people are omnipresent and continuous. The discourse of empowerment is compelling and attractive, increasingly part of policy rhetoric and website construction in multilateral and bilateral institutions. Occasionally, these institutions take what they perceive as the risky step of addressing women's political poverty, or investing in process projects that encourage outcomes that strengthen people's critical political leverage

The flaws in official and rhetorical strategies will not be overcome or criticized, however, without political engagement. In the US–Mexico borderlands, women have voices from the community councils to the board, as neighbourhood leaders, mothers and service professionals, in a poverty-alleviation agenda. The sort of gender justice expressed is one limited to women's practical interests in jobs and neighbourhood services. The local on the USA's terrain resembles the local in many places around the world.

Official rhetoric and grants do not foreclose the possibility that people could amass resources for self-sufficiency and choice, or that they could instigate and sustain a process that could ultimately change power relations. However, in a context of official policies and economic realities that disempower people, we cannot delude ourselves with the misleading language of 'empowerment'. As Lyla Mehta has convincingly argued in her analysis of the Bank's 'Knowledge Empire',' the institution's 'presentation of itself [is] nothing more than a rebottling of old modernization wine' (2001: 190). We must be wary of and watchful for the same kind of rebottling in the empowerment language on women and/or gender.

In the meantime, people struggle within the confines of existing power relations to express their interests and negotiate more balance in the unequal power relations at local, national and global levels. Only with that active engagement and struggle will their process move social relations toward more just outcomes, both on the basis of gender and class. Active agency is what will provoke the (now meagre) process levers in bilateral and multilateral agencies to negotiate outcomes with host-country governments that have some potential to move toward gender power balance. It is a long and flawed process, but a *political process* for women to exercise political power with others to achieve gender balance.

References

Baden, Sally and Anne Marie Goetz (1997) 'Who needs [sex] when you can have [gender]? Conflicting discourses on gender at Beijing', in Kathleen Staudt (ed.) *Women, International Development and Politics*, Philadelphia: Temple University Press, pp. 37–58.

Basu, Amrita (ed.) (1995) *The Challenge of Local Feminisms*, Boulder: Westview.

Bellamy, Carol (1999) Press Release posted on http://www.unicef.org. Reported in Elizabeth Olson'Free markets leave women worse off, UNICEF says', *New York Times*, 23 September 1999.

Benería, Lourdes, and Shelley Feldman (1992) *Unequal Burden: Economic Crises, Persistent Poverty, and Women's Work*, Boulder: Westview.

Charlton, Sue Ellen, Jana Everett and Kathleen Staudt (eds) (1989) *Women, the State, and Development*, Albany: SUNY/Albany Press.

Cornia, Giovanni Andrew, Richard Jolly and Frances Stewart (eds) (1987) *Adjustment with a Human Face*, vols I and II, Oxford, UK: Clarendon Press.

Development Alternatives with Women for a New Era (DAWN) (Gita Sen and Caren Grown) (1985) *Development, Crises, and Alternative Visions: Third World Women's Perspectives*, New York: Monthly Review.

Elson, Diane (1996) 'Gender-neutral. gender-blind, or gender-sensitive budgets: Changing the conceptual framework to include women's empowerment and the economy of care', presented at the Commonwealth Ministers Responsible for Women's Affairs, Fifth Meeting, Port of Spain, Trinidad, 25–8 November.

——, (ed.) (1991) *Male Bias in the Development Process*, Manchester: Manchester University Press.

Ferguson, James (1990) *The Anti Politics Machine: 'Development', Depoliticization and Bureaucratic Power in Lesotho*, New York: Cambridge University Press.

Jahan, Rounaq (1995) *The Elusive Agenda: Mainstreaming Women in Development*, London: Zed.

Jaquette, Jane S. and Sharon L. Wolchik (1998) *Women and Democracy: Latin America and Central and Eastern Europe*, Baltimore: Johns Hopkins University Press.

Kardam, Nüket (1991) *Bringing Women in: Women's Issues in International Development Programs*, Boulder: Lynne Rienner Publishers.

Mazumdar, Vina (1989) 'Seeds for a new model of development: A political commentary', in Ann Leonard (ed.) *Seeds: Supporting Women's Work in the Third World*, New York: Feminist Press, p. 217.

Mehta, Lyla (2001) 'The World Bank and its emerging knowledge empire', *Human Organization* 60(2): 189–96.

Moser, Caroline (1997) *Household Responses to Poverty and Vulnerability*, vols 1–4. Washington, DC: World Bank, Urban Management Programme.

—— (1993) *Gender Planning and Development: Theory, Practice and Training*, London: Routledge.

—— (1989) 'Gender planning in the Third World: Meeting practical and strategic needs', *World Development* 17(11): 1799–1826.

Nelson, Barbara and Najma Chowdhury (eds) (1994) *Women and Politics Worldwide*, New Haven, CT: Yale University Press.

Parpart, Jane and Kathleen Staudt (eds) (1989) *Women and the State in Africa*, Boulder: Lynne Rienner Publishers.

Prugl, Elisabeth (1999) *The Global Construction of Gender: Home-based Work in the Political Economy of the 20th Century*, New York: Columbia University Press.

Rai, Shirin and Geraldine Lievesley (eds) (1996) *Women and the State: International Perspectives*, London: Taylor & Francis.

Razavi, Shahra and Carol Miller (1995) *Gender Mainstreaming: A Study of Efforts by the UNDP, the World Bank and the ILO to Institutionalize Gender Issues*, Occasional Paper 4, Geneva: United Nations Research Institute for Social Development.

Reich, Robert B. (1992) *The Work of Nations*, New York: Vintage.

Rodríguez, Victoria E. (1998) *Women's Participation in Mexican Political Life*, Boulder: Westview.

Staudt, Kathleen (1998a) *Policy, Politics and Gender: Women Gaining Ground*, West Hartford, CT: Kumarian Press.

—— (1998b) *Free Trade? Informal Economies at the U.S.–Mexico Border*, Philadephia, PA: Temple University Press.

—— (ed.) (1997) *Women, International Development and Politics: The Bureaucratic Mire* (second edition), Philadelphia: Temple University Press.

—— (1990) *Managing Development: State, Society, and International Contexts*, Newbury Park, CA: Sage.

—— (1985) *Women, Foreign Assistance and Advocacy Administration*, New York: Praeger.

United Nations Development Programme (UNDP) (1994, 1995 and 1999) *Human Development Report*, New York: Oxford University Press.

United Nations/Division for the Advancement of Women (UN/DAW) (1994) *Technical Assistance and Women: From Mainstreaming toward Institutional Accountability*, internal document.

United Nations Research Institute for Social Development (UNRISD) (1995) *States in Disarray*, Geneva: UNRISD.

Websites

www.community scholars.org (Staudt on board, 1999–2001)
International Labor Organization, http://www.ilo.org.
United Nations Development Programme, http://www.undp.org.
United Nations Children's Fund, http://www.unicef.org.
World Bank, http://www.worldbank.org

7 Movements, states and empowerment

Women's mobilization in Chile and Turkey

Marella Bodur and Susan Franceschet

Introduction

The emergence and growth of women's movements is one of the primary means for achieving women's empowerment. By organizing and/or joining women's groups, women can become aware of their oppression and seek structural changes in power relations between men and women. The strategies through which women's movements seek empowerment, however, vary from one context to another, since women's agency is shaped by different political, historical and cultural contexts. Thus, certain theoretical insights can be gained from comparing the emergence and evolution of different women's movements. A comparison permits us to ask questions about the conditions that inspire struggles for empowerment, the strategies employed, the meaning and content of 'empowerment', and whether empowerment always implies a 'bottom-up' process, or can states also promote women's empowerment? And, perhaps most importantly, does the discourse of 'women's empowerment' include all women, regardless of class, ethnic and religious distinctions?

We advance two theoretical propositions. First, explaining the emergence of movements that promote women's empowerment requires an understanding of particular patriarchal contexts, including ways women often (creatively) draw on existing gender ideologies to expose certain contradictions and mobilize support for their demands. Attention to historical context sheds light on the construction of the term 'empowerment' by movement actors. Second, understanding the outcomes of movements requires more attention to the type of state confronting women. There are two compelling reasons for this concern. First, many states in the South are currently engaged in processes of neo-liberal adjustment, including greater integration into global economic processes. This affects their strategies and responses to the demands of women's groups. Second, empowerment is not always a 'bottom-up' process. States have sometimes taken a leading role in the promotion of (a particular version of) women's empowerment. In such cases, women's movements have had to struggle to construct their own meaning of empowerment, along with the strategies to achieve it. State–society relations also tell us much about the debates and divisions about empowerment *within* movements because they play a key role in the construction and maintenance of social, ethnic and religious cleavages that cross any society.

To that end, Chile and Turkey provide contrasting experiences for understanding the way struggles for women's empowerment are affected by state–society relations. In Chile, the transition from an authoritarian to a democratic state provided an 'opening' for women to place their demands on the public agenda of the incoming government. Consequently women in Chile have made substantial gains, although these have declined since the democratic transition, in part due to the adoption of a neo-liberal economic model that has exacerbated class differences among women. In Turkey, the 1980 military *coup*, paradoxically, enabled women to organize and set their own agenda. The history of 'state feminism' has led women's groups to seek autonomy from the state. Yet, their capacity to define and control empowerment continues to be undermined by a paternalistic state. Furthermore, state-supported initiatives to empower women have often ignored differences among women, thus empowering some while disempowering others.

Gender ideologies, states and women's movements

Amrita Basu argues that '[p]atriarchal domination is no more apt in and of itself to provide a catalyst to women's activism than class exploitation is likely in and of itself to stimulate class struggle' (1995: 10). Consequently, while an awareness of how patriarchy functions is crucial to understanding women's exclusion from social and political life in various contexts, this factor alone cannot account for why women's movements emerge at particular points in time. In other words, we need to go beyond the traditional explanations offered by feminist theory, particularly the assumption that men dominate the public realm and women the private, 'apolitical' sphere.

In fact, the gender ideology underpinning the public/private divide often plays a crucial role in women's struggles for empowerment. Women draw on existing gender discourse and ideology in order to construct sets of shared meanings and to mobilize support for their goals. The existing gender ideology forms part of the 'political opportunity structure' in which women's activism emerges, especially when there are contradictions between the prevailing ideology and women's daily life. For example, in Chile, women mobilized under the dictatorship to expose the contradiction between the violence and deprivation in their daily lives and the military regime's pro-women discourse (as mothers and wives). In Turkey, women exploited the contradictions between the official Kemalist discourse stressing gender equality in the public sphere and the daily realities of women's subordination in their homes.

In constructing a framework to explain women's activism, one needs an international or global perspective. First, the global political economy affects women in different ways. Neo-liberal restructuring and insertion into the global political economy have shifted the boundaries between public and private spheres as states increasingly rely on the private sector, including the family, for social services and basic welfare. This often occurs alongside the intensification of female labour, as states attempt to compete in the global economy.

Second, the international women's movement has profoundly affected women's movements around the world. As Nelson and Chowdury explain, '[t]he international spotlight on women, the impetus to gather and compare data, to hold their governments to account, and the occasions for international coalition building represented by the three U.N. women's conferences … all catapulted the international connections among women to a qualitatively different level' (1994: 9). In Turkey, feminist groups organized a petition campaign in 1986 urging the state to implement the United Nations Convention on the Elimination of All Forms of Discrimination Against Women (CEDAW), which Turkey had ratified in 1985, albeit with reservations. In Chile, Beijing conference preparations inspired collaboration among women's non-governmental organizations (NGOs). The resulting Grupo Iniciativa Chile, a permanent network of eleven NGOs, continues to pressure the Chilean state to honour its international agreements (Valdés 1998: 107–9; Grupo Iniciativa Chile 1994). Thus, international forces can strengthen women's groups.

We also need conceptual tools to explain the evolution of women's movements, and the impact of more institutionalized political actors on their goals and strategies for empowerment. Sometimes a more or less unified women's movement emerges out of a host of smaller groups that began to organize collectively for various reasons (e.g. economic survival, nationalism, struggles against authoritarianism, or gender or racial oppression). However, this unity is normally short lived. As certain goals are achieved, and institutionalization increases, divisions often occur. Why has this trajectory been so common?

One answer is that women's movements often emerge in times of crisis and change, which provides certain momentum and purpose. When the crises are resolved, conditions for women's activism become less hospitable. As West and Blumberg observe, '[r]ole boundaries may dissolve at the crisis stage, but later tend to be rapidly reinstated' (1990: 24). Women's incorporation into the formal political sphere on the basis of crisis-inspired activism is by no means assured. Instead, women are often expected to return to the private realm of the family once crises pass.

In addition, after key 'crisis periods', many women's movements become institutionalized and ultimately fragment. In many cases, leading activists migrate into state agencies or NGOs that either work closely with the state, or act as intermediaries between states and grassroots women's groups. Sonia Alvarez, for example, refers to the '"NGOization" of Latin American feminism' (1998: 294–5). Furthermore, many states set up ministries, bureaux or agencies specifically dedicated to women's issues and empowerment. This raises questions about the potential for 'co-optation' and highlights the need for a framework that is sensitive to gendered state processes and their impact on women's movements.

No single feminist theory of the state exists. Moreover, much feminist theorizing on the state has been grounded in Western, industrialized welfare states, and thus ignores the impact of colonialism and various interpretations of modernity (Charlton *et al.* 1989: 10; Rai 1996: 5). While liberal feminists see states as neutral, socialist feminists emphasize their class functions. Others emphasize their 'relative autonomy' and consequently their openness to political pressures (Alvarez 1990: 31; Charlton *et al.* 1989: 5; Pringle and Watson 1998). However, all feminists acknowledge the fundamentally male-biased nature of states.

Some writers emphasize the fragmented nature of states, especially in the South where state capacity may be weaker, and thereby less able to implement women's empowerment programmes (Rai 1996). Likewise, states are also constrained by global economic processes (Randall 1998: 196). The Chilean state, for example, is providing child-care support for some women workers because they enhance Chile's global competitiveness. Consequently, the strategies employed by women's movements are shaped to a great extent by the type of state(s) they deal with, the context they operate in and their willingness and capacity to respond to women's demands.

In most cases, women's movements equate women's empowerment with more inclusive politics. They concentrate on giving women a voice and presence in the centres of power. However, not all women's movements pursue this goal *through* the state. Some become institutionalized while others struggle to maintain their autonomy from the state. The resulting fragmentation undermines attempts to transform politics and empower women. As a result, women working within the state are deprived of outside support, such as public demonstrations and other forms of solidarity, which can pressure the state to be more responsive to women's demands (Waylen 1997). Concerted action from within and outside the state is required to transform political practice. Furthermore, the institutionalization of portions of the movement can increase inequalities and 'uneven power relations among women' (Alvarez 1998: 295). Women with access to the state can set the terms of citizenship, with its attendant rights and duties, in the name of all women (Schild 1997). Thus, empowerment for some women can occur at the expense of *dis*empowering others. The following case studies of Chile and Turkey illustrate these propositions.

The emergence and evolution of the Chilean women's movement

A 'first wave' of feminism swept Chile in the first half of the twentieth century. Mostly middle- and upper-class women formed study groups, women's clubs and a suffragist movement. Chilean women won the vote in municipalities in 1934 and nationally in 1949. The conservative governments granted them the vote, believing the prevailing gender ideology emphasizing women's roles as mothers would ensure their support.

Indeed, women remained socially, politically and economically subordinate to men largely due to this ideology. As Elsa Chaney notes, the 'characterization of woman as sacrificial mothers sums up what Latin Americans consider the most positive aspect of the image of woman' (1979: 47). Moreover, '[t]he suffrage movement fostered rather than challenged the feminine stereotype by emphasizing how the women's vote would infuse society with the womanly virtues' (1979: 76).

A long 'feminist silence' followed between 1953–78. Autonomous women's groups ceased as most activists shifted their allegiance to political parties. Class-based politics predominated during this period, inhibiting women from raising gender issues within the parties, especially on the left (Kirkwood 1986).

In the 1960s, the government began promoting a particular vision of women's empowerment as part of a wider social project to empower previously marginalized social groups. However, Chilean women were mobilized on the basis of their social roles rather than as citizens. For example, President Eduardo Frei's (1964–70) 'Revolution in Liberty' set up 'mothers' centres' to encourage collective organization among the poor. While these state-sponsored centres brought women together, they reinforced their subordinate social roles by focusing on domestic labour (Valdés *et al.* 1993). Under Pinochet's dictatorship (1973–90), the mothers' centres became even more explicitly ideological. They, along with a National Secretariat for Women, were headed by Pinochet's wife and staffed by a cadre of mostly upper-class women volunteers (Serrano 1992: 207). These networks and organizations reinforced a conservative gender ideology stressing women's roles in the production of another generation of patriotic (and pro-Pinochet) citizens (Molina 1989: 61–74).[1] How did this gender ideology shape the emergence of a women's movement in Chile, with its partic-ular understanding of women's empowerment?

The social and political policies of the Chilean military 'regime' and their brutal repression against the left provoked contradictions in women's roles. In order to protect and provide for their families, many women were compelled to leave the private realm to find employment. This brought unexpected changes as women began to recognize their capacities. Their new self-confidence disposed them to public actions where they demanded other rights as well, most notably the right to find out about family members who had 'disappeared' under Pinochet's rule (Molina 1989: 74–9). Eventually, they began to demand a fully democratic regime, moreover, one where women's empowerment would be based on their citizenship rights rather than their social roles. Hence, for these women, empowerment meant a transformation of the prevailing gender ideology as well as the political system.

During the 1980s a strong, fairly unified women's movement emerged, comprising human rights groups, economic organizations such as communal kitchens and producers' and shoppers' co-operatives, and feminist groups (Valdés and Weinstein 1993; Gaviola *et al.* 1994). Changes in the global political economy and Chile's place within it, as well as the brutal repression of the mili-tary regime, inspired this expansion. Moreover, when Pinochet banned all political parties, women, often for the first time, were able to organize collectively in women-only settings. They set their own goals, determined their own agendas and, perhaps most importantly, discussed and discovered their shared experi-ences of and opposition to gender subordination. Second, women could act collectively, at least initially, without fear of persecution because 'the dictatorship allowed women's organizations to survive and grow while repressing other sectors of civil society' (Valenzuela 1998: 50). Their maternalist rhetoric did not seem to challenge conservative gender ideology. After the economic collapse in 1981–2, women's groups joined other groups in a more concerted and unified opposition. Feminist goals began to coalesce with broader demands, demonstrated by the movement's slogan 'democracy in the country and in the home', which challenges the 'traditional' boundary between public and private spheres. Moreover, the movement also adopted the slogan 'without women, democracy won't work', demonstrating their belief that Chile's future as a democracy depended upon women's empowerment *as citizens*.

Opposition to the dictatorship grew throughout the 1980s, culminating in the vote against Pinochet in the 1988 referendum. Women's groups gained notoriety for their role in this victory (Valenzuela 1998; Frohmann and Valdés 1995). When the centre and left opposition parties coalesced into the *Concertación por la Democracia* (CPD), women formed the *Concertación Nacional de Mujeres por la Democracia* (CNMD). Autonomous from the CPD, it included party members, feminists and women from NGOs (Valenzuela 1998: 56). In 1989, the CNMD recommended some gender-specific policies to the incoming democratic government. Indeed, many were introduced, most notably the *Servicio Nacional de la Mujer* (SERNAM), a state agency with a ministerial-status director and a commitment to improving women's position in Chile's new democracy.[2]

SERNAM has improved the status of women in Chile. In 1993, it proposed the Equal Opportunity Plan for Women soon incorporated into Eduardo Frei's government (1994–2000). 'The Plan' promotes the redistribution of power and resources among men and women, and equal value for men and women's social roles (SERNAM 1998: 8). It focuses on legislation, family, education, culture, labour, health, participation and institutional frameworks. The recently elected government of Ricardo Lagos has adopted a second plan (2000–10). Other successes for women include laws against domestic violence, programmes for women heads of households and *temporeras* (seasonal female workers in the agrifruit industry), and more rights for women within marriage (*Comisión Interministerial para la IV Conferencia Mundial sobre la Mujer* 1995: 22).

Thus, the return of democracy has brought state promotion for women's empowerment, but with a key difference. This time women are increasingly constructed as 'citizens' with equal social, economic and political rights. However, the focus on gender equality masks the growing inequalities among women, and illustrates the need to ask, 'Empowerment for whom?' Middle- and upper-class women are, indeed, gaining from these new opportunities, while poor women, who suffer both gender and class discrimination, receive little from a discourse that ignores class and ethnic subordination. In fact, a group representing rural and indigenous women formally complained to SERNAM because the equal opportunity plan said nothing about the specific problems they faced. In sum, since 1990, the tensions inherent in seeking women's empowerment *through* a patriarchal and neo-liberal state are becoming increasingly evident.

These tensions are evident in the problems experienced by the Chilean women's movement since the return of democracy. SERNAM's efforts to improve women's lives have faced significant obstacles. Not being a ministry in its own right, it has to rely on other agencies to implement its recommendations. Given the socially conservative climate in Chile and the power of the Catholic Church, SERNAM must balance its promotion of women's rights with support for the family. Consequently, certain issues, such as reproductive rights, cannot be raised at all.[3]

Moreover, many strategies to empower women require radical reforms in state structure. Attempts in 1997 to introduce quotas for women on candidate lists for parliamentarians and in the decision-making structures of each party faced strong opposition. Women remain poorly represented in all spheres of decision-making. In the 1997 elections, women were 15 to 18 per cent of the candidates, yet only about 10 per cent were elected (Moltedo 1998: 7). The coalition parties support affirmative action but for internal rather than representative positions.[4] Few women have held executive positions although Ricardo Lagos's election as president has brought about improvements. His government has five women ministers (out of sixteen), and almost a third of his sub-secretaries are women.[5]

Attempts to promote women's participation in decision-making spheres are also constrained by the reassertion of the distinction between the political and social realms, with women dominating the latter.[6] Since the transition, women's activism has shifted back to the social or community sphere. Women hold only 10 to 15 per cent of national and municipal leadership posts but are 36 per cent of the *juntas de vecinos* (neighbourhood councils) leaders (Valdés and Gomariz 1995). Both SERNAM and PRODEMU (Fundación para Promoción y Desarrollo de la Mujer – a semi-public institution under the direction of the president's wife) promote women's leadership skills. However, most participants use these skills for community activism rather than challenging the status quo in the political arena. In 1998, 1,919 women participated in SERNAM's school for women leaders. Only seventy-five identified themselves as 'political leaders' (SERNAM, n.d.).

Women are also starting to appreciate the tensions inherent in state-supported programmes for women's empowerment when the state retains patriarchal features. For example, SERNAM has created *empoderamiento* (empowerment) programmes for women – by establishing *Centros de Información de los Derechos de la Mujer* (CIDEM – Women's Rights Information Centres). These programmes assume women's empowerment derives from knowledge of and demands for their rights (Weinstein 1997). However, knowledge about legal changes, such as the law against family violence, does not change the cultural context working against this law (Provoste and Silva 1998: 38–9). Other programmes, such as the one to help women heads of households find employment, can do little to combat the mechanisms working against women's employment. Employers can still legally ask the sex and ages of applicants, so they can avoid hiring women in their fertile years (Provoste 1997).

Women's groups are also beginning to confront the limits of achieving empowerment through a neo-liberal state. The return of democracy has increased class tensions and fragmentation within the women's movement. The professional (mostly middle- and upper-class) segments of the movement have largely migrated into state agencies, or to the numerous women's NGOs that often work for the government. At the same time, activist women, especially in rural or poor communities, have very little contact with the more institutionalized segments of the women's movement. Most contact takes place through the numerous workshops offered by SERNAM, PRODEMU and other NGOs, which aim to promote women's empowerment by providing information and technical knowledge. Despite PRODEMU's emphasis on grassroots women, its programmes largely follow a top-down model of empowerment.

However, these tensions are beginning to be recognized and steps are being taken to address them. Two umbrella organizations have been created with the hopes of rebuilding a movement based in civil society: Red de Mujeres de Organizaciones Sociales (REMOS) and Asociación Nacional de Mujeres Rurales e Indígenas (ANAMURI). Both organizations link smaller women's groups throughout the country. They are staffed by women with direct experience of the poverty, discrimination and violence lived by rural, indigenous and *pobladora* women. Both organizations are pursuing gender equality and challenge class and ethnic discrimination faced by women.[7] However, SERNAM is not adequately addressing or promoting the goals of these organizations. This is partly because their goals demand support for the very workers whose low wages are required by the government's neo-liberal economic model.[8]

The current fragmentation has led some to claim the women's movement no longer exists. This ignores the many women involved in activities both within and beyond the formal political sphere. Also, serious attempts are being made to strengthen linkages between organized women and the state. SERNAM tried to make the process of writing the second equal opportunity plan more participatory by consulting with civil society actors.[9] The process was not without problems, but represents an important step forward, given that the first plan was written without any input from organized women in civil society.

Moreover, the creation of REMOS and ANAMURI demonstrates that the process of linking various groups has begun – although in a different form. In the 1980s, women united for a common purpose – the return of democracy. Today, however, more diverse demands are being voiced. The movement is currently in transition, but conflict and some fragmentation are likely to continue as the limits of achieving women's empowerment through a patriarchal neo-liberal state become increasingly evident.

The emergence and evolution of the women's movement in post-1980 Turkey

Since the 1980s, the emergence of a women's movement in Turkey has publicized issues such as female sexuality, sexist discrimination and domestic violence against women. Women's issues, however, had been debated in the past. The 'woman question' has been central to the debates on the changing nature of the Ottoman polity and later on the question of Turkish national identity (see

Kandiyoti 1989, 1991a). The first wave of debates on women's issues and the family dates back to the mid-nineteenth and the early twentieth centuries when male intellectuals advocated women's emancipation by criticizing the practices of arranged marriages, polygamy and the segregation of the sexes. They also called for reforms in women's education, emphasizing the need for educated mothers to raise the next generation of enlightened citizens (Sirman 1989: 5). Upper-class Ottoman women, mostly the wives and daughters of the ruling class, actively participated in these debates through their writings in the daily press and women's periodicals (Sirman 1989; Zihnioğlu 1998, 1999).[10] Although they demanded equal status in the family and the right to education and employment, they did not challenge women's traditional roles as mothers and wives (Sirman 1989: 9).

The 'woman question' re-emerged in the early years of the Turkish Republic when the republican elite viewed women's emancipation as part and parcel of their modernization/Westernization and nation-building projects. They introduced a series of legal reforms to improve the status of women, such as the law for secularizing the educational system and recognizing equal rights in education for men and women. The Turkish civil code, adopted in 1926 and based on the Swiss civil code, outlawed polygamy and gender inequality regarding divorce, custody of children and inheritance. The clothing reform allowed women to abandon the veil. Women were also 'granted' the right to vote and to stand in municipal elections in 1930 and in general elections in 1934.

These reforms were an integral part of the Kemalist struggle against the political and religious structures of the Ottoman polity (Tekeli 1981; Kandiyoti 1989, 1991a), and of the attempt to create a new secular political community based on Turkish national identity. The new 'Turkish woman' not only symbolized the new Western secular Republic but also embodied the cultural essence of the new Turkish nation. Thus, the Kemalist elite assigned women two important roles/missions: to signify modernity, and to guard and transmit Turkish national culture. The new 'Turkish woman' was needed both as a modern citizen and as a mother and wife, dedicated to raising and educating the next generation of patriotic citizens.[11] Hence, while the Kemalist project of modernity introduced women to the public sphere as citizens, it did not challenge existing gender relations and sex roles in the private realm. Furthermore, the public sphere of the new republic remained a male domain and, as Kandiyoti reveals, women's entry to the male-dominated public life was 'legitimated through the projection of an "asexual" or even slightly masculinized identity' (1995: 315).[12] Turkish women had to conceal their femininity in order to take part in public life as citizens. Male domination in the public sphere was ensured by male control over female sexuality.

Likewise, the nationalist discourse both encouraged and constrained women's agency. Turkish nationalism (Parla 1995) circumscribed women's emancipation since women's (as well as men's) interests were subordinated to the needs and interests of the nation. Women had to articulate their interests within the boundaries prescribed by the nationalist discourse (Kandiyoti 1991b). During the early Republican period, before women's suffrage, a group of women attempted to establish a Women's People's Party in 1923 to struggle for their political rights. The state rejected the proposal (Toprak 1988a). In 1935, the state disbanded the Turkish Women's Union, arguing that women's full equality no longer required autonomous women's organizations (Kandiyoti 1991a: 41–2). The official discourse on gender, therefore, led to contradictions in women's identities and roles.

Until the early 1970s, few women participated in political life. During the 1970s, many young women were politicized and joined leftist movements struggling against class exploitation and domination, although ignoring gender oppression (Berktay 1995). An independent women's movement only emerged in the early 1980s. Changes in the 'political opportunity structure' (Tarrow 1994) opened up a space for the movement. When the 1980 military *coup* declared all political parties illegal and crushed the left, women activists on the left came together and started to discuss women's oppression apart from class oppression (Tekeli 1990). For these women, empowerment required organizations autonomous from the male-dominated leftist movements and traditional political actors. The elimination of the leftist movements thus provided women with the opportunity to voice their needs, to define their own priorities and organize around their own demands without being subordinated to other struggles. Furthermore, the Kemalist discourse concerning gender equality, which previously hindered women's autonomous activism, also provided a legitimate political space for women's mobilization (Y. Arat 1991). Women activists exploited the tensions within the prevailing gender discourse, thus reducing their perceived threat to state authority.

However, the women's movement attempted to break not only with the left but also with Kemalism. In the 1980s, feminist scholars and activists started to assess the limits of the Kemalist reforms for women. Some pointed to their strategic nature (Tekeli 1981). For Kandiyoti (1989: 139), the emancipation of women was one of the 'symbolic pawns' in the Kemalist struggle to break with the Islamic institutions and laws of the Ottoman polity. Gender inequalities in the civil code were also criticized, particularly articles stating that the 'husband is the head of the family', 'the wife is required to obtain her husband's permission to work' (abolished in 1992) and 'the wife uses the husband's family name' (Tekeli 1992: 140–1). The Kemalist discourse of gender equality thus obscured unequal and hierarchical power relations between men and women within the family. Since the movement developed partly in opposition to 'state feminism' (Tekeli 1986) of Kemalism, it has had little interaction with the state.

Domestic violence against women and sexual harassment occupied a central place on the agenda of the women's movement in the late 1980s. Women's groups, feminist and non-feminist, organized the campaign 'Solidarity against Battering' to draw attention to domestic violence against women. They also launched the 'Purple Needle Campaign' to stop sexual harassment of women on the streets and in the workplace. These campaigns enabled women's groups to challenge the traditional boundaries between the public and private spheres by turning so-called 'private' issues into political ones. They not only expanded the content of the political but also introduced new ways of doing politics. Furthermore, collective mobilization and political activism empowered many women through their challenges to Kemalist nationalist discourse. It allowed them to define their own priorities, set their own agendas and, more importantly, to challenge unequal power relations between women and men.

New identities emerged from these struggles as well. As Alberto Melucci argues, identities do not pre-exist movements but are constantly being formed within them through interaction with wider social and political structures, including conflict and negotiation among different actors (1996: 68–86). In Turkey, through protests, campaigns, meetings and alternative publications,[13] women's groups, especially feminist ones, have demanded full control over their bodies and sexuality. They have criticized the Kemalist project of modernity and challenged the asexual constructions and representations of the 'Turkish woman' in the public sphere. They have rejected political control over women's bodies and sexualities. However, while feminist groups have problematized the organicist, collectivist and gendered aspects of the Kemalist national identity, they have not questioned its secular and ethnic dimensions. Although they have recognized differences among women and their multiple sources of oppression, they have projected a homogeneous, essentialized identity to publicize women's oppression.[14] This has enabled feminists to challenge the dominant gender discourse, but, at the same time, it has marginalized women's groups with different agendas. This practice has been challenged of late, both by Islamist women and Kurdish feminists.

Veiled Islamist women became visible in the public sphere in the 1980s as active participants in Islamist movement(s).[15] Their demands to enter the secular public sphere in Islamic dress have challenged the principle of secularism underlining the Kemalist project of modernity (Göle 1996). Islamist women have also accused both Kemalist women and feminists of being Westernized upper-class women who do not speak for the masses of Turkish women. They rejected both Kemalist and feminist claims made on behalf of women. Yet, by stressing the feminine nature of women, Islamist women have constructed their own essentialized notion of 'womanhood'. However, it is important to note that they have gained agency through their political activism, demanding their right to participate actively in all spheres of life, asserting their difference and seeking recognition and inclusion as legitimate actors in the public sphere (Göle 1996). In other words, they have become empowered through Islamist movement(s).

However, as Göle argues:

> there is a covert tension, a paradox, in this mode of empowerment through Islamism: they [Islamist women] quit traditional life roles, making their personal life a matter of choice, pursuing a professional and/or political career, yet they acquiesce in incarnating the Islamic way of life, Islamic morality, and Islamic community. Thus, Islamism unintentionally engenders the individuation of women while simultaneously restraining it.
>
> (1997b: 73)

In other words, Islamism both encourages and constrains women's agency. Most of the time, Islamist women's discourse and activism take place within the ideological parameters established by Islamism. However, some Islamist women refuse to submerge their voices in Islamism's collectivist vision (Göle 1997b: 75–81) and attempt to renegotiate their identities and roles with Islamist men.[16]

Kurdish feminists have posed another challenge to the Kemalist national identity and to feminist representations of 'women'. During the 1990s, they started to problematize the ethnic dimension of Kemalist nationalist discourse while at the same time criticizing Turkish feminists for privileging patriarchy over ethnicity (*Roza* 1996 (1): 4; Ayşegül 1996; Kayhan 1998a). Kurdish women claim Turkish feminists ignore their double oppression from both gender and ethnic subordination. They have formed autonomous Kurdish women's groups and begun to publish their own journals, such as *Roza* and *Jujin*. However, for Kurdish feminists, autonomy means independence not only from the Turkish women's movement and male-dominated political organizations, but also from Kurdish men,[17] who want them to give priority to Kurdish national interests (Yaşar 1996; Zelal 1997). They argue that 'while Turkish women want us to forget our Kurdish identity, Kurdish men want us to give up our femininity' (Yaşar 1996; author's translation).

The 1990s also witnessed the institutionalization of some segments of the women's movement. For example, in April 1990, a group of feminists founded the Women's Library and Information Centre, which collects books, periodicals, articles, documents, statistical data and newspaper clippings related to women's issues. The Library also carries out projects such as the Women's Oral History Pilot Project. In 1990, feminists also founded the Purple Roof Women's Shelter Foundation in İstanbul, which provides shelter and protection for women exposed to domestic violence (Arat 1998). In addition, the foundation provides psychological and legal advice, and skill and vocational training. Recently, a group of female lawyers founded a consulting centre (Kadýn Haklarý Uygulama Merkezi) within the İstanbul Bar Association to provide legal advice for women.[18]

In March 1997, a group of feminist and non-feminist activists founded Kadýn Adaylarý Destekleme ve Eğitme Derneği – KA-DER (the Association for Support and Training of Woman Candidates) in İstanbul with the motto 'equality in politics, justice in representation' (*KA-DER Bülteni*, 1997 (1)).[19] KA-DER seeks to increase women's representation in political decision-making structures, especially in the parliament, by supporting women candidates who embrace its principles, including a commitment to eliminating discrimination against women and giving greater voice to women's concerns. Women supported by KA-DER must sign a contract based on these principles.[20] KA-DER also launches campaigns and organizes workshops to inform women of their political rights.

However, feminists who are sceptical about achieving women's empowerment through a patriarchal state have criticized KA-DER for helping women enter the male-dominated parliament without challenging the existing gender hierarchies

(Savran and Tura 1997: 10–11). They argue that the abstract notion of equality adopted by KA-DER ignores structural inequalities, based on gender, class and race, which constrain women's political activity. They also criticize KA-DER for lacking a clearly specified programme for women's representation (Savran and Tura 1997: 11; Bora 1997: 5). Furthermore, the diversity of women's interests complicates representation. Some critics believe the women's movement must remain autonomous in order to avoid co-optation (Bora 1997: 5). Others, however, call for affirmative action strategies, such as the introduction of quotas for women (Savran and Tura 1997), or the creation of a feminist political party.[21]

Most of the women's groups in Turkey, then, do not view the state as an agent for women's empowerment. Given the history of 'state feminism' and the male-dominated political parties and movements, they have consistently sought to defend their autonomy and distance themselves from institutionalized politics. However, this does not mean that women's groups have no relationship with the state (or with other social movements for that matter). In fact, they have engaged with the state to influence policies concerning women. In 1990, protests by women's groups led to rescinding reduced sentences for men who rape prostitutes and to the need for a husband's authorization before a woman could work. In December 1989, Aile Araştýrma Kurumu (the Family Research Institute), affiliated with the state, was set up to protect and strengthen 'the Muslim-Turkish family' from disintegration due to women working outside the home (Berik 1990: 93–4). Women's groups and associations protested the establishment of the Institute and its policies (N. Arat 1991; Koçali 1990). In 1990, thirty women applied to courts for divorce to protest the state's attempt at strengthening the traditional family (*Pazartesi* 1995 (7): 22). During the same year, feminists protested statements by state minister Cemil Çiçek, such as 'feminism is perversity' and 'flirting is not different from prostitution', by blowing whistles on the streets of İstanbul (*Pazartesi* 1995 (7): 23). In January 1998, pressure from women's groups helped bring into effect a law against domestic violence (*Resmi Gazete* 1998), although many are concerned about its effectiveness since the police often discourage victims from using the law.[22]

The state also created the Kadýnýn Statüsü ve Sorunlarý Genel Müdürlüðü (KSSGM – Directorate General on the Status and the Problems of Women) in 1990, mainly as a response to the recommendations of the Nairobi Conference of 1985. Affiliated with the Prime Ministry, KSSGM was established as a national mechanism for formulating policies and programmes to empower women and promote their equality with men in social, cultural, economic and political life. Women's groups, however, criticized KSSGM's intention to regulate and control the activities of independent women's associations and forced a revision of the original bill (see Berik 1990). However, many women's groups and associations have remained sceptical about achieving women's empowerment through KSSGM.[23] For instance, they demanded the resignation of Işýlay Saygýn, the minister of state responsible for woman's issues, who publicly supported state virginity tests, which had led some young women to commit suicide (*KA-DER Bülteni* 1998; *Pazartesi* 1998: 11).

KSSGM has carried out several important projects to enhance women's empowerment in economic and social life.[24] The Micro Enterprises Project, financed by the Japanese through the World Bank, examined the credit policies of the banking sector and the difficulties women entrepreneurs encounter when applying for credit. The Women's Employment Promotion Project (WEP), supported by the World Bank, aimed to improve policies to enhance women's employment opportunities.[25] Based on the studies conducted within the framework of WEP, the KSSGM has recommended positive discrimination for women and the elimination of legal barriers that discourage their entry into the workforce.[26] KSSGM also founded an information centre that helps women facing violence and needing marketing facilities for their handicrafts.

Despite these successes, KSSGM has not been very effective in influencing government policies and programmes to challenge structural inequalities facing women. With its small staff and budget, KSSGM lacks both the power and the means to ensure its policy recommendations are implemented. Furthermore, most of the time, KSSGM's and the state's empowerment discourse ignores women's diversity, thereby reinforcing existing social, ethnic and religious cleavages among women.

A state-initiated project called Çok Amaçlý Toplum Merkezleri (ÇATOM – Multipurpose Community Centres) is a case in point. ÇATOMs, which have been established as a part of the Southeastern Anatolia Project (Güneydoðu Anadolu Projesi – GAP)[27] by the Regional Development Directorate of GAP in co-operation with the Turkish Development Foundation, stirred a debate among women's groups. ÇATOMs are located in eastern and southeastern cities, which are mostly populated by Kurds. They emphasize women's traditional tasks, aiming to empower women through courses on household economics, maternal and child health, nutrition, birth control and income-generating activities such as handicrafts and carpet weaving.[28] Although women are claimed as participants, the declared aims of ÇATOMs, such as helping women gain self-confidence and identify their problems, imply women are passive objects requiring top-down state-led assistance.

Some feminists criticize ÇATOMs for focusing on poor women who can be exploited for regional development (Düzkan 1998). Moreover, they argue that the emphasis on women's traditional tasks perpetuates their traditional roles and subordination, rather than challenging prevailing gender hierarchies. A prominent Turkish feminist, Ayşe Düzkan, believes ÇATOMs aim to assimilate Kurds (1998: 2–3). However, she also claims that, in the long run, Kurdish women may be empowered by learning Turkish. Kurdish feminists, on the other hand, view ÇATOMs as a state vehicle for assimilating the Kurdish population (Kayhan 1998b; Sema 1998; Canan 1998). Ironically, they argue, Kurdish women's subordination in the family may have protected the Kurdish language (Canan 1996). Thus, they attach political significance to women's traditional roles as mothers within the family. Kurdish feminists criticize Turkish women for deciding on behalf of Kurdish women whether ÇATOMs are advantageous or not. Both Turkish and Kurdish feminists, however, remain sceptical about state-planned top-down development programmes. The debates about ÇATOMs are instructive since they show that particular initiatives can be empowering or disempowering depending on where particular women stand in society.

Since the 1980s, the women's movement has been struggling to carve out its place in the Turkish political scene, rejecting the identities and roles assigned to women by different social and political projects. Many women have become empowered through participation in the women's movement (as well as in other social movements). They have gained agency and established visibility in the public sphere. They have also challenged the communitarian discourses that assign women particular missions and identities. Thus, in the Turkish context, women's struggles for empowerment have also been struggles for redefining their identities. In other words, women's groups are struggling not only for a 'freedom to *act* but [also for] the freedom to *be*' (Melucci 1996: 135 [author's emphasis]). In addition, by participating in the women's movement, many women have begun to feel empowered enough to publicize gender subordination and to organize action against the dominant sexist cultural codes and norms. Thus, they have rejected the empowerment discourse promoted by the state that reinforces unequal power relations between men and women. However, the movement needs to develop strategies to reconcile women's diversity in order to challenge and transform the prevailing gender discourse. The fragmentation and institutionalization of the women's movement during the 1990s does not mean the movement has been co-opted or that it has disappeared. Rather, it has been undergoing a transformation, the effects of which remain to be seen.

Conclusion

The path toward women's empowerment clearly begins with the emergence of women's movements. Our cases illustrate the need to begin an analysis of the emergence of women's movements with an examination of the nature of patriarchy in a given context. Moreover, this analysis must understand how the prevailing gender ideology often sets up contradictions that women can exploit for their demands. In Chile, the gender ideology emphasized women's status as mothers and their roles as protectors and providers for their families. When the policies of the military regime threatened their capacity to fulfil their social responsibilities, women mobilized against the regime. However, they did so on the basis of an identity that was legitimate and (initially) non-challenging. In Turkey, the gender ideology that emerged out of Kemalism constructed women's identities in contradictory ways: they were at once the modern and emancipated symbols of the new Western secular republic *and* the guardians and transmitters of Turkish culture and morality – a morality based on patriarchal norms. Again, women exploited this tension. Because the (paternalist) state had 'given' them certain rights, most notably the right to enter the public domain, women were able to politicize the contradictions of a gender ideology supporting public emancipation with subordination in the family. Additionally, in both Turkey and Chile, the 'political opportunity structure' was shaped by the imposition of military regimes that temporarily closed the political arena and banned political party activity. This created a space for women to come together as women, without having their interests subordinated to struggles based on class or ethnicity.

However, the two cases differ. The type of state each movement encountered, as well as their particular relationship with the state, has shaped these differences. In the Chilean case, although some women's groups supported the military regime, most opposed it. However, once democracy returned, the state was no longer seen as an 'enemy'. The democratic opposition, which had been supported by the most visible parts of the movement, became the government in 1990. The state was no longer seen as a threat to the women's movement, but as an ally. This led to the incorporation of the movement into the state. In contrast, the movement's relationship with the Turkish state has been more complex. Given the history of 'state feminism', women's groups have tried to keep their distance from the state. The movement has become institutionalized in recent years, but largely outside formal state structures.

Also, in both cases, the nature of the state has affected divisions within the movements. In Turkey, the modernizing projects of the nationalist and secularist state have made ethnic and religious identity the main dividing axes within the movement. In Chile, women are confronted with a state committed to modernization based on neo-liberal principles. This exacerbates the tensions and divisions between those parts of the movement that work within the state and benefit from globalization, and those (rural, indigenous and working-class) women whose lives are negatively affected by neo-liberal social and economic policies. In both cases, neo-liberal restructuring projects have inspired state programmes aiming to further incorporate women into labour markets, programmes that often claim to be empowering. Both cases illustrate, however, that the states' goals in this respect are often aimed more at improving its global competitive position (by relying on low-wage and flexible female labour) than at empowering women as a group by challenging gender hierarchies.

However, the existence of institutionalization, division and even fragmentation does not mean that women's movements have ceased to exist in Chile and Turkey. In both cases the need to confront and address the differences among women is recognized and is being debated within the different segments comprising the movements. Thus, many women recognize the problems inherent in seeking 'women's' empowerment, without taking into account the different ways in which women experience gender subordination. The nature in which these issues are resolved is likely to determine the future shape and strength of these movements in promoting not only women's empowerment, but also class, religious and ethnic equality.

Notes

The authors wish to thank Rianne Mahon, Jill Vickers, Antonio Franceschet, Veysi T. Kondu, Kathy Staudt and Jane Parpart for their very helpful comments.

1 Much debate has taken place in Chile over the 'indoctrination' women received through the mothers' centres. Valdés and Weinstein (1993) argue that there was always a large gap between the social control the military wanted to impose through the centres and what they actually achieved.
2 The CNMD decided to fold after two years partly due to the success they had achieved and also because they did not want to become a 'ghetto' for women's issues.
3 Chile has one of the highest rates of abortion in Latin America (approximately 35 per cent of all pregnancies) (Grupo Iniciativa Chile 1994: 17), even though therapeutic abortions are illegal. A woman who aborted for health reasons was given a three-year jail sentence (Núñez 1998: 11).
4 One of the left parties has committed itself to quotas to determine candidates for representative positions as well.
5 *El Mercurio*, 29 January, 4 February, Santiago, Chile.
6 This is evident in the posts assigned to female ministers. With the exception of Soledad Alvear, External Affairs Minister, women were appointed to lead the ministries of Health, Education, Planning and Co-operation, and, of course, SERNAM.
7 Interview with Francisca Rodríguez, ANAMURI, 31 August 1999, Santiago, Chile.
8 Labour reform legislation that would have benefited these women was recently defeated in the Senate, which remains dominated by the conservative right (Molina 1999: 2).
9 Interview with Delia Del Gatto, Jefa de Sectores, SERNAM, 20 August 1999, Santiago, Chile.
10 For Ottoman women's discourses, periodicals and associations, also see Toprak 1988b; Kandiyoti 1991a; and Çakýr 1994.
11 On 'Kemalist female identity', see Durakbaşa 1987.
12 For a detailed analysis, see Kandiyoti 1988 and Durakbaşa 1998. In a similar vein, Fatmagül Berktay points to the repression of sexuality and individuality of the women active in the Turkish left (1995: 252–4).
13 During the 1980s, two feminist periodicals, *Feminist* and *Sosyalist Feminist Kaktüs*, reflected particular trends within the movement. Radical and socialist feminists gathered around the journal *Pazartesi*, which began publication in April 1995.
14 Socialist feminists, for instance, argued that ignoring differences among women and accepting any essentialist and homogenizing understanding of 'womanhood' undermines the possibility of feminist politics (*Sosyalist Feminist Kaktüs* 1988 (1): 13). For them, an autonomous women's movement is only possible when different feminist and non-feminist groups, solidarity networks, and research teams come together (1988 (1): 13).
15 For an analysis of 'the veiling movement' in post-1980 Turkey, see Göle 1996. For analyses of Islamist women's discourses and their identity, see İlyasoðlu 1994; Alankuş-Kural 1997; and Göle 1997a and b).
16 In *Kadýn Kimliği*, an Islamist women's periodical, Mualla Gülnaz (1997) criticizes Islamist men by pointing to domestic violence and injustices in Muslim families. She argues that there is a 'man's question' rather than a 'woman's question' in Muslim societies. See also Gülnaz 1996 and Toros 1997.·
17 Interview with Fatma Kayhan, 15 July 1999, İstanbul, Turkey.
18 Interview with Filiz Kerestecioğlu, 29 July 1999, İstanbul, Turkey.
19 In Turkey, women are under-represented in parliament and other decision-making bodies. In the last general elections (April 1999) only twenty-four women (4.3 per cent of the 550 MPs) were elected to the parliament.
20 For details, see Kadýn Adaylarý Destekleme ve Eğitme Derneği. *Tüzük*, March 1997
21 Interview with Ayşe Düzkan, 1 July 1999, İstanbul, Turkey.
22 Interview with Filiz Kerestecioğlu, 29 July 1999, İstanbul, Turkey.
23 Interview with Ayşe Düzkan, 1 July 1999, İstanbul, Turkey.

24 For details on these projects, see KSSGM 1996 and KSSGM, *Projects*, December 1999 (available at http://www.kssgm.gov.tr/projeeng.htm).
25 In Turkey, the economic restructuring of the 1980s did not increase female employment. Çağatay (1994) argues that even high female employment rates in home-working manufacturing do not indicate 'urban feminization'. For an analysis of structural adjustment policies and changing forms of women's labour in Turkey, see Ecevit 1998.
26 See KSSGM, *Women Employment Project*, December 1999 (available at http:// www.kssgm.gov.tr/engpro.html).
27 The GAP is the largest regional development project implemented in nine provinces of Southeastern Anatolia. It aims to redress regional disparities between Turkey's western and eastern regions.
28 For more on ÇATOMs, see KSSGM, *Periodic Reports of States Parties to CEDAW*, December 1999 (available at http://www.kssgm.gov.tr/cedeng.htm).

References

Alankuş-Kural, Sevda (1997) 'Türkiye'de Alternatif Kamular/Cemaatler ve İslamcý Kadýn Kimliği', *Toplum ve Bilim* 72: 5–44.
Alvarez, Sonia E. (1998) 'Latin American feminisms "go global": Trends of the 1990s and challenges for the new millennium', in Sonia Alvarez, Evalina Dagnino and Arturo Escobar (eds) *Cultures of Politics, Politics of Culture: Re-visioning Latin American Social Movements*, Boulder: Westview Press, pp. 293–324.
—— (1990) *Engendering Democracy in Brazil: Women's Movements in Transition Politics*, Princeton: Princeton University Press.
Arat, Necla (1991) 'Çağdýşý Ninniler!', *Cumhuriyet*, 16 January.
Arat, Yeşim (1998) 'Feminist institutions and democratic aspirations: The case of the Purple Roof Women's Shelter Foundation', in Zehra F. Arat (ed.) *Deconstructing Images of 'The Turkish Woman'*, New York: St Martin's Press, pp. 295–309.
—— (1991) '1980'ler Türkiyesi'nde Kadýn Hareketi: Liberal Kemalizm'in Radikal Uzantýsý', *Toplum ve Bilim* 53: 7–19.
Ayşegül (1996) 'Ne kadar çok Türksünüz?', *Roza* 5: 13–14.
Basu, Amrita (1995) 'Introduction', in Amrita Basu (ed.) *The Challenge of Local Feminisms: Women's Movements in Global Perspective*, Boulder: Westview Press, pp. 1–21.
Berik, Günseli (1990) 'State policy in the 1980s and the future of women's rights in Turkey', *New Perspectives on Turkey* 4: 81–96.
Berktay, Fatmagül (1995) 'Has anything changed in the outlook of the Turkish Left on women?', in Şirin Tekeli (ed.) *Women in Modern Turkish Society: A reader*, London: Zed, pp. 251–62.
Bora, Aksu (1997) 'Sözettiğiniz temsilin niteliðine ilişkin kafam karýşýk', *Pazartesi* 26: 5.
Canan (1998) 'İkinci Kez Dağ Çiçekleri Yaratýlmak İsteniyor (ÇATOM, TOKAP)', *Jujin* 7: 2–5.
—— (1996) 'Kadýn ve Anadil', *Roza* 1: 24–5.
Çağatay, Nilüfer (1994) 'Turkish women and structural adjustment', in Isabella Bakker (ed.) *The Strategic Silence: Gender and Economic Policy*, London: Zed in association with the North–South Institute, pp. 130–6.
Çakýr, Serpil (1994) *Osmanlý Kadýn Hareketi*, İstanbul: Metis Yayýnlarý.
Chaney, Elsa M. (1979) *Supermadre: Women in Politics in Latin America*, Austin: University of Texas Press.

Charlton, Sue Ellen, Jana Everett and Kathleen Staudt (1989) 'Women, the state, and development', Sue Ellen Charlton, Jana Everett and Kathleen Staudt (eds) *Women, the State and Development*, Albany: State University of New York Press, pp. 1–19.

Comisión Interministerial para la IV Conferencia Mundial sobre la Mujer (1995) Chile: Informe Nacional. Santiago.

Durakbaşa, Ayşe (1998) 'Kemalism as identity politics in Turkey', in Zehra F. Arat (ed.) *Deconstructing Images of 'The Turkish Woman'*, New York: St Martin's Press, pp. 139–55.

—— (1987) 'The formation of Kemalist female identity: A historical-cultural perspective', unpublished MA thesis, İstanbul: Boğaziçi University.

Düzkan, Ayşe (1998) 'Kürt Kadýnlara Hizmet!: Devletin eli uzanýyor mu, kalkýyor mu?', *Pazartesi* 37: 2–3.

Ecevit, Yýldýz (1998) 'Küreselleşme, Yapýsal Uyum ve Kadýn Emeğinin Kullanýmýnda Değişmeler', in Ferhunde Özbay (ed.) *Kadýn Emeği ve İstihdamýndaki Değişmeler: Türkiye Örneği*, İstanbul: İnsan Kaynağýný Geliştirme Vakfý, pp. 31–77.

Frohmann, Alicia and Teresa Valdés (1995) 'Democracy in the country and in the home: The women's movement in Chile', in Amrita Basu (ed.) *The Challenge of Local Feminisms: Women's Movements in Global Perspective*, Boulder: Westview Press, pp. 276–301.

Gaviola, Edda, Eliana Largo and Sandra Palestro (1994) *Una historia necesaria: Mujeres en Chile, 1973–1990*, Santiago.

Göle, Nilüfer (1997a) 'The quest for the Islamic self within the context of modernity', in Sibel Bozdoğan and Reşat Kasaba (eds) *Rethinking Modernity and National Identity in Turkey*, Seattle: University of Washington Press, pp. 81–94.

—— (1997b) 'The gendered nature of the public sphere', *Public Culture* 10(1): 61–81.

—— 1996. *The Forbidden Modern: Civilization and Veiling*, Ann Arbor: University of Michigan Press.

Grupo Iniciativo Chile (1994) 'Mujeres: Ciudadanía, cultura y desarrollo en el Chile de los noventa'. Santiago.

Gülnaz, Mualla (1997) 'Feminizme Müslümanca Bakýş', *Kadýn Kimliği* 23: 12.

—— (1996) 'Suyu tersine akýtanlar', *Birikim* 91: 66–9.

İlyasoğlu, Aynur (1994) *Örtülü Kimlik*, İstanbul: Metis.

KA-DER Bülteni, 1997 (issue 1) and 1998 (issue 5).

Kadýn Adaylarý Destekleme ve Eğitme Derneği. March 1997. *Tüzük*.

Kadýnýn Statüsü ve Sorunlarý Genel Müdürlüğü (1996) *Kadýn Bülteni*, 8 Mart Özel Sayýsý

Kadýnýn Statüsü ve Sorunlarý Genel Müdürlüğü. Available: <http://www.kssgm.gov.tr>

Kandiyoti, Deniz (1995) 'Patterns of patriarchy: Notes for an analysis of male dominance in Turkish society', in Şirin Tekeli (ed.) *Women in Modern Turkish Society: A Reader*, London: Zed, pp. 306–18.

—— (1991a) 'End of empire: Islam, nationalism and women in Turkey', in Deniz Kandiyoti (ed.) *Women, Islam and the State*, Philadelphia: Temple University Press, pp. 22–47.

—— (1991b) 'Identity and its discontents: Women and the nation', *Millennium* 20(3): 429–43.

—— (1989) 'Women and the Turkish state: Political actors or symbolic pawns?', in Nira Yuval-Davis and Floya Anthias (eds) *Woman-nation-state*, New York: St Martin's Press, pp. 126–49.

—— (1988) 'Slave girls, temptresses, and comrades: Images of women in the Turkish novel', *Feminist Issues* 8(1): 35–50.

Kayhan, Fatma (1998a) '8 Mart'ýn Düşündürttükleri: Türk feminist hareketin çýkmazý', *Roza* 13: 9–13.

—— 1998b. 'Kürt kadýnlarýna batýrýlan dikenler', *Roza* 13: 3–8.

Kirkwood, Julieta (1986) *Ser política en Chile: Las feministas y los partidos*, Santiago: FLACSO-Chile.

Koçali, Filiz (1990) '"Milli Gorüş" çüler ·şbaşýnda: Müslüman-Türk Kadýný Yaratýlmak ·steniyor', *Sosyalist Feminist Kaktüs* 12: 52–3.

Melucci, Alberto (1996) *Challenging Codes: Collective Action in the Information Age*, Cambridge: Cambridge University Press.

Molina, Germán (1999) 'El mundo del trabajo', informative supplement, Dirección del Trabajo. November 25.

Molina, Natacha (1989) 'Propuestas políticas y orientaciones de cambio en la situación de la mujer', in Manuel Garretón (ed.) *Propuestas políticas y demandas sociales*, vol. III, Santiago: FLACSO-Chile, pp. 33–171.

Moltedo, Cecilia (1998) *Experiencias de participación de las mujeres Chilenas en los partidos políticos: 1990 a 1998*, Santiago: Instituto de la Mujer.

Nelson, Barbara J. and Najma Chowdury (1994) 'Redefining politics: Patterns of women's political engagement from a global perspective', in Barbara Nelson and Najma Chowdury (eds) *Women and Politics Worldwide*, New Haven: Yale University Press, pp. 3–24.

Núñez, Nuria (ed.) (1998) *Actas del primer tribunal de los derechos de las mujeres Chilenas*, Santiago: Instituto de la Mujer.

Parla, Taha (1995) *Türkiye'de Siyasal Kültürün Resmi Kaynaklarý: Kemalist Tek-Parti İdeolojisi ve CHP'nin Altý Ok'u*, İstanbul: İletişim Yayýnlarý.

Pazartesi, 1995 (issue 7); 1997 (issues 26 and 27); 1998 (issue 36, 37 and 39).

Pringle, Rosemary and Sophie Watson (1998) '"Women's interests" and the post-structuralist state', in Anne Phillips (ed.) *Feminism and Politics*, Oxford: Oxford University Press, pp. 203–23.

Provoste, Patricia (1997) 'Los servicios públicos y los derechos de las mujeres: Hacia una modernización de la gestión pública', *Veredas por Cruzar*, Santiago: Instituto de la Mujer, pp. 43–64.

Provoste, Patricia and Patricia Silva (1998) 'Acciones de interés público por la no discriminación de género', in Felipe González and Felipe Viveros (eds) *Ciudadanía e interés público: Enfoques desde el derecho, la ciencia política y la sociología*, Santiago: Facultad de Derecho de la Universidad Diego Portales, pp. 9–61.

Rai, Shirin M. (1996) 'Women and the state in the Third World: Some issues for debate', in Shirin M. Rai and Geraldine Lievesley (eds) *Women and the State: International Perspectives*, London: Taylor & Francis, pp. 12–22.

Randall, Vicky (1998) 'Gender and power: Women engage the state', in Vicky Randall and Georgina Waylen (eds) *Gender, Politics, and the State*, London: Routledge, pp. 184–205.

Resmi Gazete (1998) 'Ailenin Korunmasýna Dair Kanun', no. 23233 (17 January): 15–16.

Roza, 1996 (issues 1 and 5); 1997 (issues 6 and 9); 1998 (issue 13).

Savran, Gülnur and Nesrin Tura (1997) 'Kader söylediklerini yapabilir mi?', *Pazartesi* 27: 10–11.

Schild, Veronica (1997) 'New subjects of rights? Gendered citizenship and the contradictory legacies of social movements in Latin America', *Organization* 44(4): 604–9.

Sema (1998) 'Kolonyalist "Türk feminizmi"!', *Pazartesi* 39: 14.

SERNAM (1998) *Plan de igualdad de oportunidades para las mujeres: 1994–1999*, Santiago.

SERNAM (n.d.) Cuadro 1, *Inserción organizacional de mujeres líderes por región*, Santiago.

Serrano, Caludia (1992) 'Estado, mujer y política social en Chile', in Dagmar Raczynski and Claudia Serrano (eds) *Políticas sociales, mujeres y gobierno local*, Santiago: CIEPLAN, pp. 195–216.

Sirman, Nükhet (1989) 'Feminism in Turkey: A short history', *New Perspectives on Turkey* 3(1): 1–34.

Sosyalist Feminist Kaktüs, 1988 (issue 1).

Tarrow, Sidney (1994) *Power in Movement: Social Movements, Collective Action and Politics*, Cambridge: Cambridge University Press.

Tekeli, Şirin (1992) 'Europe, European feminism, and women in Turkey', *Women's Studies International Forum* 15(1): 139–43.

—— (1990) 'Women in the changing political associations of the 1980s', in Andrew Finkel and Nükhet Sirman (eds) *Turkish State, Turkish Society*, London: Routledge, pp. 259–87.

—— (1986) 'Emergence of the new feminist movement in Turkey', in Drude Dahlerup (ed.) *The New Women's Movement*, London: Sage, pp. 179–99.

—— (1981) 'Women in Turkish politics', in Nermin Abadan-Unat (ed.) *Women in Turkish Society*, Leiden: E.J. Brill.

Toprak, Zafer (1988a) 'Halk Fýrkasý'ndan Önce Kurulan Parti: Kadýnlar Halk Fýrkasý', *Tarih ve Toplum* 51: 30–1.

—— (1988b) 'Osmanlý Kadýnlarý Çalýþtýrma Cemiyeti: Kadýn Askerler ve Milli Aile', *Tarih ve Toplum* 51: 34–8.

Toros, Halime (1997) 'Bir dönemin anlatýlmamýþ öyküsü', *Kadýn Kimliği* 23: 13–14.

Valdés, Teresa (1998) 'Las Mujeres en 1997: Ciudadanía e invisibilidad', *Chile '97: Análisis y Opiniones*, Santiago: FLACSO-Chile, pp. 103–26.

Valdés, Teresa and Enrique Gomariz (1995) *Mujeres Latinoamericanas en Cifras: Tomo comparativo*, Spain: Instituto de la Mujer.

Valdés, Teresa and Marisa Weinstein (1993) *Mujeres que Sueñan: las organizaciones de pobladoras en Chile, 1973–1989*. Santiago: FLACSO-Chile.

Valdés, Teresa *et al.* (1993) 'Mujer popular y estado: Informe de investigación', Santiago: Documento de Trabajo, FLACSO-Chile.

Valenzuela, María Elena (1998) 'Women and the democratization process in Chile', in Jane S. Jaquette and Sharon L. Wolchik (eds) *Women and Democracy: Latin America and Central and Eastern Europe*, Baltimore: Johns Hopkins University Press, pp. 47–74.

Waylen, Georgina (1997) 'Women's movements, the state, and democratization in Chile: The establishment of SERNAM', in Anne Marie Goetz (ed.) *Getting Institutions Right for Women in Development*, London: Zed Books, pp. 90–103.

Weinstein, Marisa (1997) *Políticas de equidad de género y participación de las mujeres*, Santiago: FLACSO-Chile.

West, Guida and Rhoda Lois Blumberg (1990) 'Reconstructing social protest from a feminist perspective', in Guida West and Rhoda Lois Blumberg (eds) *Women and Social Protest*, New York: Oxford University Press, pp. 3–35.

Yaşar, Hatice (1996) 'Kadýn ve Siyaset ve de Roza', *Roza* 1: 8–11.

Zelal (1997) 'Kürt Erkeklerine veya Erkek Kürtlere', *Roza* 6: 13–14.

Zihnioğlu, Yaprak (1999) 'Erken Dönem Osmanlý Hareket-i Nisvaný'nýn İki Büyük Düşünürü: Fatma Aliye ve Emine Semiye', *Tarih ve Toplum* 31(186): 4–11.

—— (1998) 'Nezihe Muhiddin: An Ottoman Turkish women's rights defender', unpublished MA thesis, Department of Political Science and International Relations, İstanbul: Boğaziçi University.

8 Political representation, democratic institutions and women's empowerment

The quota debate in India[1]

Shirin M. Rai

Introduction

This chapter examines whether the current debates about quotas for women in political institutions in India can form part of a wider debate on women's empowerment. I do this by exploring the reasons for these demands by women's groups in a country where quotas have had a problematic symbolic history of nearly forty years. The debate on quotas in India has reflected disquiet about women's engagement with state institutions, with the perceived elitism of 'the women's movement', and has challenged women's groups to address issues of difference among women based on caste and class. One of the important questions for women's groups has been whether this engagement with the state is appropriate at a time when the pressures of globalization and liberalization are increasing social inequalities and tensions within the country. Surely any debate on women's empowerment should focus on questions about improving women's life-chances rather than increasing their political representation in state institutions that are implicated, through policy-making, in the very process of globalization that is adversely affecting poor women in India?

The term empowerment has largely been ignored in mainstream Political Science. For example, it does not appear at all in the *Oxford Dictionary of Politics* (McLean 1996). On the other hand, empowerment has found great currency within feminist discourses. From early on, debates about the gendered nature of participation in local politics have been important within feminist politics (Phillips 1991). While some have taken issue with the costs of participation (Phillips 1991), the focus has been on the concept of participation rather than on empowerment. Empowerment as a concept has emerged out of debates on education and increasingly within the literature on social movements. 'The notion of empowerment was intended to help participation perform one main political function – to provide development with a new source of legitimation', writes Majid Rahnema in the *Development Dictionary* (1992: 122). Empowerment legitimates oppositional discourse as well as oppositional social movements, programmes, methodologies and policies – both macro and micro. The feminist literature on politics has re-emphasized empowerment as development. Bystydzienski, for example, defines empowerment as 'a process by which oppressed persons gain some control over their lives by taking part with others in development of activities and structures that allow people increased involvement in matters which affect them directly' (1992: 3). Feminists have used the term empowerment in preference to power for many reasons – its focus on the oppressed, rather than the oppressors, its emphasis on 'power to' rather than starting with 'power over' and its insistence upon power as enabling, as competence rather than dominance (Bystydzienski 1992: 3). In the 1990s the concept of empowerment expanded to include institutional strategies for empowerment that led to a focus on the under-representation of women in political institutions at all levels of governance. The Beijing Declaration, for example, links women's participation in institutional politics with their empowerment in social and economic life. 'The empowerment and autonomy of women and the improvement of women's social, economic and political status is essential for the achievement of both transparent and accountable government and administration and sustainable development in all areas of life' (UN 1996: 109).

Empowerment is a seductive term. It encompasses a politics that opposes the state on the one hand, and the economic forces of neo-liberal markets on the other. The actors in this oppositional politics are 'the people', variously defined and identified. This categorization is important for suggesting an alternative model of politics, one based on needs articulated by the people rather than the state, and political processes that are participatory, democratic and close to home, rather than representative and bureaucratized in far-away corridors of state power. Empowerment, then, is the knowing and the doing; the feasibility of politics that allow us to feel empowered whatever our contexts. This is the great seduction. What became obscured in this discourse of empowerment are wider political implications of the concept as well as strategies of empowerment.

While much is said about participatory politics within the empowerment framework, there is little reflection upon the machinery of social and state power. It has been argued that empowerment:

> is not a process organised from the helm of government, but it does require a strong state, that is, a state in which executive power is centralised, and departments (or provinces) are not colonised, and also one in which security agencies are not a law unto themselves …. [T]his might enable people to take greater advantage of the opportunities available to them in the existing market structures, and would in any case be a necessary condition for changes in those structures to achieve their stated aims of income or asset redistribution.
>
> (Friedman 1992: 7)

This points clearly to the importance of the state, its politics, ideology and institutions – bureaucratic as well as political (political parties, for example) – as part of the debate on empowerment. Without such a multilayered analysis, I would argue that the discourse of empowerment is not really a discourse of power. It addresses audiences as if they were all potential converts to 'the cause'. Further, there is a tendency to homogenize the actors engaged in struggles for empowerment. 'The people', or 'women', are presented without sufficient differentiation. As the debate on quotas below demonstrates, the need to focus on the politics of difference among women is important for the credibility of strategies of empowerment as well as for their long-term viability. I do not seek to de-legitimize the concept of empowerment. On the contrary, I seek to reinstate it, but taking the issue of power into account: asking empowerment of whom, by whom, through what, and for what.

The current debates on institutional strategies for women's empowerment in India are examined below. I draw on my recent work with Indian feminists engaged in this debate, as well as earlier work with women parliamentarians, to argue that social class, political ideology and communal identities are important to our understanding of this current phase of feminist politics in India. As Catherine Hoskyns and I have argued elsewhere, the issue of class is at the heart of the process of engendering development, and it is at our own peril that we forget it (1998). This is not simply to forestall a backlash, but also to address issues of difference among women, as well as among women and men, and to rethink women's empowerment.

The Indian experiments with quotas

The local, the national, the political

On 22 December 1992, the Indian Parliament passed the Constitution (73rd and 74th) Amendment Acts. These amendments 'enshrined in the Constitution certain basic and essential features of Panchayati Raj Institutions [PRI, institutions of local government] to impart certainty, continuity and strength to them' (Matthews 1997: 22). They not only responded to a growing political demand for decentralization of power after the 1990s crisis over governability, but also to the emerging voice of women's groups demanding greater visibility for women in politics. 'A unique feature of the new phase in *panchayats* [village councils] and municipalities in India is that it has ensured one-third representation for women in the local bodies and one-third of the offices of chairpersons at all levels in rural and urban bodies for them' (Matthews 1997: 25). This has created the possibility for about 1,000,000 women to be elected to village *panchayats* and urban municipalities; so far 716,234 women have held elected positions in the country, and in some states, such as West Bengal, more than the mandatory 33.3 per cent women have been elected. More remarkably, all political parties co-operated to pass this legislation.

The 1996 elections in India resulted in a parliament with fewer women members than the last three – women contested only 11 per cent of the total seats. This parliament has only thirty-six women members of parliament (MPs) out of a total of 545, as opposed to forty-four in the previous one. At the same time, the coalition that eventually returned to government committed itself to introducing legislation ensuring a quota for women of 33 per cent in future

Indian parliaments. This would ensure that out of 545 seats in the *Lok Sabha*, 182 seats go to women. Constituencies reserved for women would not be fixed, but would rotate at random. All parties, irrespective of their ideological standpoints, initially supported this legislation. The Bill was introduced in the first term of the new BJP-led government, but it has been referred to a Joint Select Committee of the Indian Parliament due to differences over details. The debate on the Bill in the Indian press reveals a lack of general political will among parties to pass the 81st Constitution Amendment Bill that would ensure the quota. Women's groups have largely supported the measure, though some important voices within the women's movements have spoken out against the Bill.

One could speculate about the reasons why the various political parties, which supported the quota for women in *panchayats*, have been more reluctant regarding similar legislation at the parliamentary level. Could it be that enhanced representation of women in the national parliament spells a far greater and immediate challenge to the gendered status quo within the party political system? The *panchayats*, while symbolic of grassroots democracy in India, have never been resourced well enough to affect the party political process in Indian politics. Or is it that the pattern of quota systems in India has shown that elite-based strategies of empowerment are less helpful to groups seeking greater recognition than those based upon grassroots institutions? The message from established political parties and state institutions is mixed. While a strong women's movement has been able to politicize the issue of gender representation successfully, mainstream political bodies have not embraced this agenda whole-heartedly.

At this point it is also important to consider the reasons for the near consensus among women's groups regarding the issue of quotas. While many women's groups have supported the move for quotas (a significant number of these are attached to political parties), some feminists have opposed this move as 'tokenist'. The first group focuses on under-representation of women in party politics; the second is concerned about the elitist character of parliamentary politics and the dangers women face in seeking inclusion into this overwhelmingly male space (Kapoor 1996: 11; Kishwar 1996: 2). Feminists who oppose the Bill do so as much on grounds of detail as principles. Kishwar, for example, also opposes reserving constituencies for women where they contest only against other women, thus ghettoizing them. She wants a system of 'multi-seat constituencies where one out of three candidates has to be a woman' (1996: 2). Concerns about co-optation and elitism worry many feminist and women's groups in India.

> The link between reservations in Parliament and 'empowerment' of women is at best tenuous, and may even be a way of closing off possibilities of further radicalization of Indian politics …. If we attempt to recover feminist politics as subversion, … we would need to move away from politics as merely seeking space within already defined boundaries of power.
>
> (Menon 1997: 41)

Women's interests, women representatives

Catherine Hoskyns and I argue that:

> policies based on a recognition that certain groups are under represented can also be seen as a means of political gate-keeping, and that in certain circumstances the recognition of gender-based groups may be seen as less disruptive of the hierarchy of power relations than the recognition of groups more clearly based on class. 'Gender' can be accommodated on this reading – but only if it loses its class dimension.

We believe 'the privileging of gender over class, together with the grip of the political parties on access to the political system, results in a particular profile of women representatives which in turn raises issues about accountability'. Moreover, 'this selective inclusion of women in the political process is important – but inadequate in challenging the established hierarchies of power relations' (Hoskyns and Rai 1998: 345–65). If development agendas are to be rearticulated, if transformation of the lives of women has to take place in tandem with the gender relations within which they are enmeshed, then the question of economic and social class relations has to be dealt with.

For the moment, the main thrust of academic research and institutional initiatives continues to focus on categories of difference other than class. The salience of class in political life remains weak and representation continues to be regarded as a strategy for reordering political hierarchies. I would argue that this political bias is reflective of what Nancy Fraser has called the politics of affirmation (1995: 68–93). She argues that while justice requires both recognition of difference and an insistence upon redistribution of socio-economic resources, currently the two have become disassociated. Representation, in this analysis, would be a strategy of recognition rather than redistribution, thus limiting its transformative potential.

Fraser distinguishes two broad approaches to remedying injustice that occur across the recognition–redistribution divide. The affirmation approach focuses on 'correcting inequitable outcomes of social arrangements without disturbing the underlying framework that generates them'. In contrast, the transformative remedy focuses on 'correcting inequitable outcomes precisely by restructuring the underlying generative framework' (Fraser 1995: 82). Whereas affirmative remedies reinforce group differences, transformative remedies tend to destabilize them in the long run. Fraser sees the combination of socialism and deconstruction as the remedy most suited to resolving the recognition–redistribution dilemma. In doing so she seems to suggest that destabilizing group difference is the long-term strategy best suited to the process of transformation. Iris Marian Young's argument with Fraser on this issue points to the problem with this binary analysis, which positions choices in a zero-sum fashion. Her position on the value of recognizing difference, and of policy outcomes flowing from this recognition in terms of group rights, suggests a different route to redistribution (Young 1997). However, Fraser's discussion of the recognition–redistribution dilemma does pose important questions for a study of gender and representation. How far can representation as a concept and strategy meet the needs of the majority of women? The debate in India about the concrete provisions of the quota legislation is salutary in this regard.

'Social backwardness' and quota politics

The introduction of the 81st Amendment Bill, and indeed the legislative changes in the form of the 74th Amendment Act, demonstrate the importance of women's political representation in Indian politics. The success of the women's movement in placing the issue of political under-representation of women on the agenda of political parties and governments begs two questions. Why has this issue become important for the women's movement in the last decade? How have women's movements been able to get recognition for this agenda? In part this is perhaps the result of the 'troubling impasse' (Omvedt 1993: 97) that the Indian women's movements faced in the 1990s. The liberalization policies have seen women increasingly being pushed into the unorganized sector of work. The decline of the trade union movement – never very sensitive to women's issues in the first place, but changing under pressure of the women's movements – has also increased the vulnerability of working-class women. Despite tremendous struggles waged by women's groups against violence against women, convictions have been difficult. The late 1980s also saw the hardening of divisions among women's groups – between 'academic' and 'activists', between right- and left-wing women, between those working with mass organizations and those working with international non-governmental organizations (INGOs). In this context the early focus of women's groups – on women's work, violence and capitalist relations, in and outside the home – became obscured. The international context of women's organizations also changed. While the demand for women's inclusion in policy-making institutions appeared first in the late 1970s, it found increasing expression in the formulations of 'women's interests' in the late 1980s and gathered momentum with Rajiv Gandhi's proposals in 1991 for the reservation of seats for women in the village *panchayats*. Reservations (or quotas) have thus had a long and chequered history in India.

A history of 'reservation' policies

When the Indian state was taking shape in the 1940s, the question of caste dominated the debates about a new constitution as well as a new social order. The arguments were cast in both philosophical and pragmatic terms. Political equality could not be realized without social and economic equality, which were attached to the whole edifice of social power. In India, the caste system is the 'steel frame' that has underpinned Hindu society despite its polytheism and plurality. The inherent inequality of birth built into this system did not allow individuals a way out of their particular positioning in the social system. Individual efforts could not therefore work as a strategy for social mobility.

The Indian Constituent Assembly decided to enshrine in the constitution a special 9th Schedule that would allow the policies of affirmative action through reservation. The Congress Party leadership recognized that ignoring the issue of caste could lead to political instability that a fledgling democracy could ill afford. The legislation was based on the idea of 'social backwardness' that was seen as a social 'placing [of] individuals/groups in particular disadvantageous position by delimiting their life chances'. The determinants of this 'social backwardness' were both the objective position of a group in terms of economic conditions in the social structure as well as the prevailing value system (Shah 1991: 601).

A further amendment to the original legislation in 1951 enabled the state to make 'special provisions' for the advancement of any socially and educationally 'backward classes' or for scheduled castes and scheduled tribes. Similar provision in Article 16(4) reserved posts for any 'backward classes' of citizens who in the opinion of the state are 'not adequately represented in the services under the state'. These clauses refer to 'classes of citizens' and not individuals; group (minority) rights were thus acknowledged as important by the Indian political elites from the start. This recognition is the basis of the quota debates and demands concerning women. However, the question of caste has posed very divisive questions for the women's groups engaged in these debates.

India's one-party dominant political system has fractured since Indira Gandhi's death in 1984. Today, coalition politics and caste interest groups are extremely visible and active in India. Parties based on regional and caste identities have gained prominence in the political process and system. At the time of the consideration of the quota legislation for women in parliament in 1993–4, the party consensus that had allowed a smooth passage of the 73rd Amendment Act broke down on the question of caste representation within quotas for women. Political parties like the Janata Party and the Samta Party argued fiercely that the quota for women should be distributed along caste lines; that the caste-based reservation already in place should be reflected in the newly proposed quota for women. On the other hand, other regional parties such as the AIDMK (All India Dravid Munetra Kadgam) have supported the Bill and given vital support to the initiative at the time when it was most needed. The saga of the non-passage of the Bill illustrates the fluidity of the Indian political situation – a fluidity that women's groups have taken advantage of, and at the same time fallen foul of.

The arguments for quotas

The arguments for quotas for women in representative institutions are fairly well rehearsed. Development policies are highly politically charged trade-offs between diverse interests and value choices. 'The political nature of these policies is frequently made behind the closed door of bureaucracy or among tiny groups of men in a non-transparent political structure' (Staudt 1991: 65). The question then arises, how are women to access this world of policy-making so dominated by men? The answers that have been explored within the Indian women's movements have been diverse – political mobilization of women, lobbying political parties, moving the courts and legal establishments, constitutional reform, mobilization and participation in social movements such as the environmental movement, and civil liberties campaigns. It is only now, however, that women's groups have come together to demand increased representation of women in India's political institutions.

Women's groups now argue that quotas for women are needed to compensate for the social barriers that have prevented women from participating in politics and thus making their voices heard. In order for women to be more than 'tokens' in political institutions, a level of presence that cannot be overlooked by political parties is required, hence the demand for a 33 per cent quota. The quota system acknowledges that it is the recruitment process, organized through political parties and supported by a framework of patriarchal values, which needs to carry the burden of change, rather than individual women. The alternative then is that there should be an acknowledgement of the historical social exclusion of women from politics, a compensatory regime (quotas) established, and 'institutionalised ... for the explicit recognition and representation of oppressed groups' (Young 1990: 183–91). This demand for quotas has been formulated first with respect to grassroots institutions (*panchayats*). It reflects the unease felt by many women's groups with elite politics and elite women (Agnihotri and Mazumdar 1995; CWDS 1994).

The National Commission for Women (NCW), set up in 1991, has consistently supported the demand for a quota for women in parliament and other representative institutions. In the 1996 elections, it called for all women voters to exercise their franchise in favour of women candidates regardless of the political party they represented. At one level this call reflected the Commission's support for quotas for women. If the purpose of the quotas is to increase the number of women in parliament, then the gender variable is the most important one to consider at the time of voting. However, women's groups in India have had close links with political parties. Consequently, the question of representativeness is also tied closely to the question of political platforms.

> In a system which is party-based, whether it is men or women, they will represent the viewpoint of the party .... Women voters while making their choice [of candidates] will have to judge which of these platforms will be closest to viewing their concerns with sympathy. They will also have to judge which of these platforms is intrinsically against women's equality and vote against the candidate regardless of whether it is a man or a woman.
>
> (Karat 1996: 8)

This concern with party politics has been exacerbated by the growing mobilization of women by the right-wing political parties in the name of cultural authenticity and the recognition of women as bulwarks against the erosion of traditions. This calls for a political response from the women's groups on the centre/left (CWDS 1994: 22–4). The consensus on the quota policy has also evolved with the successful enactment of the 73rd and 74th Amendment Acts. The feeling now is that these Acts will ensure women's grassroots political involvement; that as women become active in *panchayat* politics, their ability to participate in national politics will increase. The question of elitism will thus be answered.

The consensus on a quota for women has also gained from the support (however ambivalent) of the political parties. Here I would point out the changing character of the Indian political system. The break up of the old system of one-party domination has also led to the mobilization of new constituencies. Most parties have identified women as an important and neglected constituency that should be brought into the political mainstream. This mobilization has become an issue only because of the strength of the women's movement in India, but has taken different forms when different political parties have sought to engage women.[2] The terms of engagement of various political parties have differed. While the right wing has supported an undifferentiated quota for women, parties with significant lower-caste constituencies have been generally more ambivalent, even when reflecting upon the need to mobilize women into their parties. The pressure on political parties to support the quota has been therefore matched by their concern about the terms on which the quota is to be constructed.

As the consensus around the need for a quota has evolved, new and important issues for women's groups and movements have emerged, in particular the question of how to deal with difference among women. The current emphasis by women's groups on the representation of women in political institutions can thus be read in the light of the tension between the politics of universalism, as symbolized in the Indian debates about citizenship, and the constant and real fear of co-optation of the feminist projects by the political elites.

The arguments against

At the theoretical level, two sets of arguments have been used to oppose the introduction of quotas: first, any quota policy is against the principle of equal opportunity and, therefore, inherently undemocratic – that it is also against the principle of meritocracy. The second argument regards the nature of interest representation – whose interests are being represented? Can women be regarded as a homogenous group? How are differences among women to be acknowledged and then translated into a quota policy? The motives of those opposing the Bill have varied too. Some are moved by dilemmas that women's movements will have to face.

> It [the legislation] can either be an authentic expression of womanhood in politics, in which case it profoundly alters the way we all are, or it can be a device to co-opt women into structures of power and ways of authoritarian thinking … and yet express a vision of the universe in which the male [remains] the principal agent.
>
> (Das 1998: 1)

Others look clearly to the feasibility of such mechanisms of change. 'How can these poor women *panches* (*panchayat* members) oppose the same men whose fields they work for livelihood? First organise them and put economic power in their hands, only then can they oppose men' (Bhatt 1996: 13).

Some who initially supported the quota bills have swung into violent opposition because of the issue of minority representation. The two political parties that have derailed the passage of the Bill – the Samajwadi Party and the Rashtriya Janata Dal – have taken the position that, to be fair, the women's reservation Bill has to reflect the caste distinctions prevalent in the country. 'Gender justice, abstracted from all other forms of social justice, is an urban middle-class concept and, therefore, of little use' (*The Statesman* 1998a: 8). These parties demand that the 33 per cent quotas be differentiated by a fixed quota for women belonging to OBCs (Other Backward Castes and minorities). They argue that the quota Bill is:

> the creation of a new constituency which is not defined by social or economic criteria, strictly speaking, and whose characteristics are, in fact totally unknown – even the representatives of this [reserved] constituency would be unable to say what it is that women stand for and men don't.
>
> (*The Statesman* 1998a: 8)

Finally, there is the issue of priorities – whether the Indian political system faced with many challenges can also deal with another 'divisive' issue. 'The country is facing many serious problems ... it was not the right time to bring the women's reservation bill', said Prabhu Nath Singh of the Samata [Equality] Party in the debate over the Bill (*The Statesman* 1998b: 1).

Debate on the quota Bill has been bitter. Feminists and women's groups have come in for violent verbal abuse from those opposing the Bill. They have been caricatured as 'short-haired memsahibs' and as 'biwi [wife] brigades', and their agendas have been called divisive for the country. However, the debate has also provoked serious discussions about the requirements needed to make women's political participation meaningful, and how differences among women can be acknowledged while still demanding parliamentary quotas for women. Most of the arguments have been framed by liberal politics: an increased emphasis on education for girl children and women, gender-sensitivity training for police and bureaucrats, review of the functioning of family courts and various laws relating to issues like divorce, adoption and the share of property for women have all been aired as development policies needed to ensure women's empowerment. The question before the feminist groups in India is how this increase in women's numbers within parliament and at the local level will result in real benefits for women and women's movements.

Caste, class, gender: dilemmas for feminisms

If we examine the profile of the women representatives in the 1991–6 Indian Parliament, we find that they were mostly middle-class, professional women, with few or no links with the women's movement. A significant number of them accessed politics through their families, some through various student and civil rights movements, and some because of state initiatives to increase representation from the lower castes in India. This selective inclusion of women into mainstream politics has tended to maintain divisions within the women's movement, posing difficult questions for representation of and by women – between feminist/professionals and activists, and between women members of different political parties (Rai 1997). This is not to suggest that middle-class women cannot or do not represent the interests of women from other social categories. The party political system for one does not recognize representation of particular interests – political parties appeal to as wide a spectrum of the population as possible. However, just as party political systems do not always live up to their promises, ideological considerations do affect the policy initiatives of the parties. Consequently, women *qua* women, especially as members of mainstream political parties, are also affected by their political ideologies and careers. This influences the issues they bring to the public domain, or feel able to support. While the issue of caste/class does not translate easily into the policy debates, it continues to pose significant dilemmas for those who seek to represent, as well as those who argue for the importance of women in mainstream political institutions.

A survey of women MPs also suggests that these women have benefited from the growing strength of the women's movement, which has put the issue of women's empowerment and participation in politics on the national agenda. However, none of these women have entered political life through the women's movement. Their access to women's organizations is generally limited to the women's wing of their own parties. As party women with political ambitions, women MPs respond to the institutional incentives and disincentives that are put to them. All these factors limit the potential of women MPs to represent the interests of Indian women across a range of issues. As a result there seems to be little regular contact between women's groups and women MPs. The exception here is of course the women's wing of political parties. This does suggest the possibility that women MPs could facilitate contact between the party's leadership and its women members. They are also consulted from time to time by the party leadership on issues regarding the family and women's rights. However, non-party women's groups do not seem to be approaching women MPs (Rai 1995).

In the context of my discussion of differences among women, there are several interesting aspects of the debate about quotas in India. First, a consensus has emerged among women's groups and political parties that quotas are a valid and needed strategy for enhancing women's participation. We need more information about how this consensus came to be crafted and on what terms. Second, this consensus has been far more stable in the village and township councils, i.e. at lower levels of governance, rather than at the national level. We could ask whether this has something to do with the extent to which the *panchayat* level quotas have challenged social hierarchies, or is predictably about the reluctance of male elites to allow women into national-level institutions where power is concentrated. Third, at various points, the question of greater representation has been discussed in terms of women 'transforming politics' by representing women's interests in a deeply patriarchal society, especially in the context of high levels of political corruption (the expectation being that women are less corrupt than men). Here, we could ask, why are such burdens being placed on women and not men? More pertinently, given the discussion about differences among women, what are the philosophical reasons for greater representation of women in political institutions? Fourth, the question of differences among women was raised in the first instance by men, not the various women's groups. The result was a rather nasty and divisive debate where those demanding a quota for women were characterized as manipulative, Westernized feminists wishing to keep low-caste women out of the equation and therefore working against the interests of the 'ordinary Indian woman'. This serious charge was only partially challenged by women's groups that largely endorsed an undifferentiated quota strategy.

The high political cost that women's groups had to pay for assuming that issues of difference could be put to one side in a deeply divided social context raises questions about strategizing, and about the importance of dealing with differences among women within socio-economic contexts of great inequality. Here a consideration of the particularity of the political system becomes extremely important. In the Indian context, women's groups demanding quotas for women should have taken into account the long-standing caste-based quotas. Also, consideration should have been given to the new alliances and fractures among political parties operating in an unfamiliar context of coalition politics in a country that until recently had one political party (Congress) dominating the political system and setting political agendas. Why an alliance of strong, sophisticated and active women's movements was unable to do so is another question we could ask.

Conclusion

In making these points, I am not arguing against the need for greater representation of women in political institutions, nor denying the positive impact that such representation can have and has had. Neither am I in any sense intending to undervalue the campaigns and struggles on the part of women that have been necessary, and are still necessary, to make these advances possible. I am also not suggesting any easy correlation between class and social positioning on the one hand, and political behaviour on the other. My concern is to contribute to a more self-reflective analysis of what increasing representation on the basis of gender alone may mean in practice, and of what may be being erased in the process. For in India, and more broadly, the demand for greater representation of women in politics is taking place at a time when the conditions of women with the least access to resources and the fewest privileges are steadily deteriorating. I would argue further that this self-reflection is essential for a politics of alliances that women and women's organizations need to engage in now to be effective in a still largely male political terrain.

The Indian example offers many insights to women engaged in similar struggles in other countries and contexts. First, it points to the 'rethink' within the Indian women's movement regarding strategies of empowerment. A shift has occurred among these groups regarding an engagement with the state and its institutions. It is now increasingly seen as an essential part of women's struggles to improve their lives. This shift is so fundamental that it crosses political party lines, creating a new consensus on this issue. In the words of the doyenne of Indian Women's Studies, Vina Mazumdar, it is now accepted that 'politics is not a dirty word' for women. Changes in policy-making machineries are critical to the improvement of women's life chances (Rai 1995). Second, the Indian example points to the importance of recognizing levels of governance in crafting strategies of political empowerment when women seek to engage the state. The quota Bill in 1993, which provided for 33 per cent seats in the village and town councils, passed without a murmur from any political party. Yet similar demands at the national level tore this consensus apart. Disassociating empowerment politics from local politics provides an explanation as well as a context for this discrepancy. Third, the Indian example critically points to the importance of recognizing differences among women and women's groups. Because women's groups arguing for the quota did not think it strategically necessary to highlight the issue of differences among women on the basis of caste, they were wrong footed politically. Empowerment for whom became the issue when they had asked the question, 'Empowerment for what?' Finally, the Indian case shows that there is no simple correlation between an enhanced visibility of women in political institutions and a sense of empowerment of 'women' in the polity in general. It reminds us that the question of empowerment cannot be disassociated from the question of relations of power within different socio-political systems. In order to challenge structural impediments to women's participation in political institutions, we need to pay attention to the multifaceted power relations that contextualize that challenge. The debates on empowerment, and attempts to put them into practice, need to be opened up to these questions. Seductive as the language of empowerment is, it needs to, and can, be much more.

Notes

1 A version of this chapter was first published in *Democratization* 6(3) (autumn 1999), pp. 84–99. My thanks to the editors and anonymous referees for their comments.
2 For the particularity of right-wing mobilization of women, see U. Butalia and T. Sarkar, *Women and right-wing movements: The Indian experiences* (New Delhi: Kali for Women, 1995).

References

Agnihotri, I. and V. Mazumdar (1995) 'Changing terms of political discourse: Women's movement in India, 1970s–1990s', *Economic and Political Weekly* 30(29): 1869–78.

Bhatt, Ella (1996) 'SEWA', *The Times of India*, 23 October, p. 8.

Bystydzienski, Jill M. (ed.) (1992) *Women Transforming Politics: Worldwide Strategies for Empowerment*, Bloomington, IN: Indiana University Press.

Centre for Women's Development Studies (CWDS) (1994) *Confronting Myriad Oppressions: Voices from the Women's Movement in India*, New Delhi: Centre for Women's Development Studies.

Das, Soumitra (1998) *The Times of India*, 22 July, p. 5.

Fraser, Nancy (1995) 'From redistribution to recognition? Dilemmas of justice in "post-structuralist" age', *New Left Review* 212 (July/August): 68–93.

Friedman, J. (1992) *Empowerment*, Oxford: Blackwells.

Hoskyns, Catherine and Shirin M. Rai (1998) 'Gender, class and representation: India and the European Union', *European Journal of Women's Studies* 5 (3–4) (November): 345–65.

Kapoor, R. (1996) *The Times of India*, p. 11.

Karat, Brinda (1996) 'Vote for policies, not gender', *Indian Express*, 3 February, p. 8.

Kishwar, M. (1996) 'Do we need "biwi brigades" in parliament', *The Times of India*, 22 December, Review Section, p. 2.

McLean, Iain (ed.) (1996) *The Oxford Dictionary of Politics*, Oxford: Oxford University Press.

Matthews, George (1997) 'Restructuring the polity: The Panchatati Raj', *Mainstream* 35(22) (May), pp. 22–6.

Menon, Nandita (1997) 'Reservations and representation', *Seminar*, Special Issue on 'Empowering Women', 457 (September).

Omvedt, Gail (1993) *Reinventing Revolution, New Social Movements and the Socialist Tradition in India*, New York: M.E. Sharpe.

Phillips, Anne (1991) *Engendering Democracy*, Cambridge: Polity Press.

Rahnema, M. (1992) 'Participation', in W. Sachs (ed.) *The Development Dictionary*, London: Zed Press.

Rai, S. (1997) 'Gender and representation: Women in the Indian Parliament, 1991–1996', in A.M. Goetz (ed.) *Getting Institutions Right for Women in Development*, New York: Zed Press.

—— 1995. 'Women negotiating boundaries: State and law in India', *Social and Legal Studies* 4, pp. 391–410.

Shah, Gyandendra (1991) '"Social backwardness" and reservation politics', *Economic and Political Weekly* 26, pp. 601–8.

Staudt, Kathleen (1991) *Managing Development*, London: Sage.

The Statesman (1998a) 'Editorial', 13 July.

—— (1998b) 'Editorial', 15 July.

United Nations (UN) (1999) *1999 World Survey on the Role of Women in Development, Globalization, Gender and Work*, New York: United Nations.

—— (1996) *Platform for Action and the Beijing Declaration*, New York: United Nations.

Young, Iris Marion (1997) 'Unruly categories: A critique of Nancy Fraser's dual systems theory', *New Left Review* 222 (March–April), pp. 147–60.

—— (1990) *Justice and the Politics of Difference*, Princeton, NJ: Princeton University Press, pp. 183–91.

9 Gender, production and access to land

The case for female peasants in India

Reena Patel

Introduction

> The land goes to the men simply because they are men. Whether the son wants to cultivate the land or leave it fallow, he will still have the right over that land.
>
> It would be futile ... for a daughter to expect a share, for no matter how much one does, for as long as there is a son, parents will never give their land to a daughter.
>
> (Responses from women in the field, Orissa)

Land rights for women in India, particularly within the rural context, are crucial for women's empowerment for several reasons. First, the overwhelming dependence on agriculture for survival makes land the most crucial resource for all who depend upon it. Land ownership is vital to overcome dependence upon others for survival and subsistence needs. Second, the absence of a social security net (Guhan 1992) makes land ownership for women even more important for their economic empowerment. Third, land has significant socio-political implications, where its possession leads to power and prestige (Basu 1990). Thus, access to and control over land is vital for women's survival and empowerment in rural India.

This chapter analyses two separate legal regimes that establish women's rights over property in India – the Hindu Succession Act 1956 and the Orissa Land Reforms Act 1960. Focusing on Hindu peasant women, the discussion highlights the way these regimes *together* perpetuate women's exclusion from property rights. A deeper, critical evaluation of the law establishing Hindu women's equal property rights through succession and inheritance reveals that, although based upon liberal values of equality and fairness, it *reinforces* the religious/cultural ideology underpinning their traditional exclusion from land ownership. Land reform legislations, which explicitly seek to redistribute agricultural land and confer ownership based on the value of work, and the category of workers as male, furthers this exclusion. The chapter discusses the impact of these twin regimes on prospects for land ownership by Hindu peasant woman working on small/family-owned farms, and concludes that the regimes promote their exclusion as *Hindu* women both on the basis of succession and inheritance, and as *workers*.

Law has proved a vital site of engagement for those working toward women's empowerment in India (Kapur and Cossman 1996). The specific commitment of the postcolonial state toward social and economic transformation (Rai 1999) has enabled an active engagement with the constitutional and legal framework as a means for addressing the position of women in India (Government of India 1974). The numerous post-independence laws on dowry, *sati*, rape and areas of family law, among others, demonstrate this legal engagement.

The particular significance of property *rights* for women's empowerment has been acknowledged since India's independence. A compelling case for women's independent rights in land has been made by many, most notably by Agarwal (1994). Numerous policy formulations and official commitments, including legislation, have recognized the need to institute explicit legal guarantees of women's right to independent and absolute ownership of property. However, in a situation where acquisition of land through purchase is rare and difficult (Agarwal 1994; Basu 1990), inheritance and succession are particularly significant means for women to acquire ownership rights over land. For example, the changes introduced in 1956 by the Hindu Succession Act (HSA), established for the first time Hindu females' absolute right to acquire property through inheritance and succession. This Act not only changed Hindu women's status in respect to property ownership, it defined their share as being equal to that of a Hindu male.[1]

Notwithstanding these fundamental legal changes and the operation of redistributive land reforms, women's ability to own land has barely changed. Thus, more needs to be done if the law is to empower rural women. To that end, we need to *recognize* that legal guarantees are 'grounded' within dominant sociocultural and religious contexts. To the extent such contexts/frameworks exclude women's individual interests and place them in a subordinate position, legal guarantees are limited as a means of empowerment. Therefore, we need to re-examine the possibilities (and limitation) of empowerment through law. Such examination can lead to identifying, exploring and developing the contexts that offer increased possibilities for effective legal intervention. To do this, I explore the empowerment potential of recognizing rural women's work contribution and addressing them as workers in law. For Hindu peasant women engaged in subsistence farming, the transformative potential of law for improving access to land may begin to be realized through the recognition of women's agricultural labour. In so far as Hindu rural women believe they are entitled to certain rights as workers and contributors in agricultural production, the validation of this entitlement through law could be empowering.

However, whereas the limitations of law to bring about social change are widely understood as an outcome of the structural and institutional contexts/frameworks in which law is embedded,[2] the impact of cultural values and principles is less appreciated. Based on discussions with Hindu peasant women in rural Eastern India,[3] I highlight some of the limitations of legal entitlements founded upon religious and socio-cultural values. Taking land reform legislation in India as an example, I discuss whether there is a lack of recognition of women's work and contribution in law, reflecting a wider reluctance to recognize women's work outside the home. I conclude that a serious engagement with law as a means for empowering women through effective access to land must take account of, recognize and address women's material realities and interests as agricultural workers and producers as well as the larger socio-cultural system in which law is embedded.

This discussion aims to critically evaluate the specific contours of law's 'embeddedness' for rural Hindu women. By highlighting the principles upon which legal rights are framed, I hope to expose the conflict between avowed legal aims and prevailing norms. Further, I wish to emphasize that normative points of conflict, in so far as they are not addressed by existing law, continue to promote and entrench Hindu women's traditional exclusion from property ownership *within the law itself*. A critical reading of the legal provisions, together with voices from the field, permits a reflection upon the values, principles and norms (both implicit and explicit) that have a direct bearing on legal effectiveness, and provides insights into how to foster women's empowerment through the law.

'Personal laws' in India and the Hindu Succession Act 1956

The Indian legal framework distinguishes between different, religion-based, 'personal' laws. Consequently, an individual is governed according to her religion in certain 'personal' matters, including marriage, divorce, custody, guardianship, inheritance, succession, adoption and maintenance. The law applicable in these areas is a combination of traditional religious law, comprising of regulatory norms within religious precepts, as well as relevant statutory law. Whereas the rules derived from religious precepts are constituted by practices that have come to comprise its 'traditional' core, statutory law includes both pre and post-independence legislation and judicial decisions.

The historical processes culminating in the present regime of personal laws raise highly problematic issues regarding the engagement of the colonial regime with the native elite to establish relations of rule (Basu 1999: 249). Although the dichotomy between 'modernity' and 'tradition' defined much of the colonial project (Chatterjee 1993; Heimsath 1964; Desai 1959; Natarajan 1959), the colonial government also set up religion[4] as the determining principle for the colonized nation's future (Mani 1990; Basu 1999; Nair 1993; Sangari and Vaid 1990). The implications for gender constructions were particularly significant. Women's bodies became the site for fulfilling the colonial 'civilizing mission' while simultaneously allowing patriarchal hegemony to be retained by the native male population (Basu 1999; Nair 1993).

Lata Mani's work illustrates these processes for *sati* regulation (1990). Religious practices also defined the construction and settlement of debates on the issues of widow remarriage (Chaudhury 1990, 1993; Chakravarti 1990; Heimsath 1964) and prostitution (Oldenberg 1990; Nair 1993). In privileging religion within legal discourse, women were held up as pre-eminent signifiers in debates about 'tradition' – indeed they have been seen as its embodiment (Mazumdar 1976; Sangari and Vaid 1990; Chakravarti 1990; Chatterjee 1990; Nanda 1976).

The postcolonial state continues to adhere to this position. Witness the desire to seek legal legitimacy through religion evident in the debates in parliament during discussions about the proposed Hindu Code Bill in the 1940s and 1950s. Further, the continued existence of separate personal laws for Hindus, Muslims, Christians and Parsis within an overarching constitutional framework committed to social and political reconstruction and liberal principles is a clear contradiction. Notwithstanding guarantees of equality regardless of religion,[5] the constitutional declaration of secularism,[6] and the express objective of a Uniform Civil Code,[7] the legal framework upholds a contrary position. Thus, in 1957, the Supreme Court, in the case of *Narasu Appa Mali v. the State of Bombay*,[8] declared personal laws outside the scope of 'law' within the Fundamental Rights chapter of the constitution.[9] Thus, the foundational principle for these 'laws' continues to be religion, and not constitutional principles, even when they conflict.

The dominance of religious and traditional social structures and ideologies, combined with the liberal distinction between the private/public implicit in the Indian constitutional and legal regimes, has allowed the state and the law to limit the construction of the female subject within the discourse of religion and the family. Although it may seem that Hindu law in fact breaks down law's reluctance to enter the 'private' sphere of women's lives by addressing the family within the 'personal laws', the result of this legal regime is the exclusion of a large part of women's 'private lives' that the religious discourse ignores. Thus, the material aspect of women's 'private' lives in the domain of work and production, as agricultural workers and producers, is excluded from the purview of law.

Thus, Hindu women are governed by 'Hindu law', which today consists of 'traditional' or 'customary' Hindu law, pre- and post-independence statutes and judicial decisions (Derrett 1968; Mulla 1994). The traditional Hindu laws have been declared and interpreted through commentaries that came to be understood as the law. This dual legal system is meant to be complementary and not contradictory; traditional Hindu law may be modified or abrogated by statute (Mulla 1994), and statutory laws may create new rights and obligations or alter the existing structures in certain cases. However, a dualistic pattern has evolved, wherein people living in accordance with traditional Hindu laws, which have been incorporated within family and social structures, are faced with new norms introduced by statute.

Hindu women did not have a substantial claim to the inheritance of property under customary Hindu law, and even on the rare occasions when they could inherit, the estate was limited (Mulla 1994). The first statutory enactment to directly contradict this position was the Hindu Women's Right to Property Act of 1937. The Act awarded the widow, the predeceased son's widow and the predeceased grandson's widow a share (albeit limited) in the property of the male they survived. The provisions of the Hindu Succession Act (HSA), passed in 1956, overrode any of the matters dealt with in it and repealed all existing laws inconsistent with it.[10]

The HSA governs inheritance for Hindus today by codifying and amending the law relating to intestate succession among Hindus, giving equal rights to both female and male heirs (Mulla 1994). It sought to improve upon the earlier Hindu Women's Right to Property Act, which had for the first time awarded widows rights to an estate.[11] Further, the 1956 Act provides for the property of a female to be her absolute property.[12] Most significantly, for analysing legal empowerment strategies for women, the HSA guaranteed equal shares to males and females, and absolute estate to females.

Models, roles and identities

This section discusses some aspects of the roles, values and position accorded to Hindu women that are sanctioned and upheld by the legal framework. I argue that whereas the HSA aims to enable Hindu women to own property, Hindu cultural values undermine women's ability to own property, particularly land. These values constitute Hindu women as persons without individual self-interest, particularly in regard to property ownership, and as persons whose interests are completely submerged within the family.

In the HSA, women are addressed as daughters in respect to their interest *vis-à-vis* the father, sisters in relation to their right in conjunction with the sons, and as widows. The provisions entitle women to an individual share of property *within* each of these positions in the family. Thus, while taking the family as a relational entity, the legal provisions under the HSA nevertheless promote an individualistic notion of property, with the assumption that persons can act on their rights as individuals separate from the family (Sharma 1990). Therefore, the female addressed as daughter, sister and widow is *assumed* within the HSA to have interests and act as an individual separate from the family in at least three ways. First, as a daughter she continues to be a member of her parents' family socially, culturally and factually. Second, as a member of her parents' family, she has an interest, both perceived and legitimate, in her parents' property. Third, as a sister or widow, she has an interest in a claim even if this causes competition with her brother or son. Thus, a Hindu female's interest in property ownership is assumed to be based on her individual interests, rather than her family and/or other defining social relations.

How valid are these assumptions? Do they reflect the culture and practice within contemporary Hindu family and society? I believe they are in fact rarely borne out in the social reality of women's lives. As a daughter, a female internalizes the cultural devaluation of girls made clear by the explicit male preference in most Hindu households. A daughter's birth is not traditionally welcomed (Madan 1994; Mandelbaum 1970), and this preference continues today. At the birth of a son, drums are beaten in some parts of the country, conch shells are blown in others and the midwife paid lavishly. No such spontaneous rejoicing accompanies the birth of a daughter. Many households still perform ancient rites to encourage the birth of a male child. The practice of female infanticide and the use of amniocentesis against the birth of a female child is common

(Krishnaswamy 1996; Patel 1996). These practices also express the scriptural values, which require sons for religious rites, particularly the obligation and ability of sons only to perform ritual oblations for the soul of deceased parents (Krishnaswamy 1996).

The belief that a girl does not 'belong' to her parents' family, that she is a 'guest' for a temporary period, and that her 'real' home is with her husband's family reduces a young girl's presence in her parents' home to being a 'burden' to them. Madan, in his study of the rural *pandits* (Brahmins) in Kashmir, notes that an unmarried female (agnate) is always referred to as *amanat*, that is, as someone held in trust on behalf of her lawful owners. A young girl's upbringing is overshadowed by the fact that she is to be married and sent away to live with her husband and parents-in-law. A girl's membership in her parent's family is seen as undesirable at worst, and temporary at best. Before marriage, her parent's home is her home too, but, once married, she becomes a stranger to it. Moreover, the house of strangers, her in-laws' home, is supposed to become her home. In time, it does, as she begins to participate in domestic life. However, the position of the wife as a 'newcomer' or stranger never fully disappears, although she may acquire other positions such as mother, mistress of the house and mother-in-law over time (Madan 1994).

Marriage therefore bestows upon a woman the enduring status in her life. It requires her to relinquish her emotional attachment and expectations toward her parents' family and to develop similar sentiments toward her husband's family. The dominant role for the Hindu woman is as a wife but her position as a wife and daughter-in-law is subservient. The wife has to 'earn' her position and respect, bound by manifold duties and obligations (especially to produce a male heir), and strive to achieve the ideals inculcated in her for her 'happiness'. Her precarious position not only reinforces her insecurity, but also leaves her dependent on her brothers for defence against ill treatment by her in-laws or husband. The special bond between brother and sister is marked by this reliance.[13] Thus, from childhood to marriage and after, a woman's identity is defined in relation to others: as a daughter to parents, as a wife to her husband (and daughter in-law to his parents) and mother to her sons (and daughters)

This brief discussion highlights the social and cultural context of the 'Hindu family' in which the legal regime is embedded. This context limits Hindu females' 'individual' legal rights in practice. Although Hindu women have a statutory right to individual shares through inheritance, this right does not resonate with the cultural ideology, and women's lived realities, identities and interests. In the next section I argue that, in addition, the law also does not reflect the socio-economic reality of women's lives, as they are significant actors in agricultural production.

Women's work, contribution and access to land

The link between work, contribution and access to resources has been posed by Sen in his conceptualization of access to resources as an outcome of bargaining

(Sen 1983, 1987).[14] Within this, he argues that 'perceived contributions' affect an individual's ability to access resources. In the context of establishing a claim through bargaining, Sen points out that notions of legitimacy and reward affect an individual's access to resources. Thus, those perceived to make greater contributions to the common fund get access to a greater share of the resources. Sen makes the point that the *actual time worked* is not important, but the *value* attached to that work is. In other words, what matters is whether the work is *perceived* as contributing to the common fund or not, rather than whether it *actually* is crucial to the family's well-being and survival (Sen 1987). Agarwal (1994) extends this conceptualization to include self-perceptions as well. Adopting this framework, I will argue that the recognition or otherwise of women's work and contribution in agriculture influences their access to land as a resource. I will examine the extent to which law recognizes and values women's contribution to agricultural production thereby promoting their ability to access land.

In the broader context, the construction of the family as a separate sphere, apart from productive processes, is predicated on the assumption that women are located within the 'domestic' sphere, while men do 'productive work' in the public arena (Harris 1981: 50). Within this, the recognition and value accorded to women's contribution when they are engaged in household or home-based production is undervalued because this work is located within the domestic/private arena. The submersion of women's productive role within their role as familial nurturer exacerbates the invisibility of women's role in income creation or contribution to the family's survival and sustenance. Even when women are visibly engaged in agricultural production, the value placed on their labour and consequent contribution does not necessarily increase. In the Indian context, notwithstanding the large and varied amount of work done by women in agricultural production, the men are seen as doing the major jobs. Ploughing, irrigation and work involving physical strength are considered more difficult, and, consequently, men's work is more valued (Mencher 1993; Mies 1986). The dialectical relationship between the material context of women's relationship to agriculture and the land on one hand, and gender ideology (here related to the valuation placed on their agricultural work) assigns lower value to women's role (Mencher 1993).

The issue of land ownership and control has two very different implications in the context of women in agriculture. First, the relationship of those who do not own any land, but work on it as wage labourers for others, is a question of landlessness. Here the issue is one of redistribution or allocation of land through land reform policies establishing ownership and control for landless agricultural producers. Second, once land is owned individually, ownership may then be transmitted to heirs including females, through succession. Women's work in agriculture may be classed according to the two contexts: women working as hired labourers primarily with no land or insufficient land, and women working as cultivators on their own land or that of their fathers/husbands.

To the extent that women are engaged in agriculture as waged labourers, they are accorded legal status as their participation in agriculture is clearly identifiable and measurable, and legislation on minimum wages is readily applicable to women's as well as men's work. The evaluation of women engaged as cultivators on their own/family-owned land, on the other hand, is problematic on many counts. Is it domestic work, household work, leisure work or economically productive work in agriculture? The evaluation of their work is ambiguous, particularly its necessity for agricultural productivity and household income. No specific remuneration provides an index of the cost/benefit to the family.

In the absence of external factors separating productive labour from domestic obligations, the effect of others' perceptions based upon the prevailing cultural ideology about women's work is such that, *while women understand themselves as equal workers and contributors*, this does not ensure the visibility of their contribution. Although my informants considered themselves equal to men in providing for the family, they realized that this was not recognized as such by men or in the wider society. This, in turn, affected the *value* that they placed on their work, and undermined the legitimacy of their claim for greater access to land. Taken together, this has a direct effect on perceptions of women's agricultural contribution, which is consistently unrecognized and undervalued, and also perceived to be very low or non-existent. Hence, despite their hard work, women have little control over the primary means of subsistence, namely land (Mies 1986).

State policy and development programmes in India reflect and reinforce the non-recognition of women's contribution to agricultural production. Development programmes for women generally ignore women's agricultural work, focusing on women not as peasants or wage workers, but as property-less, petty-commodity workers (Mies 1986: 153). The fact that most rural women do not own land leads policy-makers to disregard the need for a precise recognition of women's work in agriculture. In this respect, the guarantees within the HSA and the potential for women to become independent property holders seems to have had little impact on policy-makers and implementers. In Orissa, a District Commissioner looked surprised when I asked if there were any programmes for women *as cultivators* or *peasants*. He responded by listing various programmes 'for the development of women', such as milch cattle development, milk co-operatives, basket making and the like. Women working in agriculture were clearly seen *not* as cultivators but as petty-commodity producers or engaged in allied activities.

Various studies have revealed the nature and extent of women's work participation in subsistence and agricultural labour (Saradamoni 1994; Mies 1986; Bagchi 1993) and the fact that women's involvement in agricultural labour is actually increasing (Government of India 1993). The absence of policies for women as independent providers/workers reflects the refusal to acknowledge women's agricultural work. This refusal is further reinforced by assumptions that women are 'dependants' who merely supplement family subsistence requirements. This cycle has led to women's own underestimation, not to mention the gross underestimation and invisibility of the women's work in official (and other) studies.

The non-recognition of women as cultivators and contributors to agricultural production is very closely linked to the concepts and means used to measure and enumerate women's work (Bagchi and Raju 1993; Beneria 1988; Sen and Sen 1985; World Bank 1992). Official statistics dramatically under-represent women's work. Although a complete accounting of women's work is difficult to determine (Bagchi and Raju 1993; Beneria 1988; Ahmed-Ghosh 1993), time allocation studies (Kaur *et al.* 1988; Saradamoni 1988) reveal substantial differences between women's actual work input and its enumeration in official studies (World Bank 1992; Anker *et al.* 1993). In the next section, I explore how land reform policy in India illustrates the non-recognition of women as workers and contributors in their own right within the policies of the state.

Land to the tiller: women and land reforms in India

India, like most Asian countries, is characterized by a high population density and small farm size in the agricultural sector. The average farm size is between two and four hectares, and despite redistributive land reforms (enacted through the 1960s) the distribution of farm lands remains highly unequal. The rationale behind the Indian agrarian reforms, as in many other countries, has been to give the ownership of land to the tiller. In order to improve agricultural productivity and the dynamism of the rural economy, landless peasants were given ownership rights.

In considering land reform, I am concerned mainly with land redistribution, which includes the distribution of land from households with 'excess' landhold-ings to households owning little or no land, as well as the granting of ownership rights to current tillers. The literature dealing with the merits, success and failure of land reforms in India is vast. While largely a story of failure (Appu 1996; Jannuzi 1994; Baxi 1986), there are also arguments for renewing the case for land reforms in South Asia (Quibria 1995).

Land reform policy in India illustrates the failure of state policies to recognize women as workers and contributors to agricultural production in their own right. It illustrates that the very process of under-enumeration leads to non-recognition of women's work, despite massive evidence to the contrary. Although land reforms were based on principles of *redistributive justice* (no concentration of land in the hands of a few), *empowerment* (control to workers over the productive asset, i.e. land) and *economic justice* (control over means of production to reduce severe indebtedness and poverty of a majority of the agrarian population), the principle of gender equity was ignored. The definition of 'farmers' or 'tillers' or 'tenants' was premised upon the male as the active worker/producer, built upon igno-rance of the nature and extent of women's work, particularly their contributions to the family/household's survival as a result of such work. Moreover, where women were taken into account, they were again treated mainly as 'dependants' or non-contributors to family/household income (Agarwal 1994). Further, although women play a key role, particularly in supervision of tasks on small family farms, which increases productivity through intensive use of less expensive family labour (Agarwal 1994; Quibria 1995), gender issues within land reforms have been virtually ignored. As Quibria acknowledges:

We know very little about the impact of land reform on (the) issue, a fact that ought to give us pause … faced by a lack of research directed specifically at the status of women under regimes of land reform, we are led to speculate on the status of women in peasant societies ….

(1995: 142)

The amount of land (ceiling) is awarded by family, defined as the cultivator, spouse, minor sons and unmarried minor daughters. Adult sons receive special consideration, either through additions to the total household land, or specified land in their own right. As Agarwal notes:

Underlying the ceiling specification is clearly the assumption that those who are recognised either as part of the family unit or separately (as with adult sons) will be maintained by the land allowed …. Under these enactments we thus have the extraordinary situation where *most states do not give any consideration, when fixing ceilings, for the maintenance needs of unmarried adult daughters and married minor daughters, while giving consideration to all sons, whatever their age or marital status.*

(1994: 219 [emphasis added])

Thus, a gendered analysis of land reforms demonstrates that women are absent as the target of desired goals and objectives. Land ceiling laws in many states explicitly overlook and ignore women as beneficiaries. They treat women as a 'dependent', without independent rights. Clearly, married daughters are regarded as belonging to their husbands' household. But what of the unmarried adult daughter? What is the allocation of land for her maintenance? In addition to creating a gross inequality between males and females, this practice also perpetuates the notion that the daughter is a 'burden' to her parents, while the son maintains or adds to the family resources.

Whereas the law may be considered to enshrine, legitimate and reinforce basic societal values, and yet sometimes spearhead cultural change (Baxi 1986), the land reform laws in India fail to introduce the necessary changes for women by questioning and addressing the gendered nature of land distribution. If one considers the potential of law to engender new values and generate changed expectations and attitudes, at best the land reform laws have missed the opportunity to foster more gender-equitable values, ideas and symbols. At worst, they have deepened the already entrenched notions of women as unproductive persons who have little significance for the family or nation's agricultural economy.

Conclusion

The inclusion of females' rights of succession to parental property under the Hindu Succession Act 1956 introduces a principle that significantly departs from traditional practices. At the same time, much of these successory rights remain unchanged by the Act. While the Act contravenes existing norms, understandings and attitudes by introducing a fundamental change in Hindu women's property rights, it simultaneously retains significant aspects of socio-cultural values informed by religious belief that oppose these changes. The law supports 'tradition' by locating women within the 'Hindu' family and identifying them as 'Hindu' women. In doing so, law sets up a self-contradictory position, affected by fundamentally opposite forces, which raise issues regarding the ultimate effectiveness of the changes themselves. As Parasher notes:

> Though India has not imported foreign laws for the family and religious institutions, it is nevertheless true that the modern state legislations incorporate principles that are quite contrary to the principles in traditional jurisprudence, particularly in aspects relating to women.
>
> (1992:31)

Changes in the legal provisions affirming women's equal right to parental property would require the identification of women's personhood independent of their relations to others in the family. Further, it would require the continuing identity of a woman as a member of her parents' family even after marriage. This would also require women, as sisters and widows, to compete with and thereby jeopardize their relations with brothers and sons, and the security they may expect thereby.

I have argued that, in fact, this is not the reality. The assumptions upon which the law is based continue to be unrealized, and in this the law itself plays a significant role. The law in fact upholds Hindu cultural ideology that reinforces women's subservience, dependence and familial role. There is very limited scope for the emergence of women's interests as individuals, independent of their social relations. In evaluating women's self-interest in land ownership, it would be difficult to conclude, therefore, that the law, both in its statutory expression, as well as inclusive of religious and cultural norms, fosters such an interest. While the law is ostensibly premised upon the existence of such interest, it in fact reinforces the ideology that excludes it. It is not able to overcome customary practices. Where the new provisions may be alien to a significant number of Hindu women:

> this leads to the perception of law as an imposition of alien values, and therefore makes the law ineffective in changing attitudes and values where the rightness of the law is questioned.
>
> (Parasher 1992: 31)

The issue of land ownership in India is difficult even when one considers only caste and class. Introducing gender makes it far worse, since the entire gamut of economic, social, cultural, religious and political forces that make up the patriarchal ideology are brought into play. Nonetheless, though gender bias comes into play over land ownership, I believe the separation of economic empowerment from socio-cultural and political empowerment provides a starting point for analysing the law's approach to land ownership. While these sources of empowerment overlap because land issues exacerbate other types of gender bias, a focus on land issues in their economic rather than ideological aspect may provide a starting point for critical evaluation of the law as a means for empowering women. Women's role and contribution in agricultural production could be such a starting point.

Where legislation to enable land ownership exists, as in India, to make it effective, new attitudes and expectations must be created, both on the part of women and of society in general. These in turn must be developed through tangible, material policy measures to provide a real basis for generating changes in attitudes and ultimately the effectiveness of legal guarantees. In the case of women and ownership of land within the agrarian sector, a gendered access to land requires law to create a basis of legitimacy on two counts: cultural and socio-economic. Enhancing and supporting women's role in the agrarian economy will allow for better access to the necessary inputs for growth. This in turn will provide the basis for women to negotiate control of the primary resource, land, by providing a starting point from which women can make decisions regarding resource allocation within their families due to increased recognition of their contribution to production and hence increased legitimacy of their demands.

The non-recognition of women's role in agricultural production has led to women's continued exclusion from land, which further excludes them from the view of policy-makers. Control over land by women must therefore be increased if they are to be considered by policy-makers as major actors in agricultural production, not merely 'supportive' ones. A gender-equitable land reform policy could endow hitherto landless female agricultural labourers with land as well as consolidating the ownership of those with titles to land. A precondition for the correction of the problem, therefore, is to recognize that women are in fact significant contributors to agricultural production.

The recognition of the work and contribution of women in agriculture, and as producers in their own right, not merely dependants or in supportive roles, would enhance gender equality within land reforms. A gender-balanced system of land ownership, thought to have been achieved through the Hindu Succession Act, must be established through the creation of a new basis of legitimacy. This must include the recognition of women's contribution to and role in agriculture at the same time that the entrenched cultural ideology that excludes them is replaced by new values. How this can be achieved remains a challenge to those who are committed to women's empowerment. The first step, however, is the recognition that legal change without attitudinal and material change will not empower those on the margins of society, including women.

Notes

1   Section 8, read with the Schedule, Hindu Succession Act 1956.
2   For example, in its Report, the National Committee on the Status of Women notes:

Over dependence on legislation to bring about social change is a characteristic, not only of our country, but of several modern societies, particularly those emerging from colonial rule .... *But it must be emphasised that legislation by itself cannot change society .... The judiciary has often failed to give effort to the principles under-lying legislation ... the executive has also failed to implement these laws or to spread awareness about them.*

(Government of India 1974: 39–40 [emphasis added])

3 The discussions were held with Hindu women engaged in agricultural production from three villages in two districts of Western Orissa, Jharsuguda and Sundargarh. The forty-three women included both landless agricultural labourers and peasant women from small farming households.
4 The official administrative process by which this was done included the Plan of 1772, issued by Warren Hastings, that Hindus were to be governed in (personal) matters by Hindu law, and Muslims according to Islamic law. This was rigorously enforced by the courts and administrative offices, leading to the necessity of compiling the neces-sary 'Hindu law' to be applied. For a critical account of this process, see Derrett 1968; for a formal historical account, see Basu 1983, Jain 1966 and Gledhill 1964.
5 Article 14, op. cit.
6 Preamble, *Constitution of India 1950.*
7 Article 44, op. cit.
8 ILR (1951) Bom. 775
9 In this case, the personal laws were challenged as being contrary to Article 14, the fundamental right to equality, and therefore void under Article 13, which provides that a law in contravention with the fundamental rights shall be void to the extent of the inconsistency.
10 Section 4, HSA. However, it does not touch or affect the law relating to joint family and partition, and the previous law continues to operate in such matters. Thus, for instance, the right of the mother or widow to a share on partition between the father and sons in a Mitakshara family or between the sons after the death of the father is not affected or abrogated by this Act. *Gopal Narain vs. D.P. Goenka (71) A. Delhi 61.*
11 Section 3, Hindu Women's Right to Property Act 1937.
12 Section 14, HSA.
13 The special relation between brothers and sisters, marked by the brother's duty to protect his sister and the sister's special dependence on him to do so, is celebrated by millions of Hindu males and females every year in the festival of 'Rakhee'. The festival is the celebration of the brother–sister relationship, where the ritual consists of a sister tying a piece of thread on her brother's wrist as a symbol of lifelong affection, in return for which the brother is bound by a duty to always come to her protection.
14 The 'bargaining approach' is a development of economic formulations of the bargaining 'model'. For detailed analyses and applications of the bargaining approach in various contexts, see Sen (1983, 1987); Agarwal (1994, 1995); Kabeer (1994); Hart (1995); and Folbre (1986).

References

Agarwal, Bina (1995) 'Gender and legal rights in agricultural land in India', *Economic and Political Weekly* (March 25): A-39–56.
—— (1994) *A Field of One's Own: Gender and Land Rights in South Asia*, Cambridge: Cambridge University Press.
Ahmed-Ghosh, H. (1993) 'Agricultural development and work patterns of women in a North India village', in D. Bagchi and S. Raju (eds) *Women and Work in South Asia: Regional Patterns and Perspectives*, London: Routledge.

Anker, R., S. K. Ghosh Dastidar, M. E. Khan and B. C. Patel (1993) 'Methodological issues in collecting time use data for female labour force', in A. Sharma and S. Singh (eds) *Women and Work: Changing Scenario in India*, Delhi: Indian Society of Labour Economics, Patna and B.R Publishing Corporation.

Appu, P.S. (1996) *Land Reforms in India: A Survey of Policy, Legislation and Implementation*, New Delhi: Vikas Publishing House.

Bagchi, D. (1993) 'The household and extra household work of rural women in a changing resource environment in Madhya Pradesh, India', in D. Bagchi and S. Raju (eds) *Women and Work in South Asia: Regional Patterns and Perspectives*, London: Routledge.

Bagchi, D. and S. Raju (eds) (1993) *Women and Work in South Asia: Regional Patterns and Perspectives*, London: Routledge.

Basu, D.D. (1983) *Commentary on the Constitution of India*, Bombay: Tripathy.

Basu, K. (1990) *Agrarian Structure and Economic Underdevelopment*, London: Harwood Academic Publishers.

Basu, Srimathi (1999) 'Cutting to size: Property and gendered identity in the Indian higher courts', in Rajeswari Sunder Rajan (ed.) *Signposts: Gender Issues in Post Independence India*, Delhi: Kali for Women.

Baxi, U. (1986) *Towards a Sociology of Indian law*, New Delhi: Satvahan Publications.

Beneria, L. (1988) 'Conceptualizing the labour force: The underestimation of women's economic activities', in R.E. Pahl (ed.) *On Work: Historical, Comparative and Theoretical Approaches*, Oxford: Basil Blackwell.

Chakravarti, Uma (1990) 'Whatever happened to the Vedic Dasi: Orientalism, nationalism and a script for the past', in Kumkum Sangari and Sudesh Vaid (eds) *Recasting Women: Essays in Indian Colonial History*, Delhi: Kali for Women.

Chatterjee, Partha (1993) *Nationalist Thought and the Colonial World: A Derivative Discourse*, London: Zed Books.

—— (1990) 'The nationalist resolution of the women's question', in Kumkum Sangari and Sudesh Vaid (eds) *Recasting Women: Essays in Indian Colonial History*, Delhi: Kali for Women.

Chaudhury, Prem (1993) 'Conjugality, law and the state: Inheritance rights as pivot of control in Northern India', *Feminism and Law: NLSIU Journal*: 95–116.

—— (1990) 'Customs in a peasant economy: Women in colonial Haryana', in Kumkum Sangari and Sudesh Vaid (eds) *Recasting Women: Essays in Indian Colonial History*, Delhi: Kali for Women.

Derrett, J.D.M. (1968) *Religion, Law and the State in India*, London: Faber & Faber.

Desai, A.R. (1959) *The Social Background of Indian Nationalism*, Bombay: Popular Book Depot.

Folbre, N. (1986) 'Hearts and spades: Paradigms of household economics', *World Development* 14(2): 245–55.

Gledhill, Alan (1964) *The British Commonwealth: The Development of its Law and Constitutions: India*, London: Stevens and Sons.

Government of India (1993) *Statistical Profile on Women Labour (Fourth Issue)*, New Delhi: Labour Bureau, Ministry of Labour.

—— (1974) *Towards Equality: Report of the Committee on the Status of Women in India*, New Delhi: Department of Social Welfare, Government of India.

Guhan, S. (1992) 'Social security in India: Looking one step ahead', in B. Harriss, S. Guhan and R.H. Cassen (eds) *Poverty in India: Research and Policy*, Bombay: Oxford University Press.

Harris, B. (1981) 'Households as natural units', in K. Young, C. Wolkowitz and R. McCullaugh (eds) *Of Marriage and the Market: Women's Subordination in International Perspective*, London: CSE Books.

Hart, G. (1995) 'Gender and household dynamics: Recent theories and their implications', in M.G. Quibria (ed.) (1995) *Critical Issues in Asian development: Theories, Experiences and Policies*, Hong Kong: Oxford University Press.

Heimsath, C.H. (1964) *Indian Nationalism and Hindu Social Reform*, Princeton, NJ: Princeton University Press.

Jain, M.P. (1966) *Outlines of Indian Legal History*, Bombay: Tripathy.

Jannuzi, F.T. (1994) *India's Persistent Dilemma: The Political Economy of Agrarian Reform*, Boulder, CO: Westview Press.

Kabeer, N. (1994) *Reversed Realities: Gender Hierarchies in Development Thought*, London: Verso.

Kapur, R. and R. Cossman (1996) *Subversive Sites: Feminist Engagements with Law in India*, New Delhi: Sage Publications.

Kaur, Malit, M. L. Sharma and S. Kaur (1988) 'Women and work in rural society', in T.M. Dak (ed.) *Women and Work in Indian Society*, Delhi: Discovery Publishing House.

Krishnaswamy, S. (1996) 'Female infanticide in India: A case study of Kellars in Tamil Nadu', in R. Ghadially (ed.) *Women in Indian Society: A Reader*, New Delhi: Sage Publications.

Madan, T.N. (1994) 'The structural implications of marriage in North India: Wife-givers and wife-takers among the Pandits of Kashmir', in Patricia Uberoi (ed.) *Family, Kinship and Marriage in India*, Delhi: Oxford University Press.

Mandelbaum, D.G. (1970) *Society in India, vol. One: Continuity and Change*, Berkeley: University of California Press.

Mani, Lata (1990) 'Contentious traditions: The debate on sati in colonial India', in Kumkum Sangari and Sudesh Vaid (eds) *Recasting Women: Essays in Indian Colonial History*, Delhi: Kali for Women.

Mazumdar, Vina (1976) 'The social reform movement in India', in B.R. Nanda (ed.) *Indian Women from Purdah to Modernity*, New Delhi: Vikas Publishing House.

Mencher, J.P. (1993) 'Women, agriculture and the sexual division of labour', in D. Bagchi and S. Raju (eds) *Women and Work in South Asia: Regional Patterns and Perspectives*, London: Routledge.

Mies, M. (1986) *Indian Women in Subsistence and Agricultural Labour*, Women, Work and Development No. 12, Geneva: International Labour Organisation.

Mulla (1994) *Principles of Hindu Law*, ed. S.T. Desai, Bombay: N.M. Tripathi Private Limited.

Nair, Janaki (1993) 'From Devadasi reform to SITA: Reforming sex work in Mysore state, 1892–1937', *Feminism and the Law: NLSIU Journal*: 82–94.

Nanda, B.R. (ed.) (1976) *Indian Women from Purdah to Modernity*, New Delhi: Vikas Publishing House.

Natarajan, S. (1959) *A Century of Social Reform in India*, Bombay.

Oldenberg, Veena, Talwar (1990) 'Lifestyles as resistance: The case of the courtesans of Lucknow, India', *Feminist Studies* 16(2): 259–87.

Parasher, Archana (1992) *Women and Family Law Reform in India: Uniform Civil Code and Gender Equality*, New Delhi: Sage Publications.

Patel, V. (1996) 'Sex discrimination and sex pre-selection tests: Abuse of advanced technologies', in R. Ghadially (ed.) *Women in Indian Society: A Reader*, London: Sage Publications.

Quibria, M.G. (ed.) (1995) *Critical Issues in Asian Development: Theories, Experiences and Policies*, Hong Kong: Oxford University Press.

Rai, Shirin M. (1999) 'Developing explanations for difference(s): Gender and village-level democracy in India and China', *New Political Economy* 4(2): 233–50.

Sangari, K. and S. Vaid (eds) (1990) *Recasting Women: Essays in Indian Colonial History*, Delhi: Kali for Women.

Saradamoni, K. (1994) 'Progressive land legislations and subordination of women', in L. Sarkar and B. Sivaramayya (eds) *Women and Law: Contemporary Problems*, New Delhi: Vikas Publishing House.

—— (1988) 'Women labourers, women cultivators and contribution to agriculture', in T.M. Dak (ed.) *Women and Work in Indian Society*, Delhi: Discovery Publishing House.

Sen, A. (1987) 'Gender and cooperative conflicts', *WIDER Working Papers*, WP 18, July, UN University.

—— (1983) 'Economics and the family', *Asian Development Review* 1(2): 14–26.

Sen G. and C. Sen (1985) 'Women's domestic work and economic activity', *Economic and Political Weekly* 20(17) (April 27): WS-49–56.

Sharma, P. (1990) *Hindu Women's Right to Maintenance*, New Delhi: Deep and Deep Publications.

World Bank (1992) *Report on Gender and Poverty in India*, Washington, DC: World Bank.

Part IV

The local/global, development and women's empowerment

10 Rethinking participatory empowerment, gender and development

The PRA approach

Jane L. Parpart

Introduction

The failure of development efforts to either ameliorate or eliminate poverty in much of the South has inspired numerous critiques of established development practice. In the 1960s and 1970s, dependency scholars blamed the South's underdevelopment on the North (Amin 1974). In the 1990s, another critique emerged, one more concerned with development agencies' power to control discourses and interpretations of development. Scholars and practitioners such as Arturo Escobar (1995) and James Ferguson (1991) argued that development discourse reinforced Northern, modernist assumptions about development and undervalued the knowledge and experiences of the poor, often leading to tragically inappropriate policies and practices. They called for a more people-centred approach, one that recognized the importance of local knowledge, and encouraged participation and partnership in order to empower the poor so they could challenge the status quo.

This critique inspired an interest in participation and empowerment that was initially taken up by small-scale alternative development organizations with a focus on small-scale, grassroots initiatives. These organizations evolved a participatory empowerment approach that emphasized social transformation, especially in small-scale, impoverished and marginalized communities. This approach emphasized the local and often rejected state interventions as unfriendly and even destructive (Friedmann 1992). By the mid-1990s, however, some mainstream development agencies began to adopt the language of participation and empowerment as well. Perhaps affected by the limitations of structural adjustment policies, participatory empowerment advocates in mainstream institutions argued that this approach would improve economic performance and good governance without challenging the status quo (World Bank 1995).

These different interpretations of participation and empowerment have been reflected in debates about gender and development as well. The gender initiatives of alternative development agencies, such as Oxfam and many smaller non-governmental organizations (NGOs), have generally emphasized the transformatory nature of women's empowerment efforts, particularly in grassroots, small-scale initiatives. In contrast, more mainstream institutions have tended to regard women's empowerment as a means for enhancing their productivity and efficiency within established structures and practices (Moser 1993; Rowlands 1997).

The contradictory nature of both the interpretation and practice of participation and empowerment raises several questions, both for the practice of development in general and for women's development in particular. Why, for instance, is participation and empowerment so comfortable for such diverse and even conflicting development institutions? How can the same discourse be acceptable both to advocates of social transformation and to those who favour reform within the status quo? Can such a slippery term be truly transformative? Or, paradoxically, could reform in the name of empowerment hold the promise of more transformative action at some time in the future?

In order to take up this challenge, particularly from the vantage-point of women, this chapter interrogates the practice and methodology of participatory rural appraisal (PRA). This set of methods and techniques emphasizes accessibility and practical, hands-on methods of enhancing participation and empowerment. It is popular with such disparate organizations as the World Bank, government development agencies, Oxfam and many small NGOs. Thus, PRA offers an entry point for exploring the apparent contradiction in the widespread enthusiasm for participatory empowerment approaches to development by institutions with such different and even conflicting agendas and goals. The chapter will investigate both the strengths and weaknesses of PRA and participatory empowerment, especially for women – one of the groups most often left out of development decisions and activities, and thus a group most in need of participation and empowerment. It also considers the possibility that the 'practical', experiential focus of PRA could benefit from a more explicit theoretical analysis, particularly the conceptual tools provided by political economy, with its focus on material structures, and poststructuralist debates about the discursive, relational and fluid nature of power and subjectivities.

Participatory rural appraisal: the new methodology

Participatory empowerment approaches to development have become a new mantra, promising solutions to the intensifying poverty and disempowerment in the South and to some extent in the North. The participatory methodology of Robert Chambers has found a particular niche in this approach to development. His participatory rural appraisal (PRA) methodology is currently the method of choice among a large number of development practitioners of various persuasions. Chambers's methodology thus provides a lens into the world of participatory empowerment approaches used by both mainstream and alternative development practitioners, and is an entry point for critically assessing this approach from a gender perspective (Guijt and Shah 1998; Mayoux 1995; White 1996).

Chambers has been developing his ideas and methodologies for the last fifteen years, and has had an enormous impact on the field of participatory development. His approach builds on the work of rural development specialists and the evolution of rapid rural appraisal (RRA), which emerged in the late 1970s. RRA called for greater attention to local people's knowledge, but still relied on the expert to obtain and organize this knowledge. PRA, which emerged in the late 1980s and is still evolving, shifted the focus from gathering indigenous people's knowledge to encouraging and utilizing their analytical skills. Western development experts are no longer seen as in charge of the development process. Rather, they become facilitators, aiming to empower local peoples so they can analyse and solve problems in ways that lead to sustainable development practices. This approach criticizes the top-down approach to development favoured by many Northern development practitioners, particularly more mainstream institutions. PRA advocates assert that the knowledge and analytical skills of the poor, whether formally educated or not, are crucial to both the definition and implementation of development in the South. PRA methods and techniques are designed to bring this knowledge to light, to integrate it into the development process and to empower those usually dismissed as marginal, voiceless and powerless (Chambers 1994b: 1254; 1997). As Chambers points out, 'PRA seeks to empower lowers – women, minorities, the poor, the weak and the vulnerable – to make power reversals real' (1997: 106).

PRA is above all a methodology that emphasizes experiential innovation rather than theories and abstractions (Chambers 1994a: 1263). It has developed a cluster of very assessable, easily understood techniques, usually with groups rather than individuals. For example, one group activity is called '*do it yourself*', where the PRA team learns a local skill and then participates in the activity. This provides an opportunity for local people to demonstrate their knowledge and upsets the usual hierarchy between the development 'experts', i.e. those who know and the local people, who supposedly have nothing to teach, and only need to learn from development 'experts'. '*They do it*' has local people interviewing, collecting and analysing data. This undermines the assumption that only trained experts can do this work and enhances local capabilities along these lines. '*Analysis of secondary sources*' encourages groups to evaluate information such as aerial photographs, maps of resource types and other documents. It invites collective analysis and encourages all members of the community to express opinions and be 'experts', whether able to read or not. Participatory '*mapping and modelling*' has local people draw maps and create models of social, demographic, health patterns and natural resources. The use of visual data gathering is regarded as particularly empowering 'for those who are weak, disadvantaged and not alphabetically literate' (Chambers 1997: 149).

'*Transect walks*' require local people to walk with the PRA facilitators around an area identifying local resources. Again, this destabilizes the dichotomy between the development 'expert' and local ignorance, reminding everyone in a very public way that local knowledge is often superior for discovering the problems and solutions facing particular communities. '*Time lines, trends and change analysis*' engage local folk in constructing chronologies of historical events in their communities, especially on subjects normally left out of historical discussions,

such as ecology, education and the experiences of women and girls. These techniques both raise issues that often fail to enter serious discussions and reinforce
the importance and depth of local knowledge. '*Well-being and wealth groups and
rankings*' requests groups of local citizens to identify wealth rankings of groups or
households and to point to key indicators of well-being. This is done with models
or cards for each household, so literacy is not required. This method also highlights local conceptions of power and status rather than definitions brought to
the field by outside 'experts'. The '*analysis of difference*' explores contrasts, problems and preferences by gender, age, social group and wealth. Again, it both
reveals the rich variety of local knowledge and reinforces local knowledge and
'knowers' as key informants in the development process. '*Story-telling*' and '*presentations*' of findings are also important, especially for groups, like women, who are
generally denied opportunities for public presentations.

These methods/techniques (and others) are often used in particular sequences
in order to maximize knowledge production and inclusiveness, especially among
the most marginalized. Triangulation also encourages feedback by cross-
checking sources of information at regular intervals. These methodologies are
designed to facilitate participatory data collection, analysis, planning, implementation, report writing and monitoring in order to empower broad-based
participation in development (Chambers 1994a; 1994c). At the same time, PRA
is designed 'to empower more than to extract, to start a process more than to
gather data' (Chambers 1997: 155).

Above all, PRA tries to bring the least privileged members of society into the
development process. Influenced by a liberal notion of power, Chambers
believes some people have *power over* others, but more due to past practice and
institutional structures than the inherent selfishness of those in power. The goal
for changing the powerful/powerless balance requires bringing the powerless
into the circle of the powerful and encouraging dialogue. Inclusiveness is thus a
central pillar of this approach. In order to include those with poor verbal skills,
many techniques emphasize visual as well as verbal participation. While
acknowledging the problematic potential of local power structures and practices,
Chambers argues that giving voice, whether verbal or through visual inputs, and
bringing the poor and better off together to discuss differences and identify
problems, will empower the disadvantaged and resolve conflicts. He admits that
local knowledge could be used in counterproductive and even unsavoury ways. It
could enhance biased 'traditions' and reinforce local inequality, or possibly be
appropriated by outside 'experts' for their own gain. Undeterred, Chambers
counters with the argument that sensitive, highly trained PRA experts can limit
such abuse by taking the time and care 'to find the poorest, to learn from them,
and to empower them' (Chambers 1994b: 1441, 1445).

While Chambers openly worries about the current popularity of PRA,
warning that formalism and practitioners with little understanding of PRA could
make a mockery of its goals and intentions, he believes PRA techniques can for
the most part overcome these dangers. As he points out, 'The challenge is so to
introduce and use PRA that the weaker are identified and empowered and

equity is served. Fortunately the tools available suit the task' (1997: 217). Indeed, he has developed several methods for neutralizing development practitioners' preference for top-down development and for maintaining awareness and sensitivity to power imbalances between development experts and the people (Chambers 1994a: 1256–7). While calling for more research on the 'shortcomings and strengths' of PRA, most reports of PRA, according to Chambers, have been positive (Chambers 1994c: 963).

Evaluating PRA, participation and empowerment: a gender perspective

Research on PRA has grown considerably since 1994, and we now have a better idea of both the successes and pitfalls of this methodology and approach. The World Bank has formalized its interest in participatory approaches and established a working group on the subject, although this is still hardly mainstream Bank policy (World Bank 1995). A 1990 study of fifty-two USAID projects discovered a clear correlation between participation and success (Weekes-Vagliani 1994: 31–2). More recent studies record numerous 'success' stories (Krishna *et al.* 1997). A number of scholars have reported considerable enthusiasm for participatory techniques in villages, especially mapping and transect walks (Kelly and Armstrong 1996; Tiessen 1997). Visual mapping techniques are particularly popular as they enable participation by illiterate people, who are frequently women. The mapping can reveal the gendered character of daily life. In a Zimbabwean resettlement area,[1] for example, maps illustrated women's focus on the home, nearby fields and the community while men paid more attention to roads, fields and pastures. The maps then provided a talking point for discussions of environmental use (Goebel 1998; see also Shah 1998). Group activities are also quite popular, although attendance often drops over time, especially by women who have little free time (Mayoux 1995; Wieringa 1994). Participatory methods thus often improve information gathering at the community level, and reveal gender differences, if the facilitators are sufficiently attuned to gender concerns (Mosse 1994: 498).

However, certain problems keep surfacing in reports from the field, and they raise some difficult questions about some of the methods and assumptions of this approach, particularly for women. While not wishing to undermine the very real contributions of PRA or the participatory empowerment approach, these issues need to be addressed. While many PRA advocates see such difficulties as teething problems that can be easily addressed by committed practitioners (Ngunjiri 1998), others are more gloomy about their implications. Francis Cleaver, for example, argues that:

> despite significant claims to the contrary there is little evidence of the long-term effectiveness of participation in materially improving the conditions of the most vulnerable people or as a strategy for social change. While the evidence for efficiency receives some support on a small scale, the evidence

regarding empowerment and sustainability is more partial, tenuous and reliant on assertions of the rightness of the approach and process rather than convincing proof of outcomes.

(1999: 597)

To address these concerns, we need to consider some of the problems encountered by PRA practitioners in the field.

One of the most significant limitations facing PRA practitioners comes from the methodology's focus on the local, which has encouraged facilitators to ignore or underplay the impact of national and global power structures, discourses and practices. Yet, even the smallest village has links with people and countries beyond its borders (Cleaver 1999: 603–4). Moreover, most development projects have to deal with government structures and officials at one point or another, and these dealings are often problematic. While there has been a move to bring participatory practices into government bureaucracies, most government officials have little understanding or empathy for PRA techniques, nor do they tend to believe the poor (especially women) should have a say in policy-making or programme development (Thompson 1995). This attitude is often reflected in laws. In Senegal, for example, Jesse Ribot discovered that the political administrative laws systematically disabled local representation, despite official 'support' for a community forestry project (1999: 26). Moreover, even sympathetic bureaucrats are frequently constrained by political and economic factors, such as structural adjustment programmes. Official support for a project means little when the budgetary constraints of structural adjustment programmes and economic malaise eliminate promised fiscal support (Mayoux 1998: 192–3). Moreover, male-dominated political and economic structures often inhibit women's participation in crucial decision-making processes.

The participatory 'solution' – more broad-based representation on government boards and committees – has done little to challenge national and regional power structures. An Oxfam project in Burkina Faso, for example, placed members of peasant organizations on a government/NGO participatory planning board, but discovered this had no observable impact on the board's planning agendas (Ashby and Sperling 1995: 757). Indeed, as Mayoux points out, 'the complex nature of gender subordination means that increasing women's participation may exacerbate rather than reconcile contradictions in the position of individual women' (1998: 181). The poor are rarely able to challenge national elites, and often require intervention by outside 'experts' who can insist on participatory methods and processes (interview, 20 September 1997, CIDA consultant, Masakar, Indonesia). This is particularly true when the representatives are women, as government officials often operate within a cultural context that undervalues women's opinions and contributions to public discussions (Mosse 1994: 498–9). Participation in bureaucratic structures by women, unless it addresses these rather intractable and often unrecognized assumptions, can do little to alter the gendered context in which participation occurs (Mayoux 1995).

Moreover, despite the increasing popularity of participatory approaches, development practitioners often have deeply held reservations about the knowledge and capacities of the poor, especially women. In Zambia, for example, despite strong commitment to participatory methods, the evaluation of an agricultural extension programme revealed male bias among the project leaders and difficulties dealing with gender issues (Frischmuth 1998). Goebel warns that many PRA 'experts' use the language and some of the methods of PRA 'without adequately acknowledging the complexity of social realities, or properly absorbing or practising the intended notions of "participation"' (1998: 279). Furthermore, some development practitioners believe in participatory development methods but find it difficult to give up their authority over the poor. They want to empower the poor on their terms. This heavy-handed approach is particularly apt to happen with women, as most development practitioners come from cultures where women's subordination, and need for direction, is taken for granted (Rahnema 1990: 206–7). As Heaven Crawley cautions, the language of empowerment and participation creates 'an aura of moral superiority' that can protect practitioners of PRA from criticism and 'critical self-reflection about the truth of their claims' (1998: 25).

Power structures exist at the local level as well, and these are much more complex and intractable than much PRA literature suggests. Indeed, even very poor, largely inaccessible villages have their own power brokers (Li 1999). Chambers's belief that these inequities can be transcended through persuasion, discussion and inclusion is frequently contradicted by reports from the field. Jesse Ribot, for example, discovered that local elites involved in participatory forestry projects in French West Africa had neither support from villagers nor an interest in participatory practices (1996). Local officials often reflect and support a gendered social context that dismisses women's contributions to public discussions. In such a context, simply placing women on project committees can do little to make them heard or to bring them into committee activities in a meaningful way (White 1996). Mayoux points out that 'statistics on co-operative and peasant movements indicate a continuing marginalization of women in mixed-sex participatory organizations' (1995: 240). In Zimbabwean resettlement communities, for example, Goebel discovered that in general village meetings 'women constantly had to be invited and re-invited for their views, while men regained control each time a woman had spoken' (1998: 284). Moreover, women committee members sometimes support the status quo because it legitimates their superior position *vis-à-vis* other women. A Zimbabwean participatory ecology project, operating through Zimbabwe's CAMPFIRE programme,[2] for example, was initially captured by the local elites, and the presence of women did nothing to challenge their control. When the team leader disbanded the committee and set up a more representational one, the project stalled for lack of support from the more powerful members of the community (Robinson 1996).

This example raises the issue of the relationship between the PRA team and the villages/region they are working in. Lack of familiarity with the community's power structure and cultural context may lead to problems such as those described above. The CAMPFIRE example mentioned above demonstrates the complexity of even the smallest communities, and the difficulties faced by the facilitators, particularly in the early stages of a project before community divisions are understood. However, even when the fault lines in a community are discovered, they may be very difficult to deal with (Robinson 1996). Cleaver points out that sometimes a narrow focus on establishing participatory institutions can ignore existing systems of distribution and undermine already effective distribution mechanisms (1999: 602). The specific historical experiences of communities may influence relations as well. In India, David Mosse encountered deeply entrenched suspicion about the motives of development practitioners. To his consternation, participatory methods did little to allay them (1994: 505). The informal and public nature of PRA techniques can alienate people accustomed to more formal patterns of communication. Moreover, non-directive, consultative approaches can be misconstrued, as can mapping, transect walks and wealth measurements when they suggest all too familiar interventions by government officials. These practices, when combined with ignorance of the local and national power structures, can undermine the potential for participatory work (Mosse 1994: 506–7).

As well, the collection of local knowledge and the fostering of local analytical and planning skills are a rather more complicated process than anticipated by PRA methodologies. Knowledge is not something that just exists out there, ready to be discovered and used. It is embedded in social contexts, exerted in relations of power and attached to different power positions (Scoones and Thompson 1993: 2). Control over knowledge is often an essential element in local power relations and structures. It reinforces local hierarchies and is often highly gendered. Participatory methods, with their stress on inclusiveness and voice, threaten this hierarchy of control over knowledge. As we have seen, in the Zimbabwean resettlement areas, women's voices were repeatedly ignored or silenced. This is a common report from the field around the world (Jackson 1997; Rasavi 1998). Yet the consequences of this pattern are not always easy to assess. Cleaver discovered that while few women attended meetings in a Tanzanian water use project, they spoke for the larger community of women while men spoke only for themselves (1999: 602). Clearly, the collection of knowledge is not a purely technical business; it is deeply embedded in power structures and struggles, and affected by material and cultural factors. This is particularly true in regions where development activities are well established and community leaders have learned the importance of presenting foreigners (or government bureaucrats) with the 'right' kind of information. The public nature of these transactions makes it all the more plausible that some knowledge and groups will be silenced (or forced to speak) by those leaders most able to control community discourse. Of course, the groups most apt to be silenced, or pushed into public disclosures, are the poor and women (Mosse 1994: 508–9).

Ironically, giving people voice does not always empower the poor, especially women. Control over knowledge, even through silence, can be an essential and empowering survival strategy for marginalized people (Mahoney 1996; Suski

1997). The ability to keep knowledge to yourself, to choose who you will share it with, can be deeply empowering. For example, members of secret societies gain power by their ability to decide when to speak, to whom and about what. The power associated with gossip and information, the ability to decide when, where and with whom it will be shared, reminds us that giving voice to women (or men), especially in public, is not always empowering (Gal 1991). For instance, self-control and careful speech are seen as a sign of honour and power among the Bedouin (Abu-Lughod 1999: 90–3). In Java, women's ability to control their speech and public behaviour is equated with empowerment. To speak loudly, publicly and carelessly is a sign of loss of respect and power (Brenner 1998). The public group discussions so central to PRA methods may thus be both disempowering and threatening for the more marginalized members of a community – often women.

Moreover, PRA activities do not always fit women's schedules or agendas. Mosse discovered that projects in India often assumed women would be available at central locations (away from fields and home) for lengthy periods of time. These requirements conflicted with women's work structures and limited women's participation in project activities. Collective activities often took place in spaces that were forbidden to women. Yet their lack of participation was often explained as 'natural' and so unremarkable. Indeed, at one project, women's presence at activities caused comments, but their absence went unnoticed (Mosse 1994: 512). Mapping and transect walks are often seen as men's work. The emphasis on spatial mapping in a Sierra Leone project, for example, did not fit women's concerns – they argued that 'the changes we need cannot be drawn'. Gender issues such as relations between men and women, or violence against women, were of no interest to men, and so did not get on the agenda (Welbourn 1996). Moreover, women do not all have the same interests. Social and economic hierarchies among women can undermine co-operation. Internalized notions of femininity and propriety may inhibit open discussions as well. Many women are reluctant to discuss sensitive issues like domestic violence or domestic quarrels in public forums. Indeed, consensus among women is highly problematic; many issues divide them (Mayoux 1995: 242–5). Sharing thoughts and dreams will not necessarily overcome these divisions, despite the best hopes of PRA supporters.

The need for specific skills training is also rarely discussed in the PRA literature. Yet we know women, especially poor women, often need specific skills if they are going to challenge existing stereotypes about their inability to plan and monitor activities. While gender planning has become more accepted in the literature on development planning (Kabeer 1994; Moser 1993), this literature is generally aimed at Northern experts or Southern experts trained in the North. Participatory approaches call for full participation in all phases of development projects, but they often underestimate the skills needed for such participation, especially report writing and evaluation – skills that poor women rarely have. Participatory projects, like all development projects, must submit frequent reports and budgets (Wieringa 1994). As a child-focused NGO in Uganda, Redd Barna, discovered, participatory projects require skill building and locally designed methodologies, and the time, determination and knowledge to put them in place (Guijt *et al.* 1998). Daunting as these requirements are for local people, they have been made more difficult by the current emphasis on results-based management (RBM). While designed to ensure project effectiveness, RBM creates obstacles for people who are supposedly key participants in participatory projects, whether among the rural or the urban poor. It forces project managers to employ specialists capable of obtaining base-line data and measuring project effectiveness against this data. This practice runs counter to more participatory development practices, as it requires highly skilled experts on indicators, the ability to handle figures and both numeracy and literacy. Thus, while the language of participation and empowerment spreads, development as praxis can undermine the possibilities of participatory forms of empowerment. Poor people are left outside the discussions; measurement and evaluations are once again the purview of the development 'expert' rather than local people, and women, with their lack of skills, are left outside the loop. This is a serious impediment to wholehearted, effective participation.

Conclusion

This overview of participatory empowerment approaches to development in Africa and elsewhere, especially the use of PRA, is not exhaustive. The successes of participatory empowerment approaches are undoubted, and they are important. However, the failures are also apparent and may go some way to explaining why these concepts and practices can be comfortably advocated by what appear to be conflicting perspectives on development. Mainstream development agencies have been committed to the market and reduction of the state, and any policies that shift state functions onto society without upsetting the status quo fit that mandate. Participatory empowerment approaches, with their emphasis on the local and their tendency to ignore larger political and economic structures, actually do little to challenge national power structures. It is no wonder that participation, as Rahnema (1990) points out, is no longer perceived as a threat.

This rather cynical assessment should not lead us to underestimate the very real importance of participatory empowerment approaches. Bringing the marginalized and the poor into discussions, as well as encouraging and facilitating local knowledge and analytical skills, is crucial to development both as an economic activity and as a personal and societal goal. However, the above research clearly cautions against a too-ready equation between participation and either individual or group empowerment. Gender inequalities, in particular, are deeply embedded in cultural as well as material patterns. Changing gender hierarchies and assumptions requires more than simply giving voice to women or including them in development activities. Indeed, many other inequalities are also highly resistant to change. If PRA is going to be more effective, we need to think in new ways about participation and empowerment, particularly for women. This will require the use of theoretical tools, as well as field experience, to design more effective methods and techniques to enhance women's ability and commitment to transform (or at least challenge) the cultural and material practices that reinforce gender inequalities. (For an interesting discussion on this, see Rugh and Bossert 1998.)

This rather daunting task will require melding theory with praxis in ways that address fundamental impediments to participation and empowerment while maintaining the accessibility and practicality of PRA techniques and methodologies. The challenge, it seems to me, is to develop a more nuanced and sophisticated analysis of participation, power and empowerment from a gendered perspective. This will require a thorough analysis of the way global and national power structures affect local contexts, as well as an understanding of the complexities and resilience of local power structures and relations. Power, with its discursive as well as material aspects, must be reconsidered as well. Moreover, the literature on multiple identities and subjectivities has much to tell us about the complex ways people, including women, seek to ensure their well-being in a changing world.

Participatory empowerment techniques will have to pay more attention to the way national and global power structures constrain and define the possibilities for change at the local level. Structural adjustment programmes, for example, have often hampered local and national development efforts. The participatory approach needs to develop techniques for analysing the way global and national political and economic structures and practices intersect with and affect local power structures. This will require more explicit methods for identifying these structures and their relationships with local communities. Interviews with key elites will be necessary and can only rarely be fully participatory. However, the increasingly globalized world we live in leaves no doubt that these elements must be incorporated into our analysis (Mittelman 1997). Moreover, the gendered character of these political and economic structures requires specific attention in order to understand their differential impact on the sexes (Peterson and Runyan 1993; Staudt 1990). This may seem like it is reintroducing the 'expert' and the hierarchies between 'expert' and those who do not 'know'. If carried out with due humility toward 'expert' knowledge and a belief in the importance of local knowledge, this need not happen.

Local power structures require more explicit analysis as well. One of the strengths of the participatory empowerment approach to development has been its focus on the local and its belief that even the poorest communities can understand and solve their own developmental problems. However, divisions are often ignored or underplayed by PRA advocates, who often try to avoid conflict, on the assumption that divisions can be overcome by full and frank discussion among all parties. This rather liberal, one might even say romantic, belief in democratic processes underestimates the intractable nature of many local economic and political structures. Moreover, sensitivity to existing social arrangements has often led to the uncritical acceptance of traditional inequities, especially those that relegate gender relations to the private realm, outside economic and political structures and thus to challenges to the status quo

(Fals-Borda and Rahman 1991; Guijt and Shah 1998). The wealth and status rankings and the time line techniques of PRA reveal the differential access to power and resources of men and women, but they offer little explanation for how these differences come about. To understand the forces at play, we need a more detailed exploration of the relationship between gender and local political and economic structures. We need to know how women and men participate in these structures; how some women are able to use them to their advantage, while others are silenced and marginalized. The conceptual tools of materialist feminists (Hennessy 1993) and gender and development scholars such as Kabeer (1994) and Moser (1993) offer some insights for this endeavour, particularly the emphasis on the gendered character of material and discursive forces and their role in maintaining gender hierarchies.

However, a focus on the material elements of power is not sufficient by itself. We need to understand the way belief systems and cultural practices legitimize and reinforce material structures. The link between language/knowledge and power is increasingly recognized as a central factor in development activities, particularly the power of development practitioners to define developmental 'problems' and 'solutions' (Crush 1995; Escobar 1995; Marchand and Parpart 1995). PRA techniques pick up on this critique with their rejection of top-down development practices and their desire to bring the marginalized into development discussions and plans. This is an important first step, but it is based on the assumption that giving voice to the voiceless will solve power inequities. Yet we know that the marginalized, especially women, can speak but not be heard. Moreover, speaking is not always a source of power. It can disempower if it removes the ability to control the dissemination of knowledge. To address these issues, PRA techniques need a much more sophisticated analysis of voice, and of the link between language/knowledge and power (Mahoney 1996; Suski 1997). This is particularly true in matters of gender that are deeply embedded in the unconscious and often presented as natural, unchanging cultural practices and symbols.

PRA methodology would also benefit from a more explicit integration of Foucauldian and feminist thinking on power (Foucault 1991). This thinking rejects the notion that power only happens when one has *power over* people, resources and institutions. This undergirds much of the PRA approach, with its emphasis on inclusion, on bringing the powerless into the circle of power. Many feminists argue that power has to be understood in more complex ways (Deveaux 1996; Rowlands 1997; Sawicki 1996). It includes expanded self-understanding, or *power within*. However, this kind of power does not inevitably lead to societal or even individual challenges to the status quo. For that, PRA will have to design methods that can help women to see that their lives will only improve with collective action based on *power with* others. Even more importantly, collective action will not be effective unless it considers the structural and cultural contexts in which it takes place. Participatory methods can surely be turned to this challenge, for its emphasis on participation leads readily to collective action. But action, the *power to* transform people's lives, requires a realistic assessment of material, institutional and cultural impediments to challenges to the status quo and strategic plans for overcoming these barriers.

Finally, the current interest in identity politics and shifting and multiple subjectivities offers some insights into the analysis of individual behaviour, and thus to empowerment (Grewal and Kaplan 1994; Sawicki 1996). PRA techniques are sensitive to the complexity of local conditions and the need to bring the marginalized into the centre. However, they fail to theorize the subject. Individuals are generally assumed to play a particular role in the community, when, in fact, they may play several, sometimes conflicting, roles. These conflicts can offer entry points for otherwise unexpected alliances. For example, women from the wealthier groups in a community may align more with their class than their sex, thus having little empathy for their poorer sisters. However, some women from this class may resent their treatment as women and could thus conceivably align themselves with poor women over certain gender issues. PRA techniques, with their multiple data sets, have the potential to reveal such complexities, but to do so, they must move beyond description to analysis – something that requires attention to theory as well as technique.

These rather preliminary ruminations on PRA and participatory empowerment approaches and methodologies are of necessity more an opening salvo for future discussions than a set of prescriptions. I argue that PRA techniques, particularly as outlined by Robert Chambers, and much of the writing on participatory empowerment, are under-theorized, especially in relation to power. They too readily assume participation can overcome deeply embedded material and cultural practices that legitimate and maintain social inequities. Theoretical critiques by scholars such as Scoones and Thompson (1993) and others have not been sufficiently incorporated into discussions of PRA. Indeed, Chambers seems to believe that theorizing is for scholars, but it is for the most part a waste of time for practitioners. He continues to emphasize the accessible and practical character of PRA (1997). I agree that the goals of PRA and participatory empowerment are laudable and important, particularly their accessibility for the poor and their focus on grassroots, locally constructed understandings and solutions to development problems. While often not explicitly designed to address gender issues (Guijt and Shah 1998), they have contributed to our understanding of grassroots women's daily experiences.

However, if these techniques are going to effectively challenge established power divisions, especially along gender lines, they will have to incorporate more nuanced understandings of power, particularly the connection between power, voice/silence and gender, as well as the material and structural forces at play. The challenge is to develop techniques that retain the accessibility and practicality of PRA, yet incorporate the insights of current thinking on the material and discursive nature of power. This will take time, effort and considerable experimentation. Some important efforts in this direction have been taking place (Fals-Borda and Rahman 1991; Jackson 1997; Goetz 1995; Guijt and Shah 1998; Lennie 1999; Rowlands 1997). More will be needed. However, one thing is clear. If PRA and participatory empowerment approaches do succeed in melding theory and practice in ways that successfully destabilize established power structures, they will certainly no longer be the darling of those people in the development enterprise who want to reform rather than transform the world.

Notes

1 The resettlement scheme in Zimbabwe was designed to provide land for African peasants – a key demand of the liberation war. After independence in 1980, the government set up resettlement schemes on unused or abandoned land. The programme has been a key element in the government's rhetorical commitment to land redistribution, although in practice the transfer of land to landless peasants has been depressingly slow.

2 The CAMPFIRE (Communal Areas Management Programme for Indigenous Resources) programme in Zimbabwe focuses on communal management of resources. It focuses on conservation through community-based resource management, decentralization and institution building, with due attention to ethnicity and gender. Originally focused on wildlife, CAMPFIRE projects now involve forestry and mining resources as well. Robinson was involved in the Sunungukai Tourism Project, in Mashonaland Central, which was designed to enhance the community's ability to use its natural resources through tourism. The project used PRA methods. It was CAMPFIRE's first attempt to develop non-consumptive tourism, with cultural interaction as a central focus.

References

Abu-Lughod, L. (1999) *Veiled Sentiments: Honor and Poetry in a Bedouin Society*, Berkeley: University of California Press.

Amin, Samir (1974) *Accumulation on a World Scale*, trans. Brian Pearce, New York: Monthly Review Press.

Ashby, J.A. and L. Sperling (1995) 'Institutionalizing participatory, client-driven research and technology development in agriculture', *Development and Change* 27: 753–70.

Brenner, S. (1998) *The Domestication of Desire: Women, Wealth, and Modernity in Java*, Princeton: Princeton University Press.

Chambers, R. (1997) *Whose Reality Counts? Putting the First Last*, London: Intermediate Technology Publications

—— (1994a) 'Participatory rural appraisal (PRA): Analysis of experience', *World Development* 22(9): 1253–68.

—— (1994b) 'Participatory rural appraisal (PRA): Challenges, potentials and paradigm', *World Development* 22(10): 1437–54.

—— (1994c) 'The origins and practice of participatory rural appraisal', *World Development* 22(7): 953–69.

Cleaver, F. (1999) 'Paradoxes of participation: Questioning participatory approaches to development', *Journal of International Development* 11: 597–612.

Crawley, H. (1998) 'Living up to the empowerment claim? The potential of PRA', in, I.I. Guijt and M.K. Shah (eds) *The Myth of Community*, London: Intermediate Technology Publications.

Crush, J. (ed.) (1995) *Power of Development*, London: Routledge.

Deveaux, M. (1996) 'Feminism and empowerment: A critical reading of Foucault', in S. Hekman (ed.) *Feminist Interpretations of Michel Foucault*, University Park, PA: Pennsylvania State University Press.

Escobar, A. (1995) *Encountering Development: The Making and Unmaking of the Third World*, Princeton: Princeton University Press.

Fals-Borda, O. and M.A. Rahman (eds) (1991) *Action and Knowledge: Breaking the Monopoly with Participatory Action-research*, New York: Apex Press.

Ferguson, J. (1991) *The Anti-politics Machine*, Minneapolis: Minnesota University Press.

Foucault, M. (1991) *The Foucault Reader: An Introduction to Foucault's Thought*, ed. P. Rabinow, Harmondsworth: Penguin.

Friedmann, J. (1992) *Empowerment: The Politics of Alternative Development*, London: Zed Press.

Frischmuth, C. (1998) 'From crops to gender relations: Transforming extension in Zambia', in I. Guijt and M.K. Shah (eds) *The Myth of Community*, London: Intermediate Technology Publications.

Gal, S. (1991) 'Between speech and silence: The problematics of research on language and gender', in M. diLeonardo (ed.) *Gender at the Crossroads of Knowledge*, Berkeley: University of California Press.

Goebel, A. (1998) 'Process, perception and power: Notes from 'participatory' research in a Zimbabwean resettlement area', *Development and Change* 29(2): 277–305.

Goetz, M.A. (1995) 'Institutionalizing women's interests and gender-sensitive accountability in development', *IDS Bulletin* 26(3): 1–10.

Grewal, I. and C. Kaplan (1994) *Scattered Hegemonies: Postmodernity and Transnational Feminist Practices*, Minneapolis: University of Minnesota Press.

Guijt, I. and M.K. Shah (eds) (1998) *The Myth of Community: Gender Issues in Participatory Development*, London: Intermediate Technology Publications.

Guijt, I., T. Kisadha and G. Mukasa (1998) 'Agreeing to disagree: Dealing with gender and age in Redd Barna Uganda', in I. Guijt and M.K. Shah (eds) *The Myth of Community*, London: Intermediate Technology Publications.

Hennessy, R. (1993) *Materialist Feminism and the Politics of Discourse*, London: Routledge.

Jackson, C. (1997) 'Post poverty, gender and development?', *IDS Bulletin* 28(3): 145–55.

Kabeer, N. (1994) *Reversed Realities: Gender Hierarchies in Development Thought*, London: Verso.

Kelly, P. and W. Armstrong (1996) 'Villagers and outsiders in cooperation: Experiences from development praxis in the Philippines', *Canadian Journal of Development Studies* 12(2): 241–59.

Krishna, A., N. Uphoff and M.J. Esman (eds) (1997) *Reasons for Hope: Instructive Experiences in Rural Development*, West Hartford, CT: Kumarian Press.

Lennie, J. (1999) 'Deconstructing gendered power relations in participatory planning: Towards an empowering feminist framework of participation and action', *Women's Studies International Forum* 22(1): 97–112.

Li, T. (1999) 'Compromising power: Development, culture, and rule in Indonesia', *Cultural Anthropology* 14(3): 295–322.

Mahoney, M. (1996) 'The problem of silence in feminist psychology', *Feminist Studies* 22(3): 603–25.

Marchand, M. and J. Parpart (eds) (1995) *Feminism/Postmodernism/Development*, London: Routledge.

Mayoux, L. (1998) 'Gender accountability and NGOs: Avoiding the black hole', in C. Miller and S. Razavi (eds) *Missionaries and Mandarins: Feminist Engagement with Development Institutions*, London: Intermediate Technology Publications.

—— (1995) 'Beyond naivety: Women, gender inequality and participatory development', *Development and Change* 25: 497–526.

Mittelman, J. (1997) *Globalization: Critical Reflections*, Boulder, CO: Lynne Rienner.

Moser, C. (1993) *Gender Planning and Development: Theory, Practice and Training*, London: Routledge.

Mosse, D. (1994) 'Authority, gender and knowledge: Theoretical reflections on the practice of participatory rural appraisal', *Development and Change* 25: 497–526.

Ngunjiri, E. (1998) 'Participatory methodologies: Double edged swords', *Development in Practice* 8(4): 466–70.

Peterson, V.S. and A.S. Runyan (1993) *Global Gender Issues*, Boulder, CO: Westview Press.

Rahnema, M. (1990) 'Participatory action research: The "Last Temptation of Saint" Development', *Alternatives* 15: 199–226.

Rasavi, S. (1998) 'Becoming multilingual: The challenges of feminist policy advocacy', in C. Miller and S. Razavi (eds) *Missionaries and Mandarins*, London: Intermediate Technology Publications.

Ribot, J.C. (1996) 'Participation without representation: Chiefs, councils and forestry law in the West African Sahel', *Cultural Survival Quarterly* 20(3): 40–4.

—— (1999) 'Decentralisation, participation and accountability in Sahelian forestry: Legal instruments of political-administrative control', *Africa* 69(1): 23–65.

Robinson, J. (1996) 'Searching for the "community" in community-based conservation: A case study of a Zimbabwe CAMPFIRE project', Masters in Environmental Studies, Dalhousie University, Halifax, Nova Scotia.

Rowlands, J. (1997) *Questioning Empowerment: Working with Women in Honduras*, Oxford: Oxfam Publications.

Rugh, A. and H. Bossert (1998) *Involving Communities: Participation in the Delivery of Education Programs*, Washington, DC: Creative Associates International.

Sawicki, J. (1996) 'Feminism, Foucault, and "subjects" of power and freedom', in S.J. Hekman (ed.) *Feminist Interpretations of Michel Foucault*, University Park, Pennsylvania: Pennsylvania State University Press.

Scoones, I. and J. Thompson (1993) 'Challenging the populist perspective: Rural people's knowledge, agricultural research and extension practice', IDS, University of Sussex, Discussion Paper No. 332.

Shah, M.K. (1998) 'Addressing gender issues in participatory programme implementation', in I. Guijt and M.K. Shah (eds) *The Myth of Community*, London: Intermediate Technology Publications.

Suski, L. (1997) 'Voices and absences: The subjects of development discourse', presented at the Canadian Association for Studies in International Development, St Johns, Newfoundland.

Staudt, K. (1990) *Women, International Development, and Politics: The Bureaucratic Mire*, Philadelphia: Temple University Press.

Thompson, J. (1995) 'Participatory approaches in government bureaucracies: Facilitating the process of institutional change', *World Development* 23(9): 1521–54.

Tiessen, R. (1997) 'A feminist critique of participatory development discourse: PRA and gender participation in natural resource management', paper presented at the International Studies Association, Toronto.

Weekes-Vagliani, W. (1994) 'Participatory development and gender: Articulating concepts and cases', Paris: Organisation for Economic Co-operation and Development, Technical Papers No. 95.

Welbourn, A. (1996) 'RRA and the analysis of difference', *RRA Notes* 14: 14–23.

White, S.C. (1996) 'Depoliticising development: The uses and abuses of participation', *Development and Practice* 6(1): 6–15.

Wieringa, S. (1994) 'Women's interests and empowerment: Gender planning reconsidered', *Development and Change* 25: 829–48.

World Bank (1995) *World Bank Participation Source Book*, Washington, DC: World Bank Environment Department Papers.

11 The disciplinary power of micro credit

Examples from Kenya and Cameroon

Josephine Lairap-Fonderson

Introduction

Micro credit is increasingly heralded as a means for empowering women in the Third World. Yet, these views are becoming less fashionable as the limitations of micro credit come to the fore, particularly its failure to reduce women's poverty or transform gender relations. My research on women and micro credit in Kenya and Cameroon suggests that the provision of micro credit to women in general, and to sub-Saharan African women in particular, acts more like a disciplinary power, turning them into 'efficient economic actors' to be inserted in the market economy, rather than a tool for their empowerment.

This chapter discusses the tensions between micro credit's potential to empower and to discipline. First, it explores the concept of empowerment, analysing why it came to be appropriated by the development community in general, particularly in Africa. Second, it discusses Foucault's notion of disciplinary power and highlights its relevance to micro credit and women's empowerment process. The third part uses the Foucauldian framework to evaluate the policies and practices of micro credit in Kenya and Cameroon. This is an interesting comparison, as Kenya was one of the first African countries to embrace micro credit, while Cameroon adopted it later. This difference reflects their different economic trajectories, and their impact on government and donor community efforts (or not) to fight poverty and gender subordination. The fourth section assesses the extent to which women are empowered as a result of their access to micro credit. The last part briefly compares formal micro credit schemes with grassroots ones, such as the rotating savings and credit associations, in order to evaluate their relative empowerment potential.

Appropriating the concept of empowerment

The concept of women's empowerment can be traced back to the emergence of the feminist movement. In the 1970s, increasing awareness of the deteriorating position of Third World women following the world economic recession brought the issue of empowerment to the fore. Despite its popularity, empowerment as a concept is difficult to define. Empowerment for one person is not to another, and empowerment in one part of society may not be considered as such in another. Applied to Third World women, the concept of empowerment has referred to many things: from increased participation in household decision-making and the market economy to increased capacity for self-reliance. It has been equated with women's increased ability to take over the responsibilities for social welfare services and other basic necessities needed for the survival of their families. Governments and most international financial institutions, such as the World Bank, tend to see women's active participation in the market economy as a sign of empowerment. They believe it can potentially improve women's employment opportunities, production and assets, as well as alleviating poverty and achieving sustainable economic growth. Most non-governmental organisations (NGOs), women's advocates and members of the donor community believe an increase in women's income enables them to provide for their families, reduces dependence on their husbands and, in turn, fosters self-esteem and greater participation in household decision-making. Similarly, the growing number of women's organisations has also been seen as empowerment, for organising is assumed to improve participation by enabling women's voices to be heard. Although these various conceptualizations emphasize different aspect(s) of empowerment, they nevertheless share one common feature – the belief that empowerment is above all a slow and dynamic process of women's struggle to gain power.

Micro credit emerged as one of the most widely accepted strategies for improving the position and status of Third World women. Micro credit is defined here as the small loans – often ranging from a few to a couple of hundred dollars – provided to poor women for investment in income-generating activities. Contemporary micro credit schemes are more likely to be from semi-formal financial institutions operating under government regulations. Their funding generally comes from donors and/or formal financial institutions that adopt a commercial approach to lending, i.e. they expect repayment. The popularity of micro credit is partly based on its assumed potential to improve the economic, political and socio-cultural dimensions of women's empowerment. This assumption has legitimised donors' and development practitioners' use of micro credit to promote Third World women's empowerment.

Many assessments of micro credit schemes trumpet their success. However, the experiences of sub-Saharan African women suggest that micro credit schemes rarely empower women in ways that fundamentally threaten entrenched gender inequalities (Karl 1995; Gordon 1996; Snyder and Tadesse 1995; Stichter 1985). In the market, the power of women micro entrepreneurs relative to men is negligible. In the home, despite their increased importance as providers, women are still subordinated to their husbands. In spite of their growing activism, including political activism, women and their issues remain marginalized or easily co-opted within the dominant political power structure (Wanjiku and Wanjira 1994). Despite the vague and unthreatening nature of the term, women's empowerment has been resisted until recently in sub-Saharan Africa.

African responses to women's empowerment

Some African intellectuals have considered the concept of empowerment simply another imprint of Western imperialism (Wanjiku and Wanjira 1994; Ogundipe-Leslie 1994). They argue that African women are already empowered – for the most part they have equal rights in post-independence constitutions across the continent. In Cameroon and Kenya, for instance, no laws prevent women from voting, taking office, getting involved in any economic activity, having access to credit or possessing and inheriting assets such as land. In fact, the problem for women is not legal, but one of inadequate enforcement in the face of inimical customary laws and practices.[1] In Cameroon, official rhetoric claims the sexes have a complementary relationship with equal responsibilities. In practice this is not true, and women contribute heavily to both family income and well-being. Their economic activity, however, is regarded as a duty and not a reason to end gender inequalities (Srujana 1996).

Many Africans regard empowerment, understood as a process leading to 'equality' between men and women, as a means for Westerners to interfere in their customs. As a result, while the donor community funded women's empowerment projects in Latin America and Asia in the late 1970s, projects in sub-Saharan Africa focused on promoting small-scale agricultural credits for men. Micro credit projects existed, but focused on small credit for handicraft and income-generating activities such as tie and dye, knitting, etc, implemented with a women in development approach. Micro credit schemes like the Grameen Bank, the Self-Employed Women Association (SEWA) in India, or BancoSol of Bolivia did not exist in Africa during the 1970s.

The worsening economic situation in the region since the early 1980s, compounded by the adoption of structural adjustment programmes (SAPs), highlighted the need to involve all sections of the population in the development process. More importantly, as donors increasingly channelled funds to grassroots levels, sub-Saharan African governments began to encourage the creation of women's organisations as a way to diversify their sources of funding. The concept of empowerment began to receive wide acceptance, and by the beginning of the 1990s it had become part of the political vocabulary in most sub-Saharan African countries. As a result, the number of women's groups and micro credit schemes increased dramatically in the region. Today everybody involved in development has appropriated the word empowerment: from women and their grassroots organisations, to local governments, financial institutions and the donor community.

The attractiveness of the concept of empowerment lies mainly in the fact that it legitimizes various policies and practices. Empowerment is economically, politically and socially useful. Economically, 'empowerment' is often equated with women taking responsibility for social welfare services abdicated by governments under structural adjustment programmes.[2] Women's high repayment rate has been seen as a sign of their economic empowerment. They are no longer seen as deserving special subsidies but as economic agents on whom profit can be made. Consequently, empowerment can be used to legitimatize charging women high interest rates on micro credit loans (USAID 1995; WWB 1995: 5–6; World Bank 1998). Some governments, such as Cameroon, are even trying to tax them. Politically, the concept of empowerment has enabled governments to deny polit- ical responsibility for ignoring women's issues. Instead, they make women responsible for the various insecurities facing them. Since the early 1990s, women have been urged to:

> save, create, protect and enhance their ownership in productive assets, upgrade their skills, get organised, influence decision-making, ensure that their needs are responded to in national budgets, collect, analyse and disseminate gender desegregated data on the economic contributions and needs of low income women.[3]
>
> (WWB 1994: 19)

Finally, women's empowerment, as it evolved since the 1970s, has been socially useful as it poses no serious threat to the existing status quo. In Kenya and Cameroon, for example, empowerment has provided the much-needed safety net for societies undergoing many crises: the long economic recession, the growing food problem and poverty, to mention a few. Micro credit has enabled women in Kenya and in Cameroon to take on more responsibilities without a commensurate increase in their position or status. In fact, as Sithole-Fundire and Ann Schlyter point out, while women's roles have been redefined to take on bread-winning, men's roles have also shifted from bread-winning to 'heading' the household. As a result, 'a man is still regarded as the head of the household even if he is not working' (Sithole-Fundire and Schlyter 1995: 60). This partly explains why most African men tolerate, support and/or even seek women's empowerment, especially as it reduces their own burden of providing for their families. However, empowerment is only acceptable as long as women remain fundamentally dependent on men. In Cameroon, for example, 'empowered women' are often blamed for economic and other social problems. Indeed scape- goating of 'rich, empowered' women is widespread across the continent.

Moreover, there is growing evidence not only of the precariousness of women's empowerment, but also of the increasing burden experienced by sub- Saharan African women as they take on more economic activities (Goheen 1996: 183; Gordon 1996). Yet, some researchers assume empowerment and resistance is happening in Africa because women are organising and producing more for the market (House-Midamba 1995). Just as research in the 1970s often exagger- ated African women's subordination, in the 1990s research often exaggerated sub-Saharan African women's empowerment. The danger with equating women's various survival strategies with empowerment is that little attention is paid to understanding the nature, aim and direction of women's struggles. This understanding requires a broader approach to power at both the macro- and micro-levels. It also seriously questions the nature, scope and extent of the empowerment process. Empowerment should mean more than marginal economic, social and political gains, especially when it has become clear that women rarely graduate from loans or move to more profitable businesses. It should mean more than marginal participation in the household, in the market or in politics, especially if such participation benefits men more than women. An analysis of micro credit's empowerment potential that ignores its complexity and the wider economic, political and social contexts will exaggerate its potential and ignore its limitations.

Foucault provides a framework for analysing women's empowerment. By encouraging a more individualized and localized analysis of power, Foucault's notion of power offers a good starting point for a better understanding of the way micro credit compartmentalises women from the top down and normalises them from the bottom up. His notion of disciplinary power illustrates the linkages between the macro- and micro-dimensions of power and highlights the way structures of gender and class inequalities are reproduced and, more importantly, how women struggle to resist them. The concept of disciplinary power is useful for analysing micro credit because it highlights the mechanisms of inclusion and exclusion that at a given time become politically, economically and socially useful in a power system. It also provides ways to understand the concept of resistance. Although Foucault has been criticised by feminists for ignoring resistance (see Introduction), his later work addresses resistance more directly. Foucault argues that power has two poles centred on the body. The first pole works through the 'anatomo-politics of the human body' that aims to increase docility, thus enabling more to be extracted from it (Foucault 1978: 139). The second pole of power, 'bio-politics of the populations', works through a series of interventions and regulatory controls. According to Foucault, 'bio-politics' allows governments to view their populations not as citizens, but as resources that must be efficiently linked to the requirements of capitalist development (Foucault 1978: 139–41). At the local level, micro credit works through the credit guidelines that increase extraction from women. At the macro-level, it works through lending policies and practices that exclude or include certain groups of the populations at a specific period in the development process. At closer look, micro credit reveals the characteristics of a disciplinary power, although it can be used to resist that power as well.

The relevance of the Foucauldian power framework

The regulations

At the macro-level, micro credit acts as a regulatory power, distributing citizens within countries according to their aptitudes as well as the uses that can be made of them. This regulatory power is inscribed in the policies and practices of donors, governments and financial institutions. Their biased lending policies demonstrate how credit has been used at different moments to include or exclude particular sections of the populations in the development processes. Various sections of the populations are selected and targeted with credit when their inputs are deemed necessary in the development process. Others are

ignored. Before the 1970s, for example, modernization theory focused on indus-
trialisation as the engine of growth in developing countries. Donors provided
credit for large-scale productive activities, such as manufacturing in Asia or cash-
crop production in sub-Saharan Africa. In the 1980s, worsening economic
conditions, the adoption of SAPs, food shortages, wage cuts and currency deval-
uations increased the importance of women's economic activities. Efforts to
target women were undertaken at all levels. Nationally, NGOs and government
bureaucracies supported projects to enhance women's economic productivity
and efficiency. Regionally, the Lagos Plan recommended women be 'trained for
their multiple roles as mothers, citizens and workers' (OAU 1982).
Internationally, the World Bank, Women's World Banking as well as the donor
community sought to integrate women into the development process and
supported this with credit.

   Although it is now popular to argue that micro credit empowers women,
empowerment is seldom put forward as the objective of micro credit. In fact,
poverty alleviation is the main objective for the proliferation of micro credit
lending in developing countries, and empowerment (which emerged as an unintended effect) remains a secondary rather vaguely stated objective. As the
experience in Kenya and Cameroon demonstrates, the proliferation of micro
credit programmes for women in sub-Saharan Africa is inextricably linked with
the declining economic situation, the adoption of SAPs and more specifically the
fight against poverty. Micro credit has been used as a tool to regulate women's
entrance into the market economy for the fight against economic decline.
However, the small size of the loans and the credit methodology tend to
compartmentalise women in certain sectors of the economy, further constraining
their empowerment. Because credit is provided on the basis of market rules (i.e.
creditworthiness), most women receive small loans that deny them an effective
power base.

The normalization/disciplining of women as economic actors

At the micro-level, micro credit acts as a disciplinary power, exerting a constant
pressure on women borrowers to conform to the market economy. The requirement that women's access to credit be used for the production of goods and
services for the market is not the only disciplinary mechanism. In fact, the most
potent disciplinary mechanisms of micro credit are the credit guidelines that act
as subtle mechanisms, effectively forcing women borrowers to conform to the
requirements of the market economy. The creditworthiness of the borrower,
group pressure, regular meetings, small and regular repayments, and the application of interest rates effectively work to ensure the maximum conformity to the
norm. Inclusion in a credit group is the first disciplinary force as only those who
can repay the loans are allowed to join a group. The training sessions and
compulsory savings are designed to imbue women with the values and expectations that will ensure that they take their place within the system and help

maintain it. The values of competition and achievement, both discipline and, more importantly, nurture entrepreneurial talents that will ensure women maintain good credit and participate in the market. Regular meetings provide the necessary surveillance for successful micro credit schemes. Other disciplinary mechanisms provide rewards and punishment. Images of new 'empowered' economic women are held up as models for emulation. Repayment is rewarded with new and often higher credit limits. Failure to repay often results in credit withdrawal – a powerful disciplinary mechanism.

In line with Foucault's conception of disciplinary power, contemporary micro credit schemes do not use coercion; they employ the power of normalisation to turn women into efficient market actors. Economic development based on market-based, private sector-led growth is presented as the norm. Micro credit becomes a way to promote homogeneity by encouraging women to work within the rules of the market. This makes it possible for policy-makers not only to increase the contributions of women, but also to increase, as Foucault would argue, 'the docility and utility of the elements of the system' (in this case women), thereby enabling more to be extracted from them. Without overt coercion, the market makes it possible to compare, differentiate, hierarchise, homogenise and then exclude women from access to other types of credit. Markets allocate credit on the basis of creditworthiness, and women are seen as 'micro entrepreneurs' with little or no creditworthiness. As a result, they have to be grouped and trained to become 'entrepreneurs'. Such homogenisation differentiates women from other entrepreneurs in the market and, more importantly, legitimises a hierarchy not only in the credit system, but also in the market. As a result, women are targeted with small loans and excluded from access to larger loans.

The market makes everybody visible. It individualises everyone and sets mechanisms of surveillance in motion. Within the credit groups, individual members often pressure others to repay loans so they can continue to be given credit. Successful women entrepreneurs often receive bigger loans, often with easier repayment schedules. But surveillance is not limited to individuals or women's groups. It binds the whole disciplinary system together. It works laterally between women as they observe one another, readjusting their attitudes in their quest to become good entrepreneurs worthy of credit and better financial services. Surveillance also works from bottom to top as women observe and try to respond positively to the policies of governments and lending institutions. In the community, women learn that credit only comes to those who succeed as 'micro' entrepreneurs and set up micro credit groups. Surveillance also works from top to bottom as financial institutions, governments and the donor community monitor and respond to the aptitudes and performance of entrepreneurs, as well as the various micro credit lending institutions.

Micro credit as a tool for women's resistance

It is misleading to portray micro credit entirely as a disciplinary power, determined to turn women into efficient market actors. Some improvements and gains (even if only marginal) result from access to micro credit. Although meagre, micro credit has provided the income to feed women and their children. It can make the difference between three meals a day rather than one. Foucault points out that power is not static and disciplinary power can develop a person's power. Indeed, resistance is inscribed in power as its 'irreducible opposite' (Foucault 1990: 96). Resistance is an essential part of the process through which oppression is transformed. Micro credit does have some potential for empowerment (political, economic and social). In fact, women often report reduced dependence on their husbands or male partners. As the experiences from Cameroon and Kenya show, micro credit can provide skills to negotiate within the system, even pressing for change. However, success depends on the level of resistance society mounts toward these attempts to wield more power. Consequently, we need to analyse how various strategies of resistance employed by women under certain conditions lead to different types of empowerment.

Foucault asserted that power and resistance are inextricably linked by arguing that resistance is multiple, changing and unique (Foucault 1978: 95). However, he implicitly avoided providing a theory of resistance. For him, resistance is inscribed in power as 'irreducible opposite', putting the active struggles of those at the bottom of power relations at the core of his theory of power, thereby avoiding the need to analyse them. He also argues that 'power is everywhere, not because it embraces everything, but because it comes from everywhere' (Foucault 1978: 93), thus making the concept of empowerment redundant. Nevertheless, feminists have found his approach useful not only to show how power disciplines women, but also to document the various strategies of resistance employed by women. Feminists have regarded Foucault's bottom-up, grounded and fluid approach to power as particularly useful for analysing women's empowerment.

However, it is not enough simply to document women's resistance strategies. History is full of examples showing that meaningful change is almost always resisted, especially when it seeks to reduce the relative power of individuals or groups. Empowerment should thus not be taken as automatically beneficial for women. It is not enough to define power as 'power to' or 'ability to', especially if such acts do not lead to a fundamental change in women's status relative to that of men. For example, you cannot say that the Kenyan Women Trust Funds empower women by creating additional sources of income and reducing their dependence (World Bank 1997a), if such income must be supplemented, does not feed the family properly or does not enable women to graduate from dependence on credit. This reminds us that the nature of 'empowerment' should always be analysed if we want to identify the processes that could progressively undermine gender inequality.

As we can see, although Foucault did not analyse finance or credit systems, his conceptualization of power is highly relevant to contemporary financial policies and practices, particularly their impact on women's empowerment. Based on the evolution of micro credit in Kenya and Cameroon, the next section investigates the extent to which micro credit has been used as a regulatory power both to include women in and to exclude women from struggles for power and economic development. It also questions whether micro credit empowers women and, if so, what kind of empowerment it provides and under what circumstances.

Disciplinary power of micro credit: examples from Kenya and Cameroon

Regulating women as 'producers' in the development process

The evolution of micro credit in sub-Saharan Africa has been closely related to a particular country's economic, social and political context, especially with the adoption of structural adjustment programmes. In the early 1990s, women constituted about half the total population of Kenya and about 25 per cent of its labour force. In the main, they were responsible for household costs, supplementary food, clothes and a contribution to the children's school fees (World Bank 1994). In Cameroon, women number just over half the population and about 23 per cent of the labour force. In both countries, women in rural areas were (and are) generally responsible for household food production and a substantial part of household upkeep. Moreover, female-headed households have increased dramatically in the last decade in sub-Saharan Africa. In Kenya, Thomas-Slayter and Rocheleau (1995: 14) estimated such households at 27 per cent. An additional 47 per cent of women managed the household while their husbands migrated in search of work. In 1991, women in Cameroon headed one in every twenty-five households.

This shift in women's role has inspired global efforts to increase women's economic contributions. Nation states are targeting women. In Kenya, for instance, the 1979–83 development plan identified women as a target group for income-generating activities. At the regional level, the Lagos Plan of Action (OAU 1982) and the OAU recognized women's key role in food production and recommended that they be made 'genuine economic actors' (para. 48b). At the international level, consensus that women bore the brunt of the social costs of adjustment led donors, including multilateral finance institutions such as the World Bank and International Development Association, to include women in all their projects. Grants helped set up NGOs to facilitate the flow of credit to women. Most African governments, realising that donors were increasingly directing their aid to grassroots organizations, began actively to encourage the formation of women's associations in order to attract more foreign funds. Women's organizations proliferated as a result. In Kenya, for instance, in four years, the number of women's groups grew more than five times, going from 152 in 1980 to 802 in 1984. Membership increased almost eight times from 528 in 1980 to 4,232 in 1984 (Maas 1991).

The first micro credit scheme for women in Kenya, the Kenyan Women Finance Trust (KWFT) was established in 1981, one year after the implementation of Kenya's first structural adjustment programme. The KWFT aimed 'to provide women with access to credit and technical assistance as a means of facilitating their integration into the economic development of Kenya' (World Bank

1997a: 1). Micro credit programmes have flourished in the country since then. For example, the Kenyan Rural Enterprise Program (K-rep), established in 1984, aims to promote growth and generate employment in the micro-enterprise sector by providing credit for lending and technical assistance to other NGOs. By 1996, the KWFT included 216 groups with a membership of 4,960 (World Bank 1997a). The KWFT's first loan averaged US$89 with an interest rate of 29.6 per cent.

Countries like Kenya that experienced economic difficulties and SAPs early on witnessed dramatic growth in women's organizations and micro credit schemes. During the same period, Cameroon shied away from promoting such independent women's organizations as well as 'outside-funded' micro credit schemes. In the 1980s, Cameroon's economy was still buoyant due to high oil prices. During the 1970s, Cameroon's community development plans severely restricted the formation of NGOs, especially those desiring outside funding. From 1986, Cameroon's economy deteriorated as oil profits declined and the debt burden rose. By 1988 they had taken on structural adjustment and liberalized laws governing NGOs in general and women's organisations in particular. By the mid-1990s, women's organisations and micro credit schemes were on the increase.

Kenya and Cameroon provide ample evidence of how micro credit has been used as a regulatory power to include women in the development process. Although economic decline has favoured its expansion, micro credit has not been made available to women for their own consumption needs. Women only get loans to produce goods and services for sale in the market. However, what types of economic actors are these micro-entrepreneurs and to what extent does micro credit really allow these women to enter the market economy?

Normalising women as marginal economic actors

Defining women as producers or 'genuine economic actors' places them directly in the market where they are subject to market discipline. As a result, women get small loans because of their low creditworthiness. The myth that women are non-economic actors has meant they are subjected to more disciplinary practices than other types of borrowers, especially male clients of banks.[4] There is a general belief that before giving credit to women, they have to be trained in certain skills such as banking, management and income-generating activities. The Grameen Bank's model, with its 'Sixteen Decisions', provides the most illustrative example, but few African credit schemes are so rigid. The Kenyan Women Finance Trust (KWFT) has no equivalent of the Grameen's 'Decisions'. While most African women know all too well how to work hard, women borrowers are still subjected to disciplinary practices. Potential African women borrowers must form groups. Group formation, the initial stage of market selection, constitutes another disciplinary mechanism as membership is based on the ability to repay loans.

The conversion of women into economic producers is done relatively quickly. Members in a group are more closely disciplined. Their loans must be repaid in twelve months. They have to attend weekly meetings, demonstrate their ability to save a proportion of the loans they are requesting and prove they can save for a period of time (eight weeks for the KWFT) before being eligible for their first loan. After a year and with a good repayment record, a group can graduate to bigger loans, often repayable in two years rather than the one year for first-time borrowers. As women graduate to bigger loans, the level of discipline is often reduced. Although the repayments and savings often continue on a weekly basis, the group meetings take place only twice a month. The culture of saving is a disciplinary mechanism that should be maintained throughout membership. In order to save regularly, women have to invest the loans in productive activities. The group is often used as a surveillance tool, to ensure loans are invested and repayments made. There are other procedures for monitoring loan use as well. Before the loan is approved, the micro credit institution investigates the viability of the stipulated business activities. Women often invest in familiar activities such as poultry schemes, fish marketing, beer brewing, marmalade production, hair-dressing and selling of processed or unprocessed foods. These are readily combined with household chores.

Both punishment and reward play an important role in disciplining the women borrowers or potential borrowers. A successful loan repayment, especially the first, brings graduation to bigger loans. These 'successful' micro-lenders are held up as models for emulation. Failure to repay often results in the withdrawal of credit. The same principle applies to institutions. When the KWFT repayment rate fell in the 1980s, funding was reduced until 1991 when reorganization ensured repayments rates above 90 per cent.

The impact of micro credit on women's empowerment

As we have seen, micro credit has received wide acceptance because of its assumed empowerment impact on women. This is based on the belief that credit not only enables women to enjoy economic autonomy, but also provides social and political empowerment. In most cases, women's empowerment is not only illusory but also often resisted in their societies. The impact of women micro-entrepreneurs is generally limited by the size of their activities and their markets. The magnitude of micro credit only enables them to produce marketable goods that are sold in their locality. A KWFT survey of loan use showed that about 90 per cent supported the selling of second-hand clothes and unprocessed food stuffs such as grains; the rest was spread almost equally between manufacturing (e.g. tailoring, wood workshop) and services (e.g. hairdressing, food kiosk). (World Bank 1997a: 25). Such activities use low technology, have low productivity and low returns. They offer little possibility for upgrading to more profitable ventures, particularly in the corporate world. This structural problem is exacerbated by the fact that their products are competing against cheap imports.

These micro-entrepreneurs are not entrepreneurs in the Schumpeterian sense. They can hardly be seen as agents of change, innovators who see opportunities and create markets for their products. Women's micro-enterprises seldom generate enough income to finance the technology that might lead to higher productivity, let alone to finance the new investments that would allow them to adapt their production processes and products to the imperatives of the global marketplace. Consequently, while providing women with some income, micro credit virtually excludes African women from large-scale enterprise. As a result, women micro-entrepreneurs (and many sub-Saharan women) have become highly dependent on credit agencies.

Despite this worrying situation, the discourse on micro credit is already moving away from scaling up its support for women, shifting to a focus on independent women's 'credit institutions'. It is argued that 'subsidies are not in the interest of women' (WWB 1995; World Bank 1997). The fact that women can save and repay loans, often at high rates, has been seized upon to propose that existing micro credit institutions should become self-sustaining, profitable banks. While the success of this approach is doubtful, it is based on an assumption that self-financed institutions would be more empowering than the current top-down micro credit schemes.

In general, grassroots financial associations are assumed to be capable of responding more to their needs. Around sub-Saharan Africa, there are many informal financial institutions, the most common being rotating savings and credit associations (ROSCA), known in Kenya as '*mabati*' or '*itega*' and '*tontine*' or '*njangi*' in Cameroon. Shirley Ardener and Sandra Burman argue that ROSCAs empower women 'by helping them to become to some extent economically independent of their husbands and boyfriends, and to create social standing for themselves within the community .... They are a natural vehicle for liberating and strengthening women in a very patriarchal society' (1995: 44). The Kiambu Women Beer Brewers in Nairobi-Kenya is a case in point. The beer brewers managed to acquire the initial capital and organizational skills, as well as the confidence, to deal with the formal authorities to acquire land, loans and, ultimately, substantial land-buying co-operatives (Nelson and Wright 1995). However, not all ROSCAs in Kenya or the region have the capacity to prosper like the Kiambu association, whose success was due in part to the fact that its members were 'relatively prosperous businesswomen' (Nelson and Wright 1995: 64). Before concluding, we might ask whether empowerment differs if it is an outcome of grassroots efforts or a product of a top-down (sponsored) project and if so in what way?

The dynamic of empowerment: ROSCAs versus micro credit schemes

Both micro credit schemes and the ROSCAs are often labelled in the literature as self-help organizations. However, there are two main differences between them. The first difference is in their links to formal institutions, and the second is in the purpose of the loans. Micro credit institutions such as the KWFT in Kenya or the Benevolent Community Education and Rural Development Society (BERDSCO) in Cameroon operate under government legislation. They have to register with local authorities. In addition, current micro-finance schemes in Kenya and Cameroon are closely linked to financial and donor institutions through funding and technical support. They are not, therefore, truly self-help organizations. They are to a large extent 'top-down' sponsored and fast becoming an integral part of global finance. In fact, almost all sub-Saharan micro credit schemes are heavily dependent on donors for their funds (World Bank 1997b). As such, they are often intermediaries between local communities and institutions of global finance. Unless they become sustainable banks, these links to formal institutions make micro credit schemes prone to disciplinary practices and more susceptible to co-optation. In contrast, most rotating savings and credit associations are grassroots organizations with few or no links (regulatory or financial) with their governments or other formal institutions such as the World Bank or donors. Although some ROSCAs have an account in local banks, their capital consists entirely of members' contributions. The rotating saving and credit associations are grassroots organizations formed by individuals who come together to further their interests.

ROSCAs seem to respond relatively more to their members' needs than formal micro credit institutions. Most are single-issue institutions, focusing primarily on the provision of small start-up capital to their members or performing other social functions such as financing an expensive consumption expenditure and assisting during funerals or weddings. Some ROSCAs take an integrative approach, combining their meetings with other goals such as family planning or education. However, because these associations develop in response to their members' needs, they tend to be more flexible about loan use and repayment (Ardener and Burman 1995).

I have argued that the credit guidelines in micro credit loans are disciplinary mechanisms to ensure loans are invested in market production. However, some women are able to resist this pressure by using part of their loans for unintended purposes, such as feeding and clothing their family and/or investing in the education and healthcare of their children. Because micro credit is provided for investment, using it for consumption is a form of resistance against the disciplinary power of credit guidelines. Such acts are permitted as long as the loans are repaid. I have noted that funding is often withdrawn from micro credit lending institutions with low repayment rates. Similarly, access to credit is often denied to women who default on their repayments and, in situations where group pressure is strictly observed, a whole group can be denied access to further loans if one member defaults on the repayments. In contrast, since most ROSCAs operate outside government surveillance and are free from dependence on donors' funding, they are able to show a greater degree of flexibility in responding to their members' needs.

One way to ascertain the scope and intensity of micro credit is to examine the proportion of a people who have been empowered as well as the sustainability of such empowerment. If empowerment is limited to an individual or a small group, it runs the risk of simply maintaining the status quo. It is important for many women to be empowered as collective resistance enables women to mount an effective challenge to the barriers constraining gender equality. Within this context, the ROSCA's outreach is limited to individuals or group members while micro credit schemes affect larger numbers of women. By bringing more women together, contemporary micro credit schemes also facilitate the exchange of information. Although micro credit schemes seldom assume a political identity, in the women they reach they foster a consciousness of their collective interests and the means to promote them. The weekly micro credit meetings often become the place where women learn to organize and fight for access to other resources, starting with larger loans. Most women's ROSCAs in Kenya and in Cameroon can only do so much for women. Their mobilization of funds as well as their potential for capital formation is often constrained by the group size as well as the nature and purpose of loans. Most loans provided are without interest rates or with very low interest rates. Micro credit institutions force women to save and increase capital formation by demanding high interest rates. Thus, they can reach more women. For instance, the KWFT in 1996 granted about 10,228 loans, far higher than any single women's ROSCA.

It is important to note that micro credit schemes and ROSCAs are not mutually exclusive. In fact, members of the KWFT demonstrate that both sources of finance can be complementary. The members of the Bahari group in Kilifi have used the KWFT meetings to form a ROSCA to meet immediate needs such as the buying of foodstuffs and utensils. They plan to use the ROSCA to save money and buy a lorry to transport their commodities. The K-rep also uses the Chikola schemes to provide credit to individual entrepreneurs through ROSCAs (World Bank 1997a).

Conclusion

Women's experiences with micro credit suggest that although both Kenya and Cameroon embraced empowerment and adopted micro credit at different periods, their underlying reasons for doing so remain the same. Women were offered access to micro credit due to a particular set of circumstances: the economic crises, the adoption of structural adjustment programmes, the fight against poverty, the donors' recognition of women's deteriorating status and the realisation by the Kenyan and Cameroon states that women's groups could help diversify their sources of finance and that they could no longer afford to ignore the input of women in the development process. Kenyan women have a longer experience with micro credit as well as a higher level of activism than their Cameroonian counterparts. In Kenya, micro credit has become a major issue around which women are mobilizing support for resistance to their subordination. Thus, micro credit is increasingly part of local politics. However, while such long experience has enabled Kenyan women to enjoy some economic empowerment, this has often been marginal and short term. The women's movement in Kenya is better organized and speaks more openly against gender inequalities than the rather young women's movement in Cameroon, which only started to organise in the late 1990s. However, it is progressively asserting an independent status from the dominant political party. From the foregoing discussion, five conclusions can be drawn.

First, although micro credit has often been hailed as a tool for sub-Saharan African women's empowerment, the examples from Kenya and Cameroon suggest that it works more like a disciplinary power, inserting women in the market economy as efficient producers. The point here is not to downplay the gains made by women as a result of their access to credit. However, my exami-nation of the nature and extent of such gains suggests that the empowerment potential of current micro credit is slow to advance the eradication of (or chal-lenge to) gender subordination in sub-Saharan African society. Women's empowerment is often illusory, their burdens having increased rather than diminished. Although there are successful businesswomen in Kenya and Cameroon at all levels, they still have to adhere to social norms that idealize women's roles as mothers and wives. Even when the whole family depends on the micro activities of women, the male partners rarely take on the burden of the household chores. Consequently, women cope through various organizations and especially with the help of their children. This is important for our analysis of empowerment, since future generations must build on past accomplishments. If children, especially girls, cannot benefit from their mothers' gains because they have to give up school to help, individual empowerment of the present generation holds little promise for the future.

The second conclusion flows from the myth that sub-Saharan African women are non-economic actors, in spite of strong evidence to the contrary. Such assumptions have led to the imposition of 'unnecessary' disciplinary practices on women creditors. In addition, grouping women for the purpose of ensuring loan repayment goes against the market principles that micro credit is intended to impart. Market principles are based on individual freedoms (of choice, enter-prise, etc.) as opposed to grouping women together. This new form of 'collectivisation', reminiscent of the '*harambee*' or the popular participation approach adopted by the Kenyan government after independence, raises impor-tant questions about governments' and donor agencies' willingness to truly assist women's entry into the market.

The third conclusion draws attention to the fact that the condition provided by micro credit for a rapid growth of women's empowerment has not been propitious, at least in Kenya and Cameroon. Micro credit enables women to earn or increase their income, thereby increasing their bargaining power within the households. However, this income rarely allows them to meet their social and economic responsibilities, especially since the economic decline of the 1980s.[5] The income from women's micro credit activities often does not feed their chil-dren, let alone facilitate a move to more productive activities. Most women members of micro credit schemes want more credit, both in size and outreach. Women have demonstrated their ability to repay their debts, even at high interest rates. Given access to more credit, women could potentially adopt new tech-nology and, eventually, graduate from credit, much as capitalists did in the North (Baran and Sweezy 1966). However, whatever the size of credit, the multidimensionality of women's empowerment requires that economic empowerment be consolidated by commensurate social and political empowerment.

The fourth conclusion draws attention to the crucial role played by larger economic forces, particularly as a spur to the appropriation of empowerment by African governments. Micro credit emerged within the context of structural adjustment programmes and formed part of the neo-liberal global project of integrating women in the market economy.

Last, we need to reconceptualize empowerment so it can account for the scope, direction and intensity of any empowerment process. Only then can we determine whether the outcome of a particular empowerment project or policy will be beneficial. Empowerment is defined here as the entrenched capacity of people to act individually and/or collectively in the ongoing struggle to achieve equality and social justice. This definition focuses on people's capacity to improve their social position, but more importantly their ability to successfully undertake fundamental and sustainable change in their power relations. Micro credit has been held up as a tool for women's empowerment. This chapter reminds us that empowerment cannot be achieved unless it does achieve equality and social justice for women (and men).

Notes

1   In Kenya, among the Kikuyu for example, customary laws prevent women from inheriting land (which effectively constrains their access to credit).
2   In Cameroon, for example, the population in general and women in particular, in their role as 'caretakers', must procure all drugs, bandages, syringes, etc. before they can expect medical treatment, even in an emergency.
3   The Women's World Banking (WWB) disseminates information about policies pertinent to micro-financing (WWB 1995: 11).
4   African women were producers and economic actors long before colonialism. They were important market players, exchanging their produce on the local markets for goods they could not produce.
5   In July 1991, Kenya devaluated its currency by 32 per cent, a further 37 per cent in June 1992 and again in February 1993 by 27 per cent. In 1994, Cameroon devaluated its currency by 50 per cent (World Bank 1994).

References

Ardener, S. and S. Burman (1995) *Money Go Rounds: The Importance of Rotating Saving and Credit Associations for Women*, London: Berg Publisher Ltd.

Baran P.A. and P.M. Sweezy (1966) *Monopoly Capital: An Essay on the American Economic and Social Order*, New York: Monthly Review Press.

Foucault, M. (1990) *The History of Sexuality*, New York: Vintage Books.

—— (1978) *Discipline and Punish*, trans. A. Sheridan, New York: Vintage Books.

Goheen, M. (1996) *Men Own the Fields, Women Own the Crops: Gender and Power in the Cameroon Grassfields*, Madison: The University of Wisconsin Press.

Gordon, A.A. (1996) *Transforming Capitalism and Patriarchy: Gender and Development in Africa*. Boulder, CO: Lynne Reinner Publishers.

House-Midamba, Bessie (1995) 'Traders and the struggle for economic empowerment in Kenya', in B. House-Midamba and F. Ekechi (eds) *African Market Women and Economic Power: The Role of Women in African Economic Development*, London: Greenwood Press.

Karl, M. (1995) *Women, Empowerment: Participation and Decision Making*, London: Zed Press.

Maas, M. (1991) *Women's Social Economic Projects, Report No. 37*, Leiden, the Netherlands: African Studies Centre.

Nelson, N. and S. Wright (eds) (1995) *Power and Participatory Development: Theory and Practice*, London: Intermediate Technology Publications.

Ogundipe-Leslie, Trenton Molara (1994) *Re-creating Ourselves: African Women and Critical Transformation*, NJ: Africa World Press.

Organisation of African Unity (OAU) (1982) *Lagos Plan of Action for the Economic Development of Africa 1980-2000*, 2nd revised edn, Geneva: International Institute for Labour Studies.

Sithole-Fundire, Sylvia, Agnes Zhou, Anita Larsson and Ann Schlyter (eds) (1995) *Gender Research on Urbanization, Housing, Planning and Everyday Life*, Harare, Zimbabwe and Uppsala, Sweden: Zimbabwe Women's Resource Centre and Network and Nordic Africa Institute.

Snyder, M.C. and M. Tadesse (1995) *African Women and Development: A History. The Story of the African Training and Research Center for Women and the United Nations Economic Commission for Africa*, London: Zed Press.

Srujana, K. (1996) *Status of Women in Kenya: A Sociological Study*, Delhi: Kali Publications.

Stichter, Sharon (1985) *Migrant Laborers*, Cambridge: Cambridge University Press.

Thomas-Slayter, Barbara and D. Rocheleau (1995) *Gender, Environment and Development in Kenya: A Grassroots Perspective*, Boulder, CO: Lynne Reinner Publishers.

United States Agency for International Development (USAID) (1995) *Principle of Financially Viable Lending to Poor Entrepreneurs*, Washington, DC: USAID.

Wanjiku, M.K. and M. Wanjira (eds) (1994) *The Road to Empowerment* New York: FEMNET.

Women's World Banking (WWB) (1995) *The Missing Links: Financial Systems that Work for the Majority*, New York: WWB Publication Ltd.

—— (1994) *What Works: A Women's World Banking Newsletter*, New York: WWB Publication Ltd.

World Bank (1998) *Sustainable Banking with the Poor. An Inventory of Microfinance in Western and West Central Africa*, Washington, DC: World Bank.

—— (1997a) *Kenya Women Finance Trust: A Case Study of Micro-finance Scheme*, Washington, DC: World Bank.

—— (1997b) *Sustainable Banking with the Poor. An Inventory of Microfinance Institutions in East, Central and South Africa*, Washington, DC: World Bank.

—— (1994) *World Development Indicators*, Washington, DC: World Bank.

12 Development, demographic and feminist agendas

Depoliticizing empowerment in a Tanzanian family planning project

Lisa Ann Richey

Introduction

In the post-Cairo and post-Beijing environment, 'women's reproductive health' has emerged as a crucial site for negotiation between *development, demographic* and *feminist* agendas. Because these strategies are often ambiguous and may even conflict, struggles over interpretation arise in implementation, with implications for women's empowerment. This chapter examines an NGO-run integrated family planning project in Tanzania as an entry point for illustrating how competing agendas, embedded within a web of relationships – international donors, states, non-governmental organizations (NGOs) and local recipients – manifest themselves in local implementation. The Integrated Project on Family Planning, Nutrition and Parasite Control, known as the Integrated Project, has been operating in Tanzania since 1984. It has tried to integrate family planning service provision with projects that address other community needs.[1] This 'empowerment project' has been a site of conflict between different priorities, where feminist goals have been constrained by demographic and development goals.

On the surface, one would expect that the Integrated Project would have contributed to the empowerment of Tanzanian women, thus meeting what I have labelled *feminist* goals. These goals include active participation by women in all stages of the Project – including defining its goals, objectives and scope, and an improvement of women's strategic power within the Project and its community activities. These expectations were based on the fact that the Project has operated in a changing international environment of population intervention that links family planning with a larger focus on women's empowerment. Socio-economic development issues and issues of gender inequality are receiving more attention than ever before in the international family planning community. Second, the Integrated Project is noted for its community-based approach. It is meant to be a grassroots-based project that responds to the needs of local communities. Moreover, the Project explicitly claims women's empowerment as one of its primary goals.

However, my research suggests that women's empowerment has not taken centre-place in practice. The Integrated Project illustrates how the goals of women's empowerment, fertility reduction and local-level involvement (which I have labelled *feminist, demographic* and *development*) are affected by the need to negotiate accountability, compete for economic spoils and engage in opportunist politics. I suggest that *feminist* goals have become marginalized and gender issues depoliticized by local *development* and *demographic* agendas. Thus, the dynamics of project implementation have important implications for the relationship between women's empowerment and population policies and projects.

Rowlands (1998) suggests that an 'empowerment project' may be a contradiction in terms, because while projects are usually short-term, results-driven interventions, the empowerment process requires time and flexibility (see also Staudt, this volume; Rowlands 1997). While empowerment has at its core issues of power – including what constitutes power, how power is transferred and how different kinds of power interact – politics are often disregarded. Case studies of empowerment tend to be situated firmly within the 'local' without accounting for larger, macro-level dynamics of power (see Parpart, this volume). As Vavrus points out, 'what is "local" about "empowerment" is perhaps thousands of miles away from the African villages where "empowerment" is presumed to originate' (2000: 235).

Theoretical examinations of empowerment rarely link their critiques of patriarchy and theories of personal change with political realities 'in the field'. In this chapter, I demonstrate how empowerment can be marginalized in a development project when international, national and local political realities prioritize different agendas. In order to analyse issues of empowerment in the Integrated Project, I have labelled activities that support women's empowerment goals, such as increasing women's political participation in the project and community, access to economic resources and support for fertility decisions as *feminist*.[2] This term is an amalgam of different types of feminisms, and draws on Staudt's synthesis, which argues that feminists 'recognise power and value imbalances between men and women' and 'look toward active women to foster more balance' (1998: 30).

Similarly, as the contributions in this collection exemplify, no agreed-upon conception or measurement of empowerment exists.[3] I recognize that it is problematic to use a Western, feminist gaze to evaluate the 'empowering' nature of a series of structural and discursive relationships in Tanzania. However, the Integrated Family Planning Project is itself an amalgamation of 'global' and 'local', and as such is situated across potentially differing ideas about empowerment and power. Therefore, I present my own definition of 'empowerment' in the recognition that it is neither universal nor indisputable. With these caveats in mind, I am interested in the following aspects of empowerment.

A feminist agenda would require the Integrated Project to meet the practical and the strategic gender needs[4] of its participants. 'Practical gender needs' are identified by women and men from their gendered experiences of daily life. They respond to immediate perceived necessities, such as adequate housing, food, water, healthcare and employment, which arise out of existing gender relations, but do not call them into question. In contrast, 'strategic gender needs', such as the need for credit, freedom from violence and choice over childbearing, are formulated from the analysis of women's subordination to men. They vary according to context, but require policies that improve women's status, promote equity and remove biases against women in both the public and private spheres – thus clearly challenging the gender status quo (Moser 1993; Molyneux 1985). While the strategic/practical distinction has been deployed too rigidly in some planning contexts, it is still helpful for thinking about gender relations.[5] A *feminist* agenda would require the Integrated Project to meet the practical and/or strategic needs of its female participants. In this case the label 'feminist' is my own categorization, not one used by local actors to describe their objectives.[6]

Second, I focus on empowerment in the public realm, not on the important aspects of individual women's self-perceptions, internal strength or psycho-spiritual well-being (done effectively by Rowlands 1997), nor do I examine the ways project participation affects women's empowerment within their families. I focus on how competing project agendas inhibit women's abilities to empower themselves through the Integrated Project.

Janice Stein argues that 'empowerment is a strategy designed to redistribute power and resources' (1997: 1). This assumption underlies my attempt to understand the relations of power within the Integrated Project – between men and women, but in a broader context of power dynamics emerging from imbalances between urban and rural, educated and uneducated, employed and unemployed, NGO and state, recipient and donor, and South and North. I take these parameters not as dichotomous or fixed, but as acting simultaneously as conditioning agents and as contexts for struggles and negotiations of power.

My analysis is part of a larger study based on eighteen months of fieldwork examining how global population discourse plays out in Tanzania. An East African country of approximately 31 million people, Tanzania is predominantly agricultural. It is one of the world's poorest countries with a GNP per capita of approximately US$210 (Yusaf 2000: 231). Until 1995 it was a one-party state distinguished by its rather unique brand of socialism based on the *ujamaa* [familyhood] doctrine, and a commitment to state-supported primary healthcare and education. This has crumbled in the face of increasing economic decline and the acceptance of structural adjustment programmes in the 1980s (see Turshen 1999: 100, 101; Yusaf 2000). Despite its varying economic fortunes, Tanzania has been one of the continent's most popular donor recipients. Recent government acknowledgement of a population 'problem' has increased donor interest in Tanzania's population sector.

This chapter is based on research in three project villages,[7] with the implementing of family planning organization at the regional and national levels, and with the project's international donors.[8] I explore the international, national and local contexts of the Integrated Project. I also examine its *development, demographic* and *feminist* agendas. The final section draws some conclusions about *feminist* goals and women's empowerment within the Project.

The international context of the Integrated Project

The international context is affected by international population conferences as well as by the academic and policy debates over population and development issues and 'solutions'. This arena also includes international and national aid organizations, their employees in the First and Third World, and the budgets and negotiations that channel various kinds of population assistance to countries where population is a 'problem'. The anti-natalist Tanzanian National Population Policy was adopted in 1992, and the National Family Planning Programme developed as its primary implementing arm.[9] Two international factors set the stage for these efforts: structural adjustment policies and the Cairo consensus on 'women's reproductive health'. Thus, seemingly local projects such as the Integrated Project have been affected by material and symbolic global interventions. The 'local' is increasingly constructed by 'global' forces – particularly in the realm of 'development' projects (see Escobar 1995).

The Tanzanian National Population Policy and its related projects have been implemented in the context of economic decline and structural adjustment,[10] with its attendant currency devaluation, market and trade liberalization, privatization and cuts to public spending.[11] This has increased the importance of NGOs and donor-funded projects such as the Integrated Project as, by the mid-1980s, the Tanzanian state had little money to fund the National Population Policy. Indeed, it acknowledged that 'the national population programme is mainly financed by multilateral and bilateral assistance' (United Republic of Tanzania 1994: 28). The Population Policy, from its inception, was both dependent on donor funding and shaped by donor interests. Thus, donors largely set the tone for conceptualizing and implementing solutions to the population 'problem'.[12]

During the 1980s, Tanzanian officials began to change their perceptions of population 'problems' and solutions. Of course, this shift did not come out of nowhere. It was embedded in structural adjustment programmes that reflected a shift in Tanzania's overall approach to development. Diverse organizations with different but convergent goals gained influence in Tanzania simultaneously. While this was not designed to create a common front to bombard the government with anti-natalist propaganda, it had that outcome. Tanzania's international donors and lenders promoted a problematization of population that corresponds to what I label the *demographic agenda* in the Integrated Project's implementation.

In contrast, another international factor pushed thinking about population towards *development* and *feminist agendas*. This is the concept of 'women's reproductive health'. Tanzania's population policy began when the language of 'women's reproductive health' had entered mainstream discourse at the 1994 International Conference on Population and Development in Cairo (ICPD).[13] The Conference marked an important shift in the official discourse on population. The phrase 'population control' disappeared from the official vocabulary, and with it 'several decades of policies that relied on targets or quotas, goals that often went unmet because women in poor countries had little to say in family planning' ('Population debate: The premises are changed', *New York Times*, 14 September 1994).

This so-called 'landmark consensus'[14] embraced a new approach to 'women's reproductive health'. The United Nations Population Fund describes reproductive health as:

> a positive state, not merely the absence of disease or infirmity …. [It] exists in a broader context … [which] includes action towards gender equity, including equal access for women to health care and education, income-generating opportunities, and work in the professional, academic and political spheres.
>
> (UNFPA 1994: 31)

Whether this strategy is fundamentally 'new' or not,[15] official discourse has clearly changed and gender issues are now 'legitimate' aspects of family planning projects. The post-Cairo shift to 'reproductive health' may be a significant, albeit incremental, step in promoting diverse aspects of a feminist agenda.[16] However, because feminist goals now compete with other development goals, they do not always receive high priority, as the following analysis will demonstrate.

The national context of the Integrated Project

The Integrated Project in Tanzania, initiated in 1984, was the first integrated project in Africa, and one of the longest-running Community Based Distribution (CBD) projects in Tanzania. CBD projects use members of local communities to distribute contraceptive information and supplies. CBD agents do the bulk of the project work. The criteria for their selection of agents include:

- literacy, at least in Kiswahili, the national language
- influential and respected in the community
- not be related to the community leader in order to avoid favoritism and conflicts

(Urrio 1995: 19).

In the initial phases, when only family planning education was provided, traditional birth attendants were also implementers. After 1993, only CBDs continued with the project and men were included in this role. I will discuss the implications of this below.

The project is implemented by UMATI [Uzazi na Malezi Bora Tanzania], the NGO that introduced family planning in Tanzania in 1959. The shifting role of UMATI *vis-à-vis* the Tanzanian state and other competing NGOs is a crucial part of the national-level context for the Project. The shifts in national population policy and the expansion of donor funding forced UMATI, for the first time, to justify itself as an organization.

One of UMATI's strengths, for international donors, is its local and non-governmental status, as such grassroots organizations are seen as more connected and responsive to their constituents. UMATI wisely promotes this interpretation by stressing its *voluntary* character. Its participants are referred to as 'members', not clients.[17] The Integrated Project provides evidence of UMATI's grassroots accountability and innovative approach to family planning. Bulatao (1993) argues that Northern-based NGOs generally implement their funders' agendas, not that of their clients. My research suggests that, in the Tanzanian case, even indigenous NGOs have to respond to donor priorities. Because internal funding is scarce, organizations like UMATI must be strategic and 'market-driven' (Korten 1990), regardless of their ideological orientation or values. UMATI depends heavily on foreign assistance – 60 per cent comes from the International Planned Parenthood Federation (IPPF) (Mpangile 1994: 49). This put UMATI in a precarious position when family planning shifted focus in the early 1990s. In response, UMATI began redefining itself to take advantage of an opening in the national arena by implementing potentially controversial projects that would attract donor support.

UMATI agreed to introduce long-term methods (sterilization and contraceptive implants), co-ordinate private-sector activities, deliver community-based services and establish services aimed at youth and young adults. In 1990, the Ministry of Health designated UMATI the implementing agency responsible for permanent and long-term contraception in the country. In response, UMATI agreed to implement controversial projects such as vasectomy promotion, targeting youth and unmarried women, and/or supplementing weak government health delivery.

UMATI has been confronted with a rapidly growing NGO community in family planning – all competing for their share of donor money. The Integrated Project provides proof of UMATI's grassroots character, but it has been forced to stake out a new position as a family planning 'maverick'. The need to demonstrate demographic success and promote controversial projects has undermined its ability to meet development and feminist goals.

The local context of the Integrated Project

Known as a 'more humanistic approach to family planning' (Urrio 1995: 28), the Integrated Project is designed to meet community needs first, and provide family planning afterward. Three goals of the National Population Policy affect the Project:

1 To achieve a *lower population growth rate* through reduction of birth rate by voluntary fertility regulation.
2 *Improve health and welfare for the population in general* through prevention of premature deaths and illness.
3 Promote equality of rights, opportunities and treatment in life and work for all Nationals with specific attention to *improving the status of women*.

(UMATI 1995a: 4–5 [emphasis added])

These goals articulate three different policy agendas: a *demographic agenda* (goals of fertility reduction and population control); a *development agenda* (goals of local-level involvement and improvements in the lives of villagers); and a *feminist agenda* (concentrating specifically on the needs of women and their empowerment). However, the need to prioritize scarce resources has led to conflicts at the local level.

The Project began by establishing a 'parasite control' component in an attempt to meet a 'felt need' of the communities. Once trust was gained by the Project, then family planning messages and supplies would be distributed. In fact, the initial phase went badly. Early attempts to distribute contraceptives and provide family planning education met with hostility. A local priest told parishioners that the UMATI people had no business in the village and that they 'should throw stones at them'.[18] The conflict peaked when one CBD agent was actually hit and subsequently had to be taken to the hospital. The CBDs in another village confessed that the first year was difficult. UMATI had a bad name. People feared them and pretended they were not home when a CBD appeared.[19] However, as villages began to benefit from the Project, things went more smoothly.[20]

Worms were the legitimating entry point for the Project, but as the Project became more accepted, the deworming component lost momentum.[21] CBDs told me that while they conducted community education about worms and issues of sanitation, little treatment could be done due to lack of medicines. In fact, the only sign of deworming I encountered was a lengthy intestinal worm in formaldehyde kept in a jar on the Regional Project Supervisor's desk.[22] A local doctor told me that the number of people tested and dewormed was too small to have any impact in the villages.[23] In 1992 the Integrated Project changed its strategy:

> Now you start with CBD agents [distributing contraceptives] and later continue with parasite control. Now you start with sensitization of the community and leaders, while before parasite control was used as an entry point.[24]

Deworming had lost its usefulness. It remained in Project descriptions and justifications, but very little in practice. The project's nutrition component faced similar marginalization.

In contrast, the family planning component became more central after UMATI's 1993 Strategic Plan, which stated that CBDs were to concentrate on home visits in order to deliver contraceptives and to counsel and make referrals for clients desiring a longer-term method (Mkini 1995: 4). In one village, UMATI even transported clients to its urban clinic for long-term and permanent contraception.[25]

While the Project title and philosophy suggest an 'integrated' project, the actual integration of non-family planning components has been limited. Still, these *other* aspects differentiated the Project from more narrowly defined family planning projects, and provided 'proof' of UMATI's status as a grassroots organization. The next sections analyse how the Integrated Project reflects development, demographic and feminist agendas in its local implementation.

The development agenda: local participation and communities' 'felt needs'

Local involvement is one part of the Integrated Project's development goals. The development agenda can be understood in three areas: project design should respond to locally felt needs, close links should exist between project administrators and local people, and a Local Steering Committee must control the Project. This agenda is ostensibly designed to motivate lethargic communities to accept the Project and, in the process, family planning. To the extent that the development agenda materially benefits women participants, it contributes to meeting their practical gender needs and, thus, enhances this aspect of their empowerment. However, as I show below, these development goals also conflicted with feminist goals.

The Project has capitalized on its 'community-based' status and its supposed responsiveness to local community needs. Initially, the Project administrators actually lived in rural areas, a dramatic break from the usual way projects are run from afar. A 1988 Evaluation Report claimed this as 'a turning point in the development of the project' (IPPF 1988: 25). In addition, the Local Steering Committees supposedly govern the Project through consensus (Urrio 1995: 29). In fact, important decisions were usually made in UMATI head offices, with local communities only informed later. For example, when project supervision was shifted back to town, and a new project supervisor introduced, the CBDs were only informed when the long-time supervisor was packing up to leave.[26]

In practice, relations between the village Local Steering Committee, the CBDs and UMATI have been less than democratic. For example, the village chairman of the local committee told another researcher he had *no idea* what the UMATI project did in his village.[27] I attended a Local Steering Committee meeting in one of the project villages[28], which was supposed to 'clarify the UMATI charter and review their goals', but inadvertently reinforced the Project hierarchy, with rural women at the bottom.[29] The manager of the UMATI clinic in town directed the meeting. He had driven to the village with a trainer, and the outgoing and incoming local project supervisors. The Local Steering Committee included all the important 'big men' of the village – the ward secretary, the village chairman, the village health officer, the village extension officer, the doctor in charge of the rural health centre – and two of the most active young female CBD agents. The clinic manager's dress, mannerisms and language reinforced the class divide between himself and the villagers. During the meeting, he often 'accidentally' spoke words in English; he then struggled to translate the words into Swahili. He spoke to the committee gently, but firmly, like a primary school teacher. Still, he carefully insisted that everything must be decided by consensus. Yet, the power dynamic reinforced the role of the UMATI people from town as 'experts', who could access resources for the elder committee members.[30] The CBDs, the only two rural women present, acted as workers and helpers. During a question and answer period, members of the UMATI delegation would 'call on' the CBDs to give the 'right' answer, but they never did this to the elder men. At lunch, the CBDs served everyone else with food they appeared to have prepared themselves.

Interestingly, the two female members of the UMATI delegation spoke condescendingly to the CBDs, as if it were important to distinguish themselves as urban, educated and salaried women. Women who had power as 'experts' thus distanced themselves from the local women they were supposed to empower. This served as an important reminder that notions of 'women's empowerment' can mask power relations between different categories of women (see Yuval-Davies 1994, cited in Rowlands 1998), and that we must constantly reintegrate analyses of women's class identities with those of men's gender identities (see Jackson 1998).

The development agenda of the Integrated Project, in theory, distinguishes it from other family planning projects focused solely on contraception. However, as we have seen, participation on the ground is often either minimal or driven by a desire for individual gain. Moreover, if the development focus is no longer needed to attract family planning clients, its priority declines.

Income-generating activities are also important. They provide examples of the Project's responsiveness to 'local felt needs' by providing money for goods such as milling machines or tractors. Potentially these activities could meet women's practical gender needs.[31] Income-earning projects can encourage participation in the other activities of the Project as well. Furthermore, they can raise funds to cover the costs of increased privatization, cost-effectiveness and user fees in the health sector. They also potentially reduce the Project's dependence on donor funding. A long-time Project participant explained: 'First, UMATI provides motivation. Then, they give materials such as seeds or sewing machines.' These projects are supposed to 'set examples' for individuals and, at the ward level, to 'bring the CBDs together and give them some money'.[32] Financial gain is emphasized while the gendered character of resource control is ignored.[33]

However, interviews with CBDs revealed their disappointment with the Project's income-generation activities. They criticized their lack of profitability.[34] For example, all but two pigs from the piggery project had died; half of the mosquito nets made remained unsold; most of the saplings from the afforestation project had died, and they could not sell the few that survived. Only the sale of cloth and a pottery project received approval.

The teacher at the project's nursery school left because the villagers refused to raise money for her salary. Evidently a flier posted around the village identifying the nursery school as an UMATI school meant everyone believed it was free and thus refused to pay. This calls into question the level of 'local ownership' of the Project.

Official expectations about how project income would be spent changed as well. A Project document argued that 'The income generated from IGA [income-generating activities], should be considered as sources of funds for purchase of contraceptives in future' (UMATI 1995a: 29). This new focus on sustainability potentially conflicted with community development goals and required local NGOs to prove local commitment to a project after donor money pulls out. Projects must show they need money now, but will not need it indefinitely to carry out the same objectives. Yet the idea of reinvesting local money into procuring supplies surfaced only in project documents and speeches to donors – not in practice. Income-generating projects are generally linked to individual or communal financial gains. This, of course, assumes that the projects will generate income, and that local management will be effective. Neither of these appears to have been the case for the Integrated Project.

Demographic goals: promotion of permanent and long-term contraception

In the post-Cairo environment, the Project's demographic agenda has become implicit rather than explicit. However, increasing contraceptive use to reduce population growth has remained the driving force behind the Project. For example, UMATI's 1993–5 'Three Year Plan' claims the Project is 'recording an increasing demand for long acting (e.g., Depo-Provera and IUDs [intrauterine devices]) and permanent methods of contraception', and thus assisting in population reduction (UMATI 1993: 19, 20). The 1996–8 Plan reiterates this theme (UMATI 1996: 45). The emphasis is on 'long acting and permanent methods' that will reduce fertility rates more effectively than the condoms, foam or pills distributed by CBDs.

UMATI's 1996–8 'Three Year Plan' expects '60–70 percent of clients contacted by the project's CBD agents will opt for voluntary sterilizations, Norplant, Depo Provera and IUDs' by 1998 (UMATI 1996: 45). This estimate makes little sense in a country where fewer than 12 per cent of women use modern contraception (Bureau of Statistics 1997). This figure suggests a need to demonstrate 'success' no matter how improbable.

In one project village CBDs believed incentives were being offered for agents referring women for sterilization.[35] I heard a CBD group leader inform an agent that she would get a *zawadi* [gift] for every five referrals. During an interview with all the CBDs, the leader reluctantly admitted that he had just 'heard' this and maybe no one else knew. One person dared to agree with him. They all agreed the gift was only for sterilization. Informally I learned that the 'gift' was 5,000 Shillings [approximately $8.50]. While I could *not* substantiate this rumour, it is important that the CBD agents believed it. This also demonstrates their belief in the importance of the Project's demographic agenda.

The focus on 'permanent and long-term' contraception reflects UMATI's struggle to redefine itself in a newly competitive field of family planning. By promoting the demographic goal of population reduction, UMATI has positioned itself as a complement to government service provision. Demographic goals have been highlighted to prove that UMATI can provide controversial services and remain linked to local communities. However, the consequences for women who are offered sterilization raise issues about voluntary choice in family planning.

The feminist agenda: depoliticizing gender and 'passive acceptors'

The Project implementers at the local level placed demographic goals alongside less promoted, but rhetorically important, feminist demands for improved gender relations and women's empowerment. During a presentation at the African Regional Workshop on the Project, a participant noted:

> After ICPD [the Cairo Conference] we look at the issue of larger human development and gender. In the next ten years we will be changing from 'national family planning program' to 'reproductive health program' or 'gender and development' program.[36]

The official presentations at the conference emphasized the move to embrace broader issues of women's reproductive health and their link to women's empowerment. The 'Congratulatory Address' given by the Executive Director of the project's donor agency exemplifies this rhetorical commitment:

> These global conferences have placed human beings at the centre of popu- lation and development activities, bringing our attention to the needs for comprehensive reproductive health care including family planning, and *empowerment of women.*
>
> (Kon 1995 [emphasis added])

The Integrated Project could potentially contribute to women's empowerment in different ways. First, its scope could broadly extend into health and welfare issues. A Project document states that: 'family planning is basically a welfare matter and therefore it should be linked more closely with family health and welfare than with population control alone' (Tanzania Food and Nutrition Centre 1995: 52). The Integrated Project also addresses feminist goals because it is community based rather than centred within the medical establishment. Helzner and Shepard (1997) suggest that the CBD approach, which has local villagers, mostly women, as service providers, 'fits better with a feminist ideal'. They note that 'this model significantly increases the chances that a woman's choice of family planning method will be voluntary because the relationship between her and the provider is more likely to be characterized by equality and respect' (Helzner and Shepard 1997: 177). However, they are less sanguine about other feminist concerns, such as the quality of information and service given by people with limited medical knowledge.

The third way the project could promote feminist goals is through the imple- mentation of women-specific development activities, acting as a 'supporting organization' for women's grassroots projects (Rowlands 1998). To the extent that there were material benefits to be reaped from income-generating projects, it could be argued that these activities were meeting women's strategic needs. Also, as Wieringa (1994: 843) argues, 'any project concerned with women can potentially entail a transformative element', and these projects could also have been tackling problems of women's strategic gender needs as well. In sum, the Integrated Project had the potential to contribute to women's empowerment because it was integrating larger welfare issues with family planning, providing services through a more egalitarian power structure and supporting women-specific development activities. However, as the Project evolved, its focus shifted to emphasize demographic and development goals in ways that impeded its potential for promoting feminist goals of empowerment.

The demand that local priorities benefit men as well as women and funders' desire to expand family planning has depoliticized gender issues. The Project assumes that, since most participants are women, they clearly benefit from the project. However, the competing demands of donors, and local communities, converge at project implementation in ways that reinforce existing gender inequalities and effectively allow men to usurp most of the potential benefits of the project.

One of the strategies for achieving feminist goals recommended by Urrio was 'empowerment of the community particularly women in decision making' (1995: 28). While women's empowerment was an official Project goal, the perception that UMATI was focusing unduly on women threatened to exacerbate local-level gender conflicts. For example, UMATI held a week-long seminar for training traditional birth attendants from fifteen of the surrounding villages. Local men sitting outside the seminar, were heard to say, 'These UMATI people and their money ... those women don't know anything. They're just farmers and they are getting *chai* ['tea' – idiomatic use meaning 'money'] all the time![37] The idea that women, who are 'just farmers', would receive project spoils, while men are left out, challenged local gender relations. Projects rarely succeed without support from powerful local figures – generally men. To succeed, the Project had to offer men enough benefits to ensure co-operation and reduce jealousy. At the same time, UMATI tried to appear committed to the post-Cairo emphasis on women's empowerment.

Distributing benefits became even more difficult in the context of Tanzania's economic adjustment. A 1995 report recommended that 'Local Steering Committee members and CBDs be used to sensitize the community on the need for them to share costs on the services they receive in this project' (UMATI 1995b: 10). This trend toward cost sharing in the Project reflects international donors' determination to decrease dependence on aid and increase community payment for development services. Also, the likelihood that rural women will claim their fair share is also called into question by the inclusion of more men in the Project.

In the early stages of the Integrated Project, CBDs were all women, so to the extent that there was personal gain from participation, women benefited.

However, as the Project expanded and the environment in which it operated changed, activities became more focused on cost recovery and men were included among the CBDs. Internationally, donors were calling for more 'male involvement' in family planning. By including men as CBD agents, the Integrated Project could easily show 'male involvement' to appease funders. Also by including local men as well as women, the Project could satisfy the most powerful and vocal members of the villages by offering them part of the spoils. However, were all the men receiving 'incentives' actually going to be contraceptive users? If only contraceptive users benefit directly from participation in income-generating activities, is this not coercing poor villagers to use family planning?

These issues converged in the creation of a new Project beneficiary: the 'passive acceptor'. At the African Regional Workshop on the Project, the notion of 'passive acceptors' became a mechanism for increasing the numbers of beneficiaries. 'Passive acceptors' are people who supposedly supported, but did not necessarily use, family planning. In one village, for example, there were twenty CBDs but many project-supported income-generating groups. Another village had '52 members who contribute [to an income-generating project] but only one CBD – the rest are converts of family planning'. This village gave four acres of land to males who were 'believers' and who practised family planning.[38] It seems the village leaders wanted to make the point that males as well as females could be involved in the projects and be 'family planners'.

The area service delivery manager claims to be a proponent of the notion of 'passive acceptors' and of expanding family planning to include programmes on reproductive health.[39] He gave the example of a priest in Mchanga who told his parishioners that UMATI is not as bad as they had once thought and that the projects which it supports are good for the community. He elaborated that persons who are permitted to participate in income-earning projects are not just CBDs or even necessarily family planning users, they are 'supporters'.[40] He reiterated that if UMATI only allowed family planning users to benefit from the income-generating activities, it could be interpreted as coercive. This new identity is interestingly a masculine one, expanding the realm of the project recipients to include men, without challenging male reluctance to use contraception.

The notion of passive acceptors has implications for the Project's feminist and demographic agendas. If donors want to reduce population through contraception, how can they be sure which 'acceptors' are 'real' and which are 'passive'? When seed money or project supplies are offered as incentives for participation in the Project, does this necessarily translate into contraceptive use? Are the 'acceptors' contraceptive users or just people willing to participate in a project that has family planning as one of it components? If men are legitimate beneficiaries, both as CBDs and 'passive acceptors', how can the project ensure that unequal gender relations do not translate into male dominance of the project?

The implications of the 'passive acceptor' for feminist goals are that project participation is no longer reserved either exclusively or primarily for women. For example, at CBD and Local Steering Committee meetings, men dominate conversation and continually push their own agendas to the forefront. Including men in women's groups may, in theory, expose them to more progressive ideas on women's health issues and women's empowerment. However, in practice, with no structural means of diffusing existing gender biases, men are able to use these inequalities to expand their own control within the Project.

Conclusion

This chapter has demonstrated how *development, demographic* and *feminist* agendas underlie the implementation of an integrated family planning project in Tanzania. The Project has operated in a historically specific context that has affected its relationship to the state and its policies and practices. UMATI must show that its projects are 'successful', particularly in meeting demographic goals of increased contraceptive use. Similarly, while the Cairo discourse of women's reproductive health would support an increased emphasis on feminist and some development goals, the context of structural adjustment makes Tanzania more receptive to the more demographic goals of its donors and lenders.

A development agenda, understood as 'being responsive to local communities', involves perpetuating gendered biases in those communities. A demographic agenda of fertility reduction leads to a narrow focus on the family planning component of the Project. When these two agendas compete with feminist goals to improve women's health and increase women's empowerment, the feminist goals are often ignored. At the local level, women are Project beneficiaries in traditionally 'female' spheres: by using the contraceptives provided to control their own fertility and by providing most of the labour for the Project's activities. In contrast, men receive a disproportionate amount of the spoils from income-generation activities and control over the Local Steering Committees.

Rural women, supposedly the primary beneficiaries of the Project, provide its justification – after all, it is their 'problem' of profligate fertility that family planning is meant to 'solve'. They do most of the work – going door-to-door to provide contraception. While a 'voluntary' project suggests a higher level of community responsiveness and involvement, it requires free time. Rural Tanzanian women are the most overworked members of their communities, and, in periods of economic hardship, they have even less time to 'volunteer'. Finally, they are blamed if the Project fails since they are both the primary implementers and users of contraceptives.

If local population projects such as the Integrated Project are to empower women, what interests could be expected to push for such initiatives – keeping in mind that such empowerment might spark resistance to the disempowering aspects of demographic and development agendas? The Local Steering Committee is hardly going to risk their role in the village community. 'Local' NGOs, like UMATI, which depend on donor funding, are constrained by donor requirements. Other women's groups could mobilize at the grassroots for more project accountability on empowerment issues, but they would need an independent resource base. Furthermore, these groups would have to believe that an integrated approach to family planning and gender empowerment was worth the investment of their limited time and money. Finally, should we expect resistance from local women who benefit from the Project but are vulnerable both within and outside of it?

Because the Integrated Project has been situated in a historical framework that has favoured integrating family planning with goals of women's empowerment and local-level community 'development', this Project could demonstrate the possibilities for implementing the Cairo ideals, particularly the 'fit' between feminist goals and other project activities. Instead, it illustrates the need to give feminist goals explicit priority by international donors. If 'success' at the national level is to be equated with increased contraceptive use by women, then the Cairo discourse becomes merely an auxiliary agenda. Therefore, until women's empowerment is seen as more than simply a means to decrease fertility levels, family planning projects may theoretically support a feminist agenda, but this will have little meaning in practice.

Notes

I would like to thank the Andrew W. Mellon Foundation for support during writing this piece while a fellow at the Harvard School of Public Health. The chapter has benefited from comments by Jane Parpart, Stefano Ponte and Kathy Staudt, but, as always, the author assumes responsibility for its shortcomings.
1   The Integrated Project is based on family planning experience in rural Japan, first implemented in Taiwan (1975) and then in Indonesia, Korea, the Philippines and Thailand (1976) (Tanzania Food and Nutrition Centre 1995: 2).
2   While not denying important theoretical debates over types of feminisms (see, for example, Mohanty 1991; Spelman 1988; Mikell 1997), I base my use of the term on Staudt's synthesis (1998: 30).
3   See also Moser 1989; Karl 1995; Rowlands 1997; Stein 1997; Afshar 1998).
4   'Needs' here should be understood as a political category (see Fraser 1997) constructed discursively in ways that are similar to the construction of 'interests'. However, Molyneux (1985) points out that 'interests' are more intentional and arise out of agency while 'needs' are usually 'deemed to exist' categorically.
5   Radcliffe and Westwood (1993) suggest that 'practical' and 'strategic' are often aligned with notions of 'private' and 'public', and assumed to be universal and linear so women must progress from one to the other. Marchand (1995) argues that in practice they are a continuum. Staudt (1998) suggests these distinctions are more significant for analysis than development praxis.
6   The term 'feminist' is controversial in many Tanzanian arenas, as elsewhere, no doubt partly because it is associated with aspects of white, Western ethnocentrism as much as because of its challenge to many aspects of local cultures. However, aspects of the 'feminist' agenda, such as the importance of women's control over economic resources, are discussed more concretely.
7   Village and district names are pseudonyms.
8   The villages in my study are located in two different regions and have been involved in the Integrated Project for different lengths of time. I conducted semi-structured interviews with project administrators and participants, engaged in participant observation at meetings and referral clinics, and reviewed project documentation. My larger work included non-project family planning activities as well.
9   I analyse this policy and its meaning for Tanzanian development (Richey 1999).

10 For gender critiques of structural adjustment, see Cornia *et al.* 1987; Commonwealth Secretariat 1989; Bourginon *et al.* 1991; Cagatay *et al.* 1995.
11 For IMF and World Bank domination of the African health sector, see Turshen 1995.
12 The Tanzanian case is not unique in these respects. See Warwick's (1982) eight-country study.
13 For the Cairo Conference official report, see United Nations 1995a; for a comparison with the two previous population conferences, see United Nations 1995b.
14 However, Hartmann (1995: 148) argues that this 'consensus' was manufactured by a few powerful actors and reflects a top-down strategy rather than the grassroots.
15 My research supports Bandarage's (1997) critique of the rather liberal, unthreatening character of the Cairo consensus and the Beijing Platform for Action. However, to say the shift to 'reproductive health' was purely cosmetic would be premature at this stage.
16 Helzner and Shepard (1997) present a thoughtful description of how feminists can achieve incremental change working in large population institutions.
17 UMATI's membership is over 200,000 and its volunteer structure includes 800 Branch Committees, eighty-three District Committees, twenty Regional Committees and a National Executive Committee (USAID 1990: 44). UMATI emphasizes healthier children and families more than simply family planning (Kihamia and Maro 1984: 1).
18 Interview 95NO18, 5/4/96.
19 Interview 95NO10, 3/5/96.
20 Participant observation 95GM14, 7/3/96.
21 UMATI's 1996–8 'Three Year Plan' claims 'through showing concern for an immediate health problem (worms) as perceived by the communities, the project staff manage to boost their personal images and create appropriate rapport that then becomes instrumental in ensuring project success' (UMATI 1996: 43–4).
22 The worm came from a child during their school deworming. This illustrates the need to 'show', in tangible, physical and measurable terms, the project's accomplishments. The worm represented the project's responsiveness to the 'felt needs' of villagers. Of course, it says nothing about the reliability, continuity or accountability of the Project.
23 Interview 95NO13, 10/17/96.
24 Interview 95NO15, 10/14/96.
25 By the time I got there, the car had broken down and no replacement had been sent, but a handful of women had been taken to the town clinic for sterilization or Norplant.
26 Furthermore, the incoming supervisor had attended a closing ceremony of a training seminar, and did not even introduce herself to the local CBDs in attendance (participant observation 95GM14, 7/3/96).
27 Personal communication, 95GM14, 5/7/96.
28 These meetings are supposed to be held four times per year to run the local project.
29 All data in this section come from participant observation 95GM14, 7/3/96.
30 For a critique of the notion of 'expertise' from a gender perspective, see Parpart 1995.
31 However, Stamp (1990) questions the value of small income-generating activities because they trivialize their main work as food producers and reinforce stereotypes of women's labour as supplementary.
32 Interview 95NO15, 10/14/96.
33 The UMATI Eastern Zone Annual Report (1994) suggests that incentives ensured project participation: 'By the end of the year all the 30 CBDs and all the young volunteers and TBAs [traditional birth attendants] were still with the project.' This was due to offers of bicycles, materials for constructing the UMATI office, the guest

house and the clinic/pharmacy, as well as seed money for a forestry programme (Mkini 1995: 19).

34 CBD Interview 95NO16, 5/3/96.
35 The use of incentives has been called into question both for its incompatibility with a 'user perspective' that believes in client's rights, and also for its management conse-quences for health sector workers; see, for example, Staudt 1991.
36 From participant observation 95NO12, 7/17/95.
37 From participant observation 95GM14, 5/7/96.
38 From participant observation 95NO12, 7/12/95.
39 He linked 'passive acceptors' with the expansion of family planning to include a larger reproductive health agenda. This may suggest a self-conscious attempt to inte-grate a women's empowerment agenda with demographic and development agendas.
40 From participant observation 95NO12, 7/12/95.

References

Afshar, H. (ed.) (1998) *Women and Empowerment: Illustrations from the Third World*, New York: St Martin's Press.

Bandarage, A. (1997) *Women, Population and Global Crisis*, London and New Jersey: Zed Books.

Bourginon, F., J. de Melo and F. Stewart (1991) 'Adjustment with growth and equity', *World Development* 19(11): 1527–44.

Bulatao, R. (1993) *Effective Family Planning Programs*, Washington, DC: World Bank.

Bureau of Statistics, Planning Commission and the EVALUATION Project (1997) *Tanzania Service Availability Survey 1996*, Dar es Salaam: Bureau of Statistics, Planning Commission.

Cagatay, N., D. Elson and Caren Grown (eds) (1995) 'Gender, adjustment and macroeco-nomics', *World Development* 23(11) (special issue).

Commonwealth Secretariat (1989) *Engendering Adjustment for the 1990s*, London: Common-wealth Secretariat.

Cornia, G., R. Jolly and F. Stewart (eds) (1987) *Adjustment with a Human Face*, Oxford and New York: Clarendon Press.

Escobar, A. (1995) *Encountering Development: The Making and Unmaking of the Third World*, Princeton: Princeton University Press.

Fraser, N. (1997) *Justice Interruptus: Critical Reflections on the 'Post Socialist' Condition*, London: Routledge.

Hartmann, B. (1995) *Reproductive Rights and Wrongs: The Global Politics of Population Control*, Boston: South End Press.

Helzner, J. and B. Shepard (1997) 'The feminist agenda in population private voluntary organizations', in K. Staudt (ed.) *Women, International Development, and Politics: The Bureaucratic Mire*, Philadelphia: Temple University Press, pp. 167–84.

International Planned Parenthood Federation (IPPF) (1988) *Evaluation of JOICFP Integrated Projects in Tanzania and Zambia*, London: IPPF.

Jackson, C. (1998) 'Rescuing gender from the poverty trap', in C. Jackson and R. Pearson (eds) *Feminist Visions of Development: Gender, Analysis and Policy*, London and New York: Routledge, pp. 39–64.

Karl, M. (1995) *Women and Empowerment: Participation and Decision Making*, London and New Jersey: Zed Books.

Kihamia, C.M. and J.J. Maro (1984) 'The UMATI Integrated Family Planning, Nutrition and Parasite Control Project (IP)', in *Masama & TPC Localities in Moshi District of*

Kilimanjaro Tanzania: Report on Baseline Data and Preliminary (IP) Activities, Dar es Salaam: UMATI.

Kon, Y. (1995) 'Regional workshop on the Integrated Project (PANFRICO V) congratulatory address', PANFRICO V, Dar es Salaam: UMATI.

Korten, D.C. (1990) *Getting to the 21st Century: Voluntary Action and the Global Agenda*, West Hartford, CT: Kumarian Press.

Marchand, M.H. (1995) 'Latin American women speak on development: Are we listening yet?', in J.L. Parpart and M.H. Marchand (eds) *Feminism/Postmodernism/Development*, London, New York: Routledge, pp. 56–72.

Mikell, G. (1997) 'Introduction', in G. Mikell (ed.) *African Feminism: The Politics of Survival in Sub-Saharan Africa*, Philadelphia: University of Philadelphia Press, pp. 1–52.

Mkini, A.H. (1995) 'Background paper on Integrated Project in Morogoro region', PANFRICO V, Dar es Salaam: UMATI.

Mohanty, C.T. (1991) 'Introduction: Cartographies of struggle: Third World women and the politics of feminism', in C.T. Mohanty, A. Russo and L. Torres (eds) *Third World Women and the Politics of Feminism*, Bloomington and Indianapolis: Indiana University Press.

Molyneux, M. (1985) 'Mobilization without emancipation? Women's interests, the state, and revolution in Nicaragua', *Feminist Studies* 11(2): 227–54.

Moser, C.O.N. (1993) *Gender Planning and Development: Theory, Practice and Training*, London: Routledge.

—— 1989. 'Gender planning in the Third World: Meeting practical and strategic gender needs', *World Development* 17(11): 1799–1825.

Mpangile, Gottlieb S. (1994) *Review of the 1989–1993 Plan of Operations of the National Family Planning Program*, Dar es Salaam: World Bank.

Parpart, J.L. (1995) 'Deconstructing the development "expert": Gender, development and the "vulnerable groups"', in J.L. Parpart and M.H. Marchand (eds) *Feminism/postmodernism/development*, London, New York: Routledge, pp. 221–43.

Radcliffe, S.A. and S. Westwood (1993) *Viva: Women and Popular Protest in Latin America*, London: Routledge.

Richey, L. (1999) 'Family planning and the politics of population in Tanzania: International to local discourse', *The Journal of Modern African Studies* 37(3) (September).

Rowlands, J. (1998) 'A word of the times, but what does it mean?: Empowerment in the discourse and practice of development', in H. Afshar (ed.) *Women and Empowerment: Illustrations from the Third World*, New York: St Martin's Press, pp. 11–34.

—— (1997) *Questioning Empowerment: Working with Women in Honduras*, Oxford: Oxfam.

Spelman, E. (1988) *Inessential Woman: Problems of Exclusion in Feminist Thought*, Boston: Beacon Press.

Stamp, P. (1990) *Technology, Gender and Power in Africa*, Ottawa: International Development Research Centre.

Staudt, K. (1998) *Policy, Politics and Gender: Women Gaining Ground*, West Hartford, CT: Kumarian Press.

—— (1991) *Managing Development: State, Society, and International Contexts*, Newbury Park, CA: Sage Publications, Inc.

Stein, J. (1997) *Empowerment and Women's Health: Theory, Method and Practice*, London and New Jersey: Zed Books.

Tanzania Food and Nutrition Centre (1995) *Nutrition Situation Analysis on Integrated Family Planning, Nutrition and Parasite Control Project in Morogoro and Kilimanjaro Regions June–August 1993*, Dar es Salaam: Tanzania Food and Nutrition Centre and UMATI.

Turshen, M. (1999) 'The ecological crisis in Tanzania', in J. Silliman and Y. King (eds) *Dangerous Intersections: Feminist Perspectives on Population, Environment, and Development*, Cambridge, MA: South End Press, pp. 89–107.

—— (1995) 'The World Bank eclipses the World Health Organization', *ACAS Bulletin* 44/45 (winter/spring): 25–8.

UMATI (1996) *Three Year Plan 1996–1998*, Dar es Salaam: UMATI.

—— (1995a) 'The Integrated Family Planning, Nutrition and Parasite Control Project: Tanzania country paper', PANFRICO V, Dar es Salaam.

—— (1995b) *The Annual Workshop on the Integrated Parasite Control, Nutrition and Family Planning Project (IP) in Tanzania*, Morogoro, Tanzania: UMATI.

—— (1994) *Eastern Zone Annual Report*, Dar es Salaam: UMATI.

—— (1993) *Three Year Plan 1993–1995*, Dar es Salaam: UMATI.

United Nations (1995a) *Report of the International Conference on Population and Development*, Cairo: United Nations.

—— (1995b) *Population Consensus at Cairo, Mexico City and Bucharest: An Analytical Comparison*, New York: United Nations.

United Nations Population Fund (UNFPA) (1994) *Quality of Family Planning Services*, New York: UNFPA.

United Republic of Tanzania (1994) 'Country report on population and development to the International Conference on Population and Development to be held in Cairo, Egypt, September 5–13, 1994', Dar es Salaam.

Urrio, T. D. O. P. (1995) 'IP development in Tanzania', the regional workshop on the Integrated Project (PANFRICO V), Dar es Salaam, UMATI.

USAID (1990) *Project Paper: Family Planning Services Support'*, Dar es Salaam: USAID.

Vavrus, F. (2000) 'Governmentality in an era of "empowerment": The case of Tanzania', in T.S. Popkewitz (ed.) *Educational Knowledge: Changing Relationships between the State, Civil Society, and the Educational Community*, Albany, NY: State University of New York Press, pp. 221–42.

Warwick, Donald P. (1982) *Bitter Pills: Population Policies and Their Implementation in Eight Developing Countries*, Cambridge: Cambridge University Press.

Wieringa, S. (1994) 'Women's interests and empowerment: Gender planning reconsidered', *Development and Change* 25: 849–78.

Yusaf, Shahid (2000) *Entering the 21st Century. World Development Report 1999/2000*, New York: Oxford University Press for the World Bank.

Yuval-Davies, N. (1994) 'Women, ethnicity and empowerment', *Feminism and Psychology* 4(1): 179–97.

13 Informal politics, grassroots NGOS and women's empowerment in the slums of Bombay[1]

Vandana Desai

Introduction

The reach of global capital shows no sign of diminishing its impact on developing nations and their people. Indeed, in the past fifty years, the developing world has undergone major structural changes (Potter and Lloyd-Evans 1998) with drastic implications for social, economic and political life. There is a crucial gender dimension to such economic restructuring (Elson and Pearson 1981; Joekes 1985; Wilson 1993). Women are increasingly drawn into employment in globalized industries. The consequences of this change continue to be debated. Some scholars reject the notion that employment can empower women (Joekes 1985; Lawson 1995; Wilson 1993). Nevertheless, it is important to point out that women, even poor women, are sometimes developing strategies to cope with new situations. Indeed, even a small income can become the basis for challenges to existing social roles, norms, values, traditions and boundaries.

Poor urban women have their own daily, diverse and subtle strategies to bring about change and enhance their lives within the context of the household and its restrictions. Scheyvens (1998) defines 'subtle strategies' as attempts to achieve profound, positive changes in women's lives without stirring up wide-scale dissent. Subtle strategies can be a form of informal politics, which represent women's citizenship in action, and are important for the empowerment of communities and individuals. They build on social capital[2] – the 'networks of norms and trust which govern societal interactions'. Empowerment and social capital are inherently linked through the informal networks forged between households at the community level. Non-governmental organizations (NGOs) have a crucial role to play in encouraging the transferability of such informal networks into organized community groups that will be key players in civil society and municipal and national politics.

Women-focused NGOs have expanded dramatically since the 1975 declaration of the United Nations' International Decade for Women. Over time, many have also shifted from welfare-oriented strategies based on women's customary domestic roles to more transformative empowerment projects. International donor agencies have followed a similar pattern, becoming increasingly focused on women's empowerment. To that end, some donor agencies have provided direct support to indigenous or local women-focused NGOs as part of the neo-liberal agenda to reduce state power and shift the burden of service delivery on to local stakeholders. Grassroots NGOs have been seen as key players in the reordering of political space and a revitalization of the 'local'. Yet the focus on local and women's empowerment is often constrained by donor concern with overt, measurable action rather than the more indirect and subtle moves that often lead to social transformation.

This chapter aims to inject a much-needed dose of realism into the new civil society and development discourse. Healthy democracy depends on a strong and vibrant civil society. NGOs have a central role to play in this process, especially those that empower disadvantaged and under-represented groups such as women. However, we need a thorough organizational and political under-standing of NGOs in the South in order to comprehend both their potential and their limitations. Examples from Bombay highlight the difficulties faced by NGOs trying to enhance women's empowerment.

The chapter draws on evidence from ten gender-oriented NGOs[3] within a diverse larger sample of sixty-seven mainly small- and medium-sized grassroots NGOs[4] working with the urban poor in the slums[5] of Bombay. Bombay has recently experienced economic adjustment and liberalization; moreover, it is a rapidly expanding metropolitan centre with a distinctive urban profile. Its indus-trial base has become increasingly feminized under pressure from global competition. The findings are drawn from interviews in 1995 with women in slums, NGO staff and from participant observations. The chapter contributes to debates on informal strategies, NGOs and women's empowerment.[6]

Women's informal politics

Women's informal politics represents women's citizenship in action, a different politics that needs to be understood and valued, especially at the grassroots level. This informal politics exists in the form of 'subtle strategies' – actions that attempt to improve women's lives without stirring up wide-scale dissent. They are thus defined more by process and outcomes than by content. Subtle strate-gies are an important way for women to assert or reassert themselves in their communities rather than resigning themselves to unpalatable circumstances (Scheyvens 1998: 237).

My research reveals a rich and inspiring nexus of activities at the grassroots level; a lot of unstructured and fluid activism escapes the net of even more broadly trawled research into political or community participation. The case for viewing such activism as informal politics is two-fold:

1   It represents an interconnecting network of community life, maintaining informal networks and generally sustaining the personal, public and political lives of poor neighbourhoods.

2   It contributes to individual women's self-development. For many women, informal politics is more personally rewarding than engagement in formal

politics which is often more alienating than empowering. 'Accidental activism' can transform previously apolitical women into political activists.

There is perhaps a danger here of idealizing women's informal activism, often born of deprivation, exhaustion and disadvantage. Nevertheless, informal politics contributes to women's conscious sense of political agency. It helps to break the chains of victimhood and facilitates women's emergence as full and active citizens. Poor women in the city of Bombay are forging a different way of doing politics – generally less hierarchical, more participatory, more informal and, importantly, more sustainable on a daily basis, within and outside their own households. These practices can provide new role models for active political citizenship at a time of growing disenchantment with conventional politics in many developing countries. Moreover, the value of such politics lies in the process as well as the result.

The involvement of individuals in a particular informal strategy might be motivated initially by self-interest, but the outcome could benefit the wider community and even the individual. For example, a mother might join a campaign for decent crèche facilities for her own children but the campaign could benefit the whole community. If it increases her mobility and participation in employment it may have broadened her own concerns and actions.

When we think of ourselves as citizens, we are adopting a shared understanding of the rights and duties of participants in our community. Yet citizenship in a poor society often requires support from organizations such as NGOs to make a difference. This support has to value difference and recognize the fluidity of political identities. It also has to recognize that disadvantaged women face difficulties moving from the private to the public sphere. This is easier to theorize than practise for it requires acknowledging differences as well as commonalities. It also requires listening to the 'previously silenced women's voices' and acknowledging 'their interpretation of the world they inhabit, their successes and failures and their desire for change'. In order to do so, we need a thorough understanding of women's multiple realities and strategies for survival (Parpart 1993: 457). Thus, if women choose to support subtle, informal strategies rather than judge their efforts as conservative or 'politically immature', we should perhaps consider why they support them and to what extent they effectively challenge oppressive relations.

NGOs in developing countries are often central to empowerment efforts and are thus a good starting point for examining the relationship between informal politics, gender, empowerment and NGOs. Such an analysis must of course be placed in the context of global restructuring. Yet, despite prolific writings on empowerment (Afshar 1998; Elson and Pearson 1981; Mayoux 1998), little substantial research has been conducted on the strategies of the women involved – *their own 'subtle strategies'* (Scheyvens 1998). By exploring the subtle strategies of urban poor women, we can begin to understand how empowerment operates at the grassroots through informal networks. It will improve our understanding of the extent to which sources of social capital emerge from such grassroots empowerment and informal politics, and the role of NGOs in this process.

Empowerment of women: experiences of NGOs

Poor women's aspirations have been dramatically affected by the impact of global economic change on urban life in the South. Yet these women are often challenging, implicitly or explicitly, the existing hierarchies, social norms and boundaries that control them. I discovered that women within the slums of Bombay were more effective in using subtle strategies than confrontational ones. While these strategies may seem like soft options to casual observers, they can profoundly change and enhance women's lives. I spoke to many young women in the slums (between 18 and 25 years) who were involved with NGOs, either as community workers or as participants in other activities. These young women were confident and quite determined in their own way about choosing their partners. One young woman said 'I want a husband who will help me to be economically independent, not be like my father and brothers.' Another told me, 'I want my husband to support me in doing various vocational courses so that I can get a better job and we can both bring in income to raise a family.' Another insisted that 'I will choose my own husband, try and know the person well before I get married, I don't care what other people think or my parents think, I have to live with him, if things go wrong nobody will help me, there is no point crying later.' These statements reflect their visions and expectations. Some were actually dating young men within the slums or at work. Of the six who were Hindu, two were dating and wanted to marry their Muslim boyfriends. They recognized they would encounter opposition from the religious communities of the slum and from their own families, but were patiently saving money and building up networks of friends in their generation to counter the opposition. They realized that NGOs would not be willing to interfere in cultural or traditional issues, yet these are the kind of changes that are taking place at the grassroots level and for which the younger generation receive little support. After all, culture is not static but dynamic and susceptible to change, especially for the young. They are the ones most apt to confront traditional/religious values and rituals.

Seven NGOs involved in the study were aware of these changing attitudes and aspirations at the grassroots, especially among the younger generation. Yet NGOs in the Bombay slums are unable to encourage this transformation. This limits their ability to encourage change and enhance women's empowerment. While all ten NGOs support women's empowerment, many have demonstrated an inability to understand the many complex ways women pursue empowerment. NGOs emphasize participation and the codification of local knowledge for inspiring social change. However, NGOs working in urban slums also need to know more about the changing nature of gender relations and resource use within slum households, as well as women's decision-making and coping strategies within these households. They also need to understand the extent to which networks have formed between households within the community and whether these informal networks (social capital) are allowing women to access resources to empower themselves.

There is a critical gender dimension to some of the household adjustment and/or survival strategies in post-liberalization India. In many societies urban women have borne a disproportionate amount of the cost of the adjustment process (Elson 1989; Elson and Pearson 1981). With rising unemployment levels and declining real wages, women increasingly have to bring in an income so they can provide food for the family.

For example, I interviewed Parvati, a woman in her fifties living in the slums of Asalpha village near Ghatkopar. She worked as a domestic servant, while her daughter (Rani), 20 years old, worked in a nearby garment industry. Parvati's husband had worked in the textile mills of Bombay but economic liberalization eliminated his job and, at the time of the interview, he worked as a garage attendant in a nearby petrol station. An alcoholic, he contributed little to the household income. Parvati's 22-year-old son drove a hired auto-rickshaw and used most of his small income to buy fashionable clothes and hang around with friends. Parvati and Rani were thus the main breadwinners. Rani told me she is saving for the future, wants to do vocational training courses and regrets her poor school performance in the past. She does not want to be a domestic helper, preferring the long hours at the garment factory, which pays more. She recently changed jobs due to sexual harassment. She had expected support from her co-workers but received none, so she found a new job. It is further away unfortunately. She knows there is legislation about harassment but it offers little help to women like her who work in the informal economy.

Rani was quite critical of the local NGO, which overlooks the needs of women like her. She thinks it does not recognize the value of quiet, yet challenging, initiatives taken by individuals. NGOs have failed to support the younger generation of women who are taking initiatives at a personal level to change the role of women. They have failed to capture and build on the enthusiasm for change and empowerment aspired to by this group of women.

The case study illustrates the way women are trying to shape different social relationships by taking several small initiatives in their particular social and cultural contexts (see Wieringa 1994: 833). These subtle strategies often catalyse changes in women's lives and improve gender relations more appropriately than more confrontational means. They sometimes involve short-term compromises in order to reach long-term objectives. Subtle strategies can make practical improvements to women's lives, as in the examples given above, but they can also be forms of resistance. While their attempts may not seem particularly innovative or effective to outsiders, to the women involved, the resulting changes are significant. These strategies provide evidence of the many ways in which a feminist consciousness can manifest itself despite lack of support from NGOs and other institutions.

However, some NGO programmes do promote women's empowerment. NGOs such as Apnalaya[7] have used health promoters' and pre-school teachers' training programmes to meet practical needs for health and childcare and, in the process, enhanced women's skills and knowledge. This has led to personal empowerment manifested by more confidence and independence in daily life. Similarly, women from the Mahila Milan group of the NGO Society for the Promotion of Area Resource Centres (SPARC) learned how to build low-cost housing. Some even travelled to South Africa for a South–South interaction. One woman said she was surprised by the similarity of their problems. 'They have no security of housing, they also hear a lot of promises from their politicians, but see no money, situations are getting worse day by day and women spend all day trying to get some money to feed their children, it is all so much like us.' She spoke at length discussing the differences and similarities, confidently placing it in a global context. With their newfound skills and self-confidence, these women have spoken at conferences and to the media and have participated in a national campaign for low-income housing. Similarly, experiences have reinforced SPARC's credit disbursement (Mahila Milan programme). While the savings and loan programme initially attracts women to establish groups, the regular meetings and savings eventually give the relationship a more proactive character.

Another NGO, Stree Mukti Sangathana developed a Marathi drama, *Mulgi Zali Ho* (A Girl is Born), which highlights the inequality and discrimination a girl child faces from birth to old age. It is entertaining and often humorous, and attracts large audiences, including men. The drama conveys a powerful educational message (both in rural and urban areas of Maharashtra) through entertainment, both disseminating information to women and sensitizing men. Other NGOs in Bombay use theatre, song, dance, puppetry or other appropriate methods to convey important and controversial messages to the community.

These examples demonstrate how development education can empower women by challenging their ideas and expanding their knowledge. However, this education has often focused more on facilitating dialogue than inciting effective responses to the dilemmas facing women in slums. Women who participated in these initiatives were profoundly moved by them and gained a clearer perception of their life opportunities and of their own worth. They challenged customary norms by travelling away from home without their husbands and their traditional roles by becoming leaders in their communities. But what about those women who do not participate in the public arena or training programmes? They still have strategies for coping and surviving in the changing gender relations within society and their particular household.

Moreover, the question remains whether women actually want to become empowered, to be opened up to new opportunities and to make their own life decisions. For as Wieringa highlights, 'to empower women to critically and creatively reshape their worlds, women's own concept of themselves has to be decoded and reinscribed. This is a difficult and often painful process' (1994: 834). Many women fear the 'new', 'for although the old may be painful and uncomfortable, it still provides the security of tradition and of the consent of one's social surrounding' (Wieringa 1994: 834).

Here it is important to investigate the behaviour of gender-oriented NGOs who are confronted with women's strategic needs. Half the NGOs[8] in this study provide legal aid for women in distress (compared to 19 per cent of NGOs generally; see Desai 1999). They have found themselves in very difficult moral/ethical situations. Some women who suffered domestic violence, disputes over Muslim women's right to maintenance, rape incidents, alcoholism, sexual abuse, harassment, divorce, separation, dowry harassment, even teasing and other such issues, have been willing to take legal advice and help from NGOs. Meetings with family members are arranged, court petitions filed and summonses issued, often with the help of police escorts. Initially these problems are shrouded in silence or denial as they affect the family's honour. Families often blame woman for not 'suffering in silence'. Supportive relationships with NGO staff help break down this silence.[9] Women are increasingly willing to seek help confronting these situations. Thus, issues that had previously been private have acquired a public and political status in the eyes of many slum women.

Women who took the initiative to resolve distressing situations were, most of the time, ostracized from their family or marital home, with no financial or emotional support or shelter. Most NGOs willingly helped in the short term with legal advice, but court cases in India can be long and tedious.[10] Moreover, four of the ten helped with food and shelter, compared with only 16 per cent of NGOs generally (Desai 1999). In these interim periods, NGOs often find it difficult to maintain ongoing emotional and material support due to their own precarious financial circumstances.[11] According to the NGOs, many women return to previous situations, such as abusive husbands, although one woman said she would rather commit suicide.

This example highlights the interdependence between different categories of needs, particularly in the lives of poor urban women. Women's lives cannot be compartmentalized or insulated from each other. Problems in one arena have implications for others. They require ongoing input from NGO staff who are hemmed in by the demands of their donors, including development agencies and government bureaucracies.

Self-esteem is an important element here as well. To speak in one's own voice and put forward one's own views in the polity requires self-esteem, a stable sense of one's own separate identity and a confidence that one is worthy to participate in political life. This has particular resonance and difficulty for poor women. Attempts at empowerment have to take note of the trade-offs women make in order to cope with the oppressive relationships in their lives. The empowerment approach tends to assume women are aware of their needs and options, that they are mobile and that they have adequate support systems to help in the process of empowerment.

In fact, none of the NGOs interviewed provide a full range of support services to women who have left home, such as shelter, counselling, legal advice and support, job placement and so on. Children who accompany these women have needs as well. Most NGOs try to restore the self-esteem and autonomy of the women badly damaged by their inner experiences. This is neither automatic nor quick. Many women are unaccustomed to fending for themselves in public spaces such as NGO shelters or centres, and even fewer have dealt with public officials.

Occasionally NGOs have to help women referred to them by police, welfare departments, hospitals or other NGOs, but most expect women to approach them on their own. This ensures the clients are fully aware of the consequences of their actions and prepared to make the choices and trade-offs facing them. Patience is also required when working with younger unmarried women who may be forced into marriage, abused by step-parents, having conflicts at home because of unemployment and so on. Gaining the trust and confidence of such women is a difficult task.

NGOs that identify with the empowerment approach acknowledge it is often a difficult process, requiring time and patience. However, they are often caught in a bind because of their donors: 'development planners are searching for easy schedules, quantifiable targets and simplicity, while addressing enormously complex situations – planners want to fix, with projects of a few years' duration, problems which have grown over ages' (Wieringa 1994: 835). Consequently, most NGOs within Bombay prefer taking on more straightforward health and education projects. As Sharada Sathe (from the NGO Stree Mukti Sangathana) pointed out, NGO programmes that increase women's assertiveness are labelled 'feminist' and frequently encounter hostile, negative reactions. This has led many NGOs to disassociate themselves from feminism, despite the fact that 'gender planning is a political process with feminism at its heart' (Wieringa 1994: 844).

Most poor urban households demonstrate the complex strategies women have to adopt to cope with the combined effects of poverty in an increasingly competitive global economy. Issues relating to food, employment and the lack of provision of basic services are often seen as more important than the informal politics of gender relations in the household and society. Women-centred NGOs have begun to realize the need to integrate broader issues with women's concerns. For example, a feminist group in Bombay, the Forum Against Oppression of Women, has campaigned against issues such as rape and bride burning since 1979. However, the Forum soon realized that over half the women slum dwellers were more concerned with housing, so they shifted focus to that issue. Lack of housing for women exacerbates domestic violence and the provision of women's hostels provides a critical, practical gender need. Mobilization around homelessness also revealed the patriarchal bias in inheritance legislation and provided the basis for wider, cross-sex alliances. To enhance this, the Forum has become part of a nation-wide alliance of NGOs lobbying for a National Housing Charter. Consequently, women's housing needs have been placed on the mainstream political agenda. They are no longer simply a woman's issue.

These examples highlight the integration of separate but interlinked issues – NGOs, gender, empowerment, culture and politics. If women's informal politics involves grappling with issues at the heart of 'culture', then how does this map on to NGO agendas? The following section looks at the role of NGOs in raising gender issues in Bombay, and discusses the possibilities, constraints and dilemmas facing NGOs and their staff. It explores ways in which informal politics lead to various issues for NGOs and for grassroots activism.

The role of NGOs

The pace of social change in developing countries shows no signs of diminishing as Third World lives are caught up in a system of global restructuring. This process has three dimensions: economic, social and political. The NGO sector is bound up in all three. NGOs are increasingly being drawn into welfare state service provision as a means of reducing state fiscal crises and institutional constraints. The NGO sector is being transformed into a shadow state apparatus, filling the gaps left by the state. But what do these changes mean for the grassroots NGO sector, especially for gender equality? Local politics of NGOs can be just as volatile and variable as the sector's economic structure and patterns.

Development practice of late has moved towards 'participation' and 'empowerment'. Actors and institutions on the 'left' and 'right' applaud this shift. In particular, the local has emerged as *the* site of empowerment and hence as a locus of knowledge generation and development intervention. Some scholars and development practitioners (for example, Whaites 1998) believe NGOs should strengthen the capacity of the state as part of their localized, grassroots work, rather than creating parallel or alternative welfare delivery systems. Others are more sceptical about the state. However, NGOs also have to be sensitive to the complexity and particularity of change, especially in regard to gender relations and practices. They cannot determine where the space for social change is going to emerge or what form it will take.

Activities of NGOs

We need to look at more concrete experiences to evaluate this dilemma. Fifteen per cent of the NGOs interviewed in Bombay targeted poor women as a specific group of beneficiaries. Of those, most focused on women's health (compared to 52 per cent of NGOs in general focusing on health; see Desai 1999). This is especially important because the shame and embarrassment associated with women's bodies in many societies gives rise to a 'culture of silence' around women's sexual, reproductive and general health questions.[12] Education is also seen as a means to help women, especially through adult education. Income generation projects such as *papad* making, sewing, pickle making and handicrafts are less popular as many NGOs recognize such projects may increase women's workload for little return. They cannot compete with the increasingly competitive global market, especially in Bombay, which has lots of small informal-sector activity. Some NGOs no longer see credit as the answer to women's empowerment (see chapter by Lairap-Fonderson). More interventionist measures such as niche marketing may be necessary (Desai 1999). However, even apparently successful income-generating projects rarely transform a woman's position in the household (Goetz and Sen Gupta 1996). Indeed, some argue that micro-finance programmes divert women from other more effective strategies for empowerment (Ebdon 1995) and/or the resources of donors from more effective poverty alleviation (Rogaly 1996).

Many NGO[13] projects for women have failed, often due to lack of technical knowledge or poor planning. Moreover, NGO projects tend to stay in relatively 'safe' service delivery areas that do not always relate to women's concerns, such as health and education. NGOs often avoid activities that preoccupy women because these activities require a lot of patience and emotional support. Yet, economic changes or reforms affect social gender relationships within the household. Unfortunately, the problems stemming from these changes often receive little attention from, or cannot be handled by, NGOs.

Gender participation within NGO activities

Although participation has become a buzzword throughout development practice, the NGO sector has been its most ardent champion. Normally, three steps are taken to ensure 'popular participation'. First, People's Committees are set up, usually at the behest of external project leaders, elected by the community using customary methods. Hence they are usually entirely male, thus confirming the position of local notables (Desai 1995). Women's participation is usually established separately. Many women are reluctant to act outside their patriarchal cultural traditions, making initial involvement very difficult. Slum communities are stratified by factors such as income, housing, religion, caste and class, so the homogeneity of project committees can undermine the project's acceptability and credibility later on. Furthermore, societies that protect and seclude women are generally suspicious of any training given to women as it may encourage immoral activities (interview with Apnalaya staff).

Moreover, men within the community often exert considerable control over the activities of their wives and daughters. They resent time spent away from household duties, and worry that female involvement in the 'public' world of community development will threaten patriarchal power structures. Male community leaders also restrict women's potential for exercising control over the design, practice and outcome of participatory projects. This is true of slum settlements in Bombay. Male slum leaders sometimes block and circumscribe NGO staff interactions with female residents. Although women often recognized community problems more readily and accurately than men, they found it difficult to discuss their concerns with NGO staff. Consequently, NGOs often bypass women leaders, and fail to recognize their contribution to the organization and to the improvement of urban settlements. This is all the more alarming considering the quotas for female representation at the village *panchayat* level (73rd Constitutional amendment), municipal councils in cities and metropolitan areas (74th amendment) and in the Lok Sabha (People's Assembly) and state legislative assemblies (84th amendment).[14]

Moreover, in many cases women's full and active participation in project design, implementation and management is more restricted than that of their male counterparts. Practical constraints such as timing and workloads reduce women's participation so they may even seem 'invisible'. Women's projects frequently fail to arouse male support as well. Men tend to dismiss women's abilities and resent having to share their skills and expertise with them (for similar evidence in Sri Lanka, see Fernando 1987).

By and large, policy-makers see poverty alleviation as a male problem. Women are rarely treated as knowing what they need; rather, agencies seek to think and act on their behalf. Women's needs and priorities are either subsumed (and then forgotten) within those of the household collectivity or, when addressed (separately), tend to focus on women as mothers, wives and care-givers within the family (Kabeer 1994: 230). Furthermore, policy-makers often assume women have time to participate in empowerment projects.

There are two contradictory trends concerning women's seclusion and social mobility. In cities such as Bombay, girls attending school and women's employment are gradually becoming a recognized option, and for poorer families it is an economic necessity. However, many men dislike women having opportunities for income generation and want to keep them in their more traditional roles.[15] The new position of women in urban Bombay has created conflicts within households and between older and younger generations of women. Development agencies such as NGOs and their staff need to understand these changes and to support both women and men in their new roles and relations. For this, the role of NGO staff is critical.

NGO staff

Discriminatory attitudes of male NGO project staff sometimes limit women's active and visible participation. At the slum level, women react to male hostility by downplaying their interest in women's issues. However, beneath the overt rhetoric and behaviour I discovered that women NGO staff, at the field and mid-management levels, had learned from their work experiences and held quite strong positions on gender justice. This was particularly so among field workers, one of whom reported that 'They [NGO management] want us to talk to women in slums, but women want so many different things which we cannot ever deliver.' Another complained that:

> Our support for these poor women is short term, we do not want to take a risk when a women is abused or is suffering domestic violence, we keep saying they should not be dependent on us; in fact they will always be dependent on us for some time. I don't see what sort of help we are offering.

Field workers wanted to provide space where women could talk about their emotional needs and daily problems. They rejected the (usually male) notion that this was soft, unimportant work. Indeed, many women NGO staff criticized the gender-based inequities in their own organizations and the biases in service provision. Of course, these women often failed to act on their critiques and avoid taking risks, getting personally involved in domestic situations or providing long-term emotional/counselling support for women in need. Nor were they often able necessarily to visibly change their work culture,[16] or to change their male colleagues' behaviour. Conformity is safer and carries more tangible rewards, a point supported by the experiences of many senior women in bureaucratic organizations (Goetz 1992: 14). However, subtle and internal changes can sometimes provide the basis for organizational change.

As Sheela Patel (founder and director of SPARC) told me, the degree of backlash against women's organizations, and the capacity of women staff in NGOs to create positive environments for gender equity or feminist concerns, depends on the culture of the organization and on attitudes about gender equity in the broader culture. Government bureaucracies in the Philippines, for example, demonstrate that women can transform both the internal culture of bureaucracies and the policies and work of these institutions (Valdeavilla 1995; del Rosario 1995). In Bombay, many people believe women no longer face discrimination, especially since they are well represented in high levels of business and government. This is despite statistical indicators showing women well behind men, and evidence that issues such as sexual harassment are ignored despite their widespread occurrence.

However, NGOs in Bombay for the most part recognize women's crucial role in society and their many real needs. Nevertheless, to work with women you need appropriate tools. You cannot simply use tools and methods designed for men. This is evident in the credit programmes in Bangladesh, where women's duties and cultural practices have undermined attempts to empower them through credit (Goetz and Sen Gupta 1996; Hashemi *et al.* 1996; Schuler *et al.* 1998). NGOs have to adopt a proactive role to deal with such impediments.

Hence the issue of NGO staffing is critical. Most NGO staff are from educated middle-class families whose ideas of equality, empowerment and gender awareness differ dramatically from that of the communities they serve. Class is, or can be, a barrier between women (also caste in the Indian context). Class is inherent in NGOs, as in most things, and so we need to distinguish between the aims of grassroots NGOs, the perceptions and capabilities of NGO staff, and issues facing poor urban women. Class is an important part of our development analysis, and we should not discard it when it comes to the development of women. At the same time we must remain responsive to the needs and concerns of different women, defined by them for themselves (Sen and Grown 1987; Mehta 1991).

Structural issues within NGOs

NGOs face a number of structural issues that influence their attitudes and behaviour toward gender and empowerment. These issues explain why many NGOs have failed to capture and build upon the subtle strategies and informal politics operating at the grassroots level. Many small- and medium-sized NGOs (which constitute most of the sample from the NGO sector in Bombay), especially those facing funding uncertainties, tend to operate in a day-to-day short-term crisis management mode. In this environment, organizational purpose and goals may become submerged, to be replaced by frantic resource searches from various donor agencies and implementation of stop-gap measures. Long-term goals are rarely translated into practice. Transformative goals are forgotten in the rush to come up with quantifiable targets and short-term goals – the net result being a rather diluted effort at empowering women (Wieringa 1994).

The crisis management mode of NGOs is often associated with a failure to predict problems and devise strategies for attaining organizational goals. Many NGOs see planning either as a luxury or as an exercise in futility given their dependence on external funding and uncertain future. Although the NGO sector is becoming increasingly professionalized, planning to reduce uncertainty is a foreign concept. The diversity of NGO clients also mitigates against planning (Desai 1999). The complex and lengthy problems besetting many women in the slums further complicate NGO response. Additionally, high staff turnover, a shortage of management and planning skills, and the inability to fund highly qualified staff also inhibit planning.

Women's NGOs within Bombay have focused a lot of energy on influencing state policy; they have also had widely varying attitudes toward the state, ranging from support and collaboration, to mediation and direct confrontation. They have worked with the women's movements[17] to bring issues such as dowry deaths and rape into the public arena. While NGOs and the women's movements do not always agree, they have managed to collaborate effectively to increase government commitment to women's issues.

For example, work around violence against women is carried out by very few NGOs who obviously cannot satisfy the needs of the entire city of Bombay. This work includes public awareness campaigns and demonstrations lobbying the government for legal reform, taking up individual cases and extending support to women victims, confronting perpetrators of violence against women and organizing social boycotts of offenders. Demands for changes in police structures and practices have also featured strongly, resulting in the creation of special women's units and all-women police stations in some Indian cities. However, the women-only focus is being questioned and a more broad gender-aware policy is being encouraged (as in Maharashtra state).

Bureaucrats and politicians tend to treat NGOs as 'junior partners'. They are never involved in the formulation of policies or plans, but are expected to implement them. Suggestions by NGOs are mostly accepted in a piecemeal manner or distorted or reformulated. Government often tries to pressure its 'partners' into taking on work they may oppose. This works against the nature and best interests of NGOs. They function better as autonomous bodies, experimenting with new ideas and building models as well as monitoring official activities. Some organizations, such as Annapurna, link to government without losing their independence,[18] but most are not as lucky. Moreover, government officials have rather 'traditional' notions of gender roles and relations, and some do not understand or sympathize with NGO gender-oriented programmes or their transformative agendas.

Conclusion

This chapter reflects on the question of empowerment and its relation to women's (strategic) informal politics. Though the evidence is largely from Bombay, some generalizations can advance our broader understanding and inform research and debates on the role of NGOs in promoting women's empowerment. The data reveal the need to enhance the transformatory potential of women through strategies that seek to open up rather than foreclose possibilities available to women. Transformation often depends on the extent to which NGOs are able to provide women with access to new kinds of resources, thereby signalling new potential and possibilities rather than merely reinforcing old roles and constraints. This will only happen if NGOs understand how subtle strategies can encourage and support women's empowerment.

The value of informal politics does not constitute an alibi for the continued under-representation of women and 'minority groups' in the formal structures of power. This remains important. However, a more inclusive formal political system also needs to welcome the kinds of informal strategies and politics that many women will probably continue to prefer. At the same time, better links between informal (NGOs) and formal political institutions might encourage more women to move from one to another. Opening up formal to informal modes of politics could legitimate and enhance the latter as a form of political citizenship. NGOs can be considered a form of political organization through which women can outline a space for themselves. The activities of such organizations at the grassroots can be seen as feminist expressions without a feminist discourse.

Working with women, at whatever level, raises the possibility of changing women's position in society, yet this is rarely acknowledged by NGOs. It is incumbent on NGOs to open the debate, particularly on the extent to which it is appropriate to attempt to reshape the social order. NGOs working in conservative, patriarchal societies have to face several questions. Should the long-term implications of development work for women be addressed? Should the underlying strategic aim of fundamental social change be disclosed? Should NGOs encourage communities to strive for development when it might lead to a substantial shift in social values and a degree of social disintegration? These questions raise moral and ethical dilemmas for NGOs. They require acknowledging the diverse visions for empowering women, especially in societies undergoing rapid change but where women are still expected to conform to customary norms. Moreover, it is crucial to acknowledge that gender transformation affects men too, and effective change, without too much opposition from men, may require subtle strategies rather than overt confrontation. Both informal and formal politics are important for women and deserve NGO support.

I have argued that the effectiveness of the NGO sector is at risk if it does not support the young women and their emerging gender issues in the changing world of cities such as Bombay. NGOs need to overcome internal obstacles that inhibit their ability to support the informal and formal politics required to address the challenges of progressive social transformation. Working within informal politics and supporting subtle strategies of women require long-term commitments to achieving empowerment, even when output or success cannot be quantified (especially for donors). This raises some important questions for the NGO sector regarding the sustainability of empowerment programmes/projects in the context of economic liberalization and the shadow-state role of the NGO. However, NGOs cannot afford to ignore women's informal politics. If they do, they will lose their constituency and their grassroots effectiveness.

Aware of changes in attitudes and expectations, NGOs have encouraged some programmes, such as training, health and childcare, to enhance women's skills and knowledge, and have collaborated with governments on legislative changes. However, they have shown an inability to understand the complexity of women's strategic adaptations and a limited capacity to support them. Most NGOs have come to the sad realization that, although they have achieved many micro-level successes, the systems and structures that determine power and resource allocations – locally, nationally and globally – remain largely intact. More recent interventions have begun to address the need to connect the local more deliberately to the national and global. Participatory development is being undertaken in less utopian ways. NGOs increasingly recognize that change will not occur through localized action alone. Participatory approaches must be linked to the more complex and difficult processes of democratization, anti-imperialism and feminism. Obsessive concern over internal organizational practices and problems can prevent NGOs from effectively interpreting the larger political economic landscape (both formal and informal) and its implications for organizational funding, goals and praxis. This wider vision, including a reassessment of the political role of the NGO sector, is required before NGOs, even grassroots NGOs, become an effective means for empowering women and transforming gender relations.

Notes

My sincere thanks to all the NGOs for their valuable time, for funding from the Department for International Development (DFID), UK, and for comments by Ramya Subrahmanian and Professors Rob Imrie, Jane Parpart, Tulsi Patel and David Simon as well as the external reviewer.
1   The state government of Maharashtra has declared that the city should be renamed Mumbai.
2   Social capital refers to 'features of social organisation such as networks, norms and social trust that facilitates co-ordination and co-operation for mutual benefit' (Putnam 1993: 67). Definitions vary, and the term has acquired a particular World Bank popu-

larity. See Ben Fine's (1999) very useful deconstruction in *Development and Change* 30: 1–19.

3 NGOs that concentrate on gender issues and projects.

4 For a description of the sector with regard to activities, target groups, funding base and linkages, see Desai (1999). Desai and Preston (2000) use this data to construct a typology of Bombay NGOs using statistical classification techniques.

5 The term 'slum' is used here, as in much of the literature, to denote an area of poor-quality housing, deficient maintenance and inadequate infrastructure; no derogatory connotation is intended. There is considerable diversity within such settlements in terms of type and quality of housing, extent of infrastructure and services, tenure, site-specific hazards and so on.

6 Empowerment has been identified as a key goal of feminist grassroots organizations that want to move beyond the women in development (WID) focus on formal equality with men. The major international development agencies now routinely refer in their policy declarations to the empowerment of the poor and of women. However, there is no consensus on the meaning of the term, and it is frequently used in a way that robs it of any political meaning; sometimes it merely substitutes for integration or participation. I adopt Staudt's definition that empowerment is a process by which people/individuals acquire the ability to act in ways to control their lives (Staudt 1990).

7 Apnalaya is a grassroots NGO working with slum dwellers in five different areas of Bombay. It tries to respond to local needs using local resources with local participation. It focuses on community health, pre-school facilities, vocational training, para-professional training for community workers and a drug relief programme (see Desai and Howes 1995).

8 NGOs involved in legal aid in this research sample are: Annapurna Mahila Mandal, Ashankur, BUILD, Hamara Club, Jagruti Kendra, Majlis, Mahila Dakshata Samiti, Pragati Kendra, Streehitkarni, Stree Mukti Sangathana, Swadhar, Women's Center and YUVA.

9 Sharada Sathe (Stree Mukti Sangathana) drew my attention to this point.

10 Judicial gender bias is not unusual in India. It has periodically provided the women's movement with major rallying points. While the Indian women's movement has managed to prompt legislative reform, it has done little to monitor violations of women's rights in both civil and criminal court proceedings. The meagre benefits of progressive legislations often get neutralized by the prejudices and hostility women encounter in law courts.

11 Personal communication with Aruna (Women's Center) and Flavia Agnes (Majlis).

12 In the slums of Bombay, inadequate sanitation facilities require women to use open spaces or unmaintained, filthy public toilets. Moreover, in the interests of modesty, they are used under cover of darkness, either late in the evening or early in the morning. This leads to bowel and bladder problems. Furthermore, limited availability of water exacerbates problems faced during menstruation.

13 Some women's organizations do not consider themselves NGOs, but autonomous women's groups with various funding sources. Some NGOs refused to disclose their funding sources.

14 Almost all the women who figure in electoral politics seem to be someone's wife, daughter, daughter-in-law or other close relation. Few follow male political career patterns. Elections in India have become very complicated, violent, dirty and expensive. Women find it hard to fit into this matrix. All political parties subordinate women's participation and concerns to the interests of the party.

15 Emerging political parties like the Shiv Sena and RSS consistently portray traditional gender roles under the disguise of *Hinduthva*.

16 Organizational culture means the way NGO offices operate and the leadership's attitude toward its staff. Very few men worked on gender issues within NGOs. NGO

male staff could be unsympathetic to the emotional and support needs of women within the organization and also in the field.

17 After the formation of the National Commission for Women, Maharashtra was the first state to establish a state commission for women in 1993 (Sujata *et al.* 1994). The Commission has progressive policies and was established after widespread consultation.

18 Annapurna Mahila Mandal (AMM) is a grassroots organization of self-employed women in the informal sector. Established in 1975, it has over 60,000 women members. To circumvent labour laws, the mill owners stopped recruiting women workers. Faced with starvation, these women had to resort to income-generating activities in their own homes. They began providing cheap, home-cooked meals for single mill workers and became known by the Marathi word *Khanawallis* (meaning an inn for eating food). These women were financially exploited by their grocers/suppliers and moneylenders. They started a credit programme with a group loan from the nationalized banks, thus ending their dependency on moneylenders. AMM has now expanded its activities and set up two training centres with units for vocational training, catering, tailoring, handicrafts, health and legal aid.

References

Afshar, H. (1998) *Women and Empowerment: Illustrations from the Third World*, Basingstoke: Macmillan.

del Rosario, Virginia (1995) 'Mainstreaming gender concerns: Aspects of compliance, resistance and negotiation', *IDS Bulletin* 26(3) (July): 102–9.

Desai, V. (1999) 'Anatomy of the Bombay NGO sector', *Environment and Urbanization* (11)(1) (April): 247–65.

—— (1995) *Community Participation and Slum Housing: A Study of Bombay*, London, New Delhi: Sage Publications.

Desai, V. and M. Howes (1995) 'Accountability and participation: A case study from Bombay', In Michael Edwards and David Hulme (eds) *NGO Performance and Accountability: Beyond the Magic Bullet*, London: Earthscan Publications, pp. 83–93.

Desai, V. and I. Preston (2000) 'Urban grassroots non-governmental organisations in Bombay: a suggested typology', *Government and Policy (Environment and Planning, Series C)* 18: 453–68.

Ebdon, R. (1995) 'NGO experience and the fight to reach the poor: Gender implications of NGO scaling-up in Bangladesh', *IDS Bulletin* 26(3): 49–53.

Elson, D. (1989) 'The impact of structural adjustment on women: Concepts and issues', in B. Onimode (ed.) *The IMF, the World Bank and the African Debt*, vol. 2, London: Zed Books.

Elson, D. and R. Pearson (1981) 'Nimble fingers make cheap workers: An analysis of women's employment in Third World export manufacturing', *Feminist Review* 7: 87–107.

Fernando, Marina (1987) 'New skills for women: A community development project in Colombo, Sri Lanka', in Caroline Moser and Linda Peake (eds) *Women, Human Settlements and Housing*, London: Tavistock, pp. 88–112.

Goetz, A.M. (1992) 'Gender and administration', *IDS Bulletin* 23(4): 6–17.

Goetz, A.M. and Sen Gupta (1996) 'Who takes the credit? Gender, power and control over loan use in rural credit programs in Bangladesh', *World Development* 24(1): 45–64.

Hashemi, S., S.R. Schuler and A.P. Riley (1996) 'Rural credit programs and women's empowerment in Bangladesh', *World Development* 24(4): 635–53.

Joekes, S. (1985) 'Working for lipstick? Male and female labour in the clothing industry in Morocco', in H. Afshar (ed.) *Women, Work and Ideology in the Third World*, London: Tavistock.

Kabeer, N. (1994) *Reversed Realities: Gender Hierarchies in Development Thought*, London: Verso.

Lawson, V. (1995) 'Beyond the firm: Restructuring gender divisions of labor in Quito's garment industry under austerity', *Environment and Planning D: Society and Space* 13: 415–44.

Mayoux, L. (1998) 'Women's empowerment and micro-finance programmes: Strategies for increasing impact', *Development in Practice* 8(2): 235–41.

Mehta, Mona (1991) 'Gender, development and culture', in Candida March (ed.) *Changing Perceptions: Writings on Gender and Development*, Oxford: Oxfam.

Molyneux, M. (1985) 'Mobilisation without emancipation: Women's interests, state and revolution in Nicaragua', *Feminist Studies* 11(2): 227–54.

Parpart, J. (1993) 'Who is the "other"? A postmodern feminist critique of women and development theory and practice', *Development and Change* 24: 439–64.

Potter, R.B. and S. Lloyd-Evans (1998) *The City in the Developing World*, New York: Longman.

Putnam, R. (1993) *Making Democracy Work: Civic Traditions in Modern Italy*, Princeton: Princeton University Press.

Rogaly, B. (1996) *Micro-finance Evangelism, 'Destitute Women', and the Hard Selling of a New Anti-poverty Formula*, Oxford: Oxfam.

Scheyvens, R. (1998) 'Subtle strategies for women's empowerment: Planning for effective grassroots development', *Third World Planning Review* 20(3): 235–53.

Schuler. S.R., S.M. Hashemi and S.H. Badal (1998) 'Men's violence against women in rural Bangladesh: Undermined or exacerbated by micro-finance programmes?', *Development in Practice* 8(2): 148–56.

Sen, G. and C. Grown (1987) *Development, Crisis and Alternative Visions: Third World Women's Perspectives*, New York: Monthly Review Press.

Staudt, K. (ed.) (1990) *Women, International Development and Politics: The Bureaucratic Mire*, Philadelphia: Temple University Press.

Sujata, Gothoskar, Gandhi Nandita and Shah Nandita (1994) 'Maharashtra's policy for women', *Economic and Political Weekly* 29(48) (26 November): 3019–22.

Valdeavilla, Ermelita (1995) 'Breakthroughs and challenges of making the Philippine government work for gender equality', *IDS Bulletin* 26(3) (July): 94–101.

Whaites, A. (1998) 'NGOs, civil society and the state: Avoiding theoretical extremes in real world issues', *Development in Practice* 8(3): 343–53.

Wieringa, S. (1994) 'Women's interests and empowerment: Gender planning reconsidered', *Development and Change* 25: 829–48.

Wilson, F. (1993) 'Workshops as domestic domains: Reflections on small-scale industry in Mexico', *World Development* 21(1): 67–80.

Part V
Conclusion

14 Concluding thoughts on (em)powerment, gender and development

Kathleen Staudt, Shirin M. Rai and Jane L. Parpart

This volume is about power, in its multiple meanings, and about shifts in gender power relations. As we have learned from all the contributors, this is no simple topic to understand or document. Power relations are deep, but fluid and elusive; power relations change, and from contributors to this volume, it appears that women have gained some leverage in these shifts through organizing, earnings, internal strength, awareness, policies and laws that legitimize their rights and claims. We learn in this volume that power shifts involve changes in *processes* – in how people relate to one another – and in the concrete *outcomes* that result from these processes.

Throughout the volume, we have moved from global to national to local, so local as to include migrants' personal narratives. Contributors moved across the boundaries of nation, jurisdiction and cyberspace. Power relations can hardly be understood without grounding knowledge in the personal and local while at the same time recognizing how global forces shape these relations. In the broadest brush overview, these chapters affirm that institutional and male *power over* women is still formidable, but that women's *power within* gets expressed in individual negotiation and agency as well as in collective organizations that challenge discourse, interpretation and the status quo. The *power to* make change as individuals, in groups and with coalitions, is thereby enhanced. Yet the chapters illustrate more change in process than in outcomes. Ultimately, gender justice should provide concrete results, whether getting there is quiet and subtle or noisy and confrontational. Several chapters offer analyses of gendered power relations that strengthened men's voices and benefits, in the name of women's empowerment.

Contextualizing chapters: challenges ahead

In the introduction, we began with the all-too-comfortable word 'empowerment'. Disparate people use this terminology, from local grassroots activists to officials, crafting their schemes and dreams with and upon people. The empowerment word has a noble history, with power, after all, at its core. Only in the last decade has empowerment talk appeared in official discourse. In international organizations, empowerment has become the new adjective that embellishes many education, income-generation, and service projects. Contracts with non-government organizations (NGOs) are re-titled empowerment projects. We must be wary of 'business as usual' in the development industry. If empowerment is everything, then nothing distinguishes it from 'development' as usual. Contributors to this volume demonstrate how institutions have managed to neutralize radical concepts of power and of power relations.

From this volume, we draw out the themes and conditions under which activities can acquire an honest and transparent use of the word empowerment for people. Official institutions exercise a great deal of power and authority that shape, compel and induce particular relationships of power among people in space. Global finance and corporations exercise as much or more. Can a few power crumbs make a dent in this big feast?

Both the editors and Nelly Stromquist unpack the word power in all sorts of ways. We learn that power has many dimensions: material and economic; expertise, knowledge and strategic position; psychological; political awareness, mobilization and organization. We learn that power emerges from within, with a sense of personal autonomy apart from, though not an elimination of, cultural and kinship relationships. We understand that power is exercised in both action and resistance, but that changes in power relations operate in concert with others and in ways that challenge a status quo that privileges men.

From Stromquist, we gain global perspectives on the potential (and limits) of formal and informal education to empower girls and women. The potential often goes unrealized in formal education as girls and boys learn 'their place' in society with a pedagogy that rarely provides protected spaces to challenge the status quo and act toward its change. One is aghast to read about empowerment projects that teach girls their wifely 'duties'.

Informal education, including some adult education, offers more potential for empowerment. Stromquist describes lots of projects that delink from the 'dynamics of patriarchy'. They provide *protected places* where women can acquire a sense of their autonomy, raise consciousness about their similarities, network, organize and mobilize for change. In some cases, women reduce their dependency on husbands. (But do they create new dependencies on banks or the state, to which Lairap-Fonderson's chapter calls attention?)

Stromquist's chapter offers extensive insight on *process* in empowerment, mainly in NGO-funded informal adult education. Outcomes that change power relations probably represent the exception more than the rule among women and in formal education budgets. Formal education, we must remember, is increasingly universal at the primary school level. Empowerment activities, through which *power within*, *power to* and *power with* processes occur, need more secure funding sources like those for public education generally. NGOs must exert pressure in the politics of the budgetary process.

From the global big picture, we turn to Barber's local, even personal, analyses of migrant women. The spatial dimensions of her chapter transcend national boundaries, indeed span half the global in connecting the Philippines and Canada. Through narratives, we get the sense that women are aware of and act upon their autonomy, even as outsiders (like the media, or even academic researchers) interpret them as victims. Women interpret their decisions to migrate and return in calculating ways. Many take risks to work 'illegally' or to work at a second job despite the rules.

But who makes these rules? And what sorts of options are available to these skilled women, formally educated, who work largely as live-in care-givers? Migrants have little collective voice in the nations where they work or from global civil society. Their ability to change the rules depends on the power of nationals who likely challenge the power, however diminished, of the often national-protectionist organized labour.

Ali examines the potential of human rights law as a tool to empower women in both global and trans-Islamic nation states. Through comparing CEDAW with alternatives that arise from Islamic human rights instruments, she finds no universally ascribed norms. Yet commonality exists: first, the history of human rights law separates women's rights and human rights. Second, legal tools acknowledge a public–private dichotomy. Outside the public, women have little to no personal autonomy. Third, laws are hardly enforced. Rights are 'violated with impunity ... in the name of Islam'. The same occurs in the name of supposed constitutionally driven, rights-oriented democracies.

Imbalanced gender power relations are clearly at work here. One must ask again, who makes, interprets and enforces these laws? The lack of protection in personal and public space calls into question any delusions that ratification of equality or human rights laws are 'outcomes' of empowerment. If the process was gained whereby women acquired inner power, consciousness and the skills to challenge these laws or their lack of enforcement, perhaps then outcomes could lead toward empowerment. For now, they are not enforced, as Patel's chapter further elaborates at the national level.

Youngs analyses the enormous, protected space available to women's networks in cyberspace. She connects the personal with the global from her experience in the UNESCO Women on the Net (WoN) project. UNESCO, unlike many international organizations cited in this volume, provided a protected space in which women could learn, connect, network, organize and create a discourse that challenged the status quo through cyberactivism. Youngs talks about the quick and close touch of online communication. She ties the extensive ability to transmit information through uploading, downloading and printing – reducing the cumbersome (and more easily controllable) faxing and posting of hard copies – to global protests.

Not a 'naïve futurist', as she says, Youngs does pose the daunting obstacles to access among four-fifths of the world's population not in the OECD countries (where computers are plentiful, with 91 per cent of Internet users). Both national and gender digital divides undermine the potential of this strategy to encompass and include the majority. The power to alter gender relations, through cyberspace, is still a 'distant dream'.

In Part II, we look at empowerment, gender and development themes through a national lens, where accountability ostensibly exists both to the governed and to the international institutions to which governments contribute. Staudt traces the global to local through a partial national lens, wherein women's *power to* engage with supposed democratic institutions does not begin to approach the strategic capacities and position of men's power. She highlights the clever alteration of multilateral institutional discourse toward women's empowerment amid massive policies that disempower many women and members of poor communities. While warning about co-optation, Staudt nevertheless encourages continued engagement in the real and messy political world of long-term change.

Bodur and Franceschet compare women's organizations and state feminism in two world regions, focusing on Chile and Turkey. Women interact with and acquire power from the state quite differently in both countries. Here, too, co-optation is always a threat and occasionally a reality. Together, these comparisons remind us that victories for middle- and upper-class women, often better organized to engage with the state, do not always imply victories for working-class and poor women. Privileged women can neutralize, even undermine, gains for all women. At the same time, many privileged women have played crucial roles in broad-based struggle for women's rights and gender equality.

Rai's chapter on political representation follows two chapters calling for political engagement and illustrating the process complexity of women organizing to change power relations. For which women are these actions? And what outcomes ensue from successful organization? Will critical masses of women in parliament transform power relations? Rai discovers that women gain and women lose from some gender struggles, depending on their class and caste.

In the early 1990s, India's Parliament passed a constitutional amendment to ensure that one-third of village *panchayats* were women. Over three-fourths of a million women have held those positions. Rai takes up the late 1990s debates to institute a similar quota in Parliament and sets it in the historical context of 'reservation' politics. Many disagreed, including some women's groups, for fear that women would be co-opted by elite politics, still a very 'male political terrain'. Female politicians could themselves neutralize the potential power to transform the men's institutional house from within.

Patel takes up 'rights' considerations, but, unlike Ali, looks at land within a nation state. Like the global and trans-Islamic rights debates, illusions are created in dual-legal systems of traditional/customary laws and statutory law that acknowledge a public and private dichotomy. After the Hindu Succession Act (HSA) of 1956, women's ability to control land would seemingly have enlarged. However, as Patel points out, HSA assumes individualistic property notions while cultural values undermine women's ability to control land. While a sense of autonomous self-interest *is* compatible with culture, in situational kinship relationships (daughter, sister), all-pervasive cultural values often devalue girls' and women's sense of the *power within*. Women *are* farmers, but most discourse, cultural and official, constructs women's work as sidelines to farming, even under the guise of 'women's development'. *Power within* is a prerequisite to even learning about and acting on abstract 'rights', which are claimable only with the power and wherewithal to engage a status quo system of gender relations that makes women and land ownership seemingly incompatible.

In this, the second of the chapters on rights, one wonders about connections with education, whether the formal education system, or the informal and adult processes. Do legal literacy projects empower women? To what extent is value rethinking and critical challenge part of girls' (and boys') education?

Part III goes explicitly to the local in a wide range of global contexts. Parpart analyses a seemingly empowering methodology known as Participatory Rural Appraisal (PRA). In PRA, local people have a voice and utilize local knowledge in ways that ought to address both process and eventually outcomes. PRA should address power relations, heretofore imbalanced in a way that privileges outsider experts compared with local insiders. Yet the conceptualization of PRA has been virtually oblivious to imbalanced gender relations. Parpart's review of PRA-in-practice shows that local men's voice tends to become expert and privileged. If knowledge construction is to have a protected space for women to exert their expertise and voice, it does not always happen through PRA.

Lairap-Fonderson provides an eloquent and chilling analysis of micro-enterprise projects in Kenya and Cameroon. Using insights from Foucault, she suggests that projects extract productive labour from women, thereby empowering the market economy, rather than empowering women who are subject to rules and discipline in meetings, timetables for loan repayment and possible fines.

In this sort of analysis, *power over* women seems complete. It is the sort of power that makes micro-enterprise rules and discipline seem normal rather than a late twentieth-century invention spread through the World Bank and various NGOs. Lairap-Fonderson uses outcome-like figures of 'the' Bank's own reports, figures we might challenge.

Power over women is no new invention across the continent, or globally for that matter. Rules and discipline have historically made violence and other subordinate experiences 'normal' for women. Indeed the discipline of group meetings and loan repayments has been documented in grassroots and indigenous women's efforts.

Richey looks at an ostensible family planning project in Tanzania, framing her analysis in feminist context, a word as contested as empowerment should be. Her focus is the public rather than women's self-perceptions and spiritual strengths. Globally, official discourse in family planning has changed, and few are sorry that the language of top-down 'population control' is no longer in vogue. Instead, empowerment language is used, emanating from the 1994 UN International Conference on Population and Development in Cairo. Once translated from the global to the local of Tanzanian villages, we learn of a practice that is far from empowering. NGOs are obliged to document success in meeting their goals, not women's goals. Implementation turned women into targets, selectively benefiting women who obliged them and granting men more spoils and voice. If empowerment is about, as Richey says, redistributing power and resources, then this project seems to have empowered men more than women.

Desai's analysis of NGOs in Bombay illustrates the ways in which women acquire power within in order to have power to make individual, programme and policy changes. Desai reminds us that the quiet, subtle strategies can be as effective as the noisy and confrontational. Yet the range of NGOs illustrates a range of protected and unprotected spaces for women to acquire this power. The dangers of NGOization abound in various regions, and accountability within the groups is part of the democratic process

The chapters in this volume illustrate several themes to future thinking and practice in empowerment. First, empowerment may be sequential, moving from a process that develops power *within* to the *power to* act on one's own and with others to engage publicly in action for change, which produces a redistribution of power and resources toward women and resulting in gender balance. Second, gender balance alone cannot be the process or outcome in a world ridden with poverty and class inequality. All classes of women must occupy protected public space, whether they seize it and settle in or have it reserved. Third, we should use the empowerment language, but contest the way it has been neutralized and even abused.

We have consciously tried to connect the global and the local, including the personal in the local. In the introduction we noted theory on how globalization erodes boundaries, yet how localization strengthens boundaries. Political institutions have divided us into complicated jurisdictions that make public engagement easily transformable into struggle against one another, even women, in our 'own' spaces. It remains a challenge to build solidarity across class, local and gender boundaries. However, we must recognize that engagement begins at and is grounded in the local.

Challenges to globalization and unfettered capitalism use slogans to remind us of the global–local connections: 'resistance must be as global as capitalism'; 'resistance must be as local as capitalism'. James DeFilippis echoes the work of our contributors: 'social movements need places in which to develop and prosper, and the privileging of the global scale over other, smaller scales of organizing threatens to undercut the ability of the protests to realize the transformative changes that are its goals' (2001: 2).

This volume behoves us as writers (and readers, we hope) to rethink our own participation in the local. It is up to us all to de-neutralize what institutions (and some people) have, in practice, done to the discourse of empowerment. Power must be restored as the centrepiece of empowerment, through global, national and local lenses.

References

DeFilippis, J. (2001) 'Our resistance must be as *local* as capitalism: Place, scale and the anti-globalization protest movement' (http://comm-org.utoledo.edu/papers2001/defilippis.htm).

Index

CPSIA information can be obtained
at www.ICGtesting.com
Printed in the USA
LVHW080244100620
656226LV00006B/153

9 780415 277693